Learning from the Student's Perspective

Learning from the Student's Perspective

A Sourcebook for Effective Teaching

Alison Cook-Sather

*with Brandon Clarke, Daniel Condon,
Kathleen Cushman, Helen Demetriou, Lois Easton,
Peter M. Evans, Jossi Fritz-Mauer, Darla Himeles,
Jessica Mitra Mausner, Marsha Rosenzweig Pincus,
and Bernadette Youens*

Paradigm Publishers
Boulder • London

Copyright © 2009 Paradigm Publishers

Published in the United States by Paradigm Publishers, 3845 Wilderness Place, Suite 200, Boulder, CO 80301 USA.

Paradigm Publishers is the trade name of Birkenkamp & Company, LLC, Dean Birkenkamp, President and Publisher.

Library of Congress Cataloging-in-Publication Data
Cook-Sather, Alison, 1964–
    Learning from the student's perspective : a sourcebook for
effective teaching / Alison Cook-Sather.
        p. cm.
    Includes bibliographical references and index.
    ISBN 978-1-59451-693-1 (hardcover : alk. paper) — ISBN 978-1-59451-694-8
(paperback : alk. paper)
    1. High school teaching.   2. Effective teaching.   3. Learning, Psychology
of.   4. High school students—Attitudes.   I. Title.
    LB1737.A3C66 2009
    373.1102—dc22

                                2009017108

Printed and bound in the United States of America on acid free paper that meets the standards of the American National Standard for Permanence of Paper for Printed Library Materials.

Designed and Typeset by Mulberry Tree Enterprises.

14   13   12   11   10   09   2   3   4   5

To Jean Rudduck, 1937–2007,
Cambridge University's first female professor of education
and a pioneer of student voice research

Contents

Introduction

Learning from the Student's Perspective: Why It's Important, What to Expect, and Important Guidelines

Why This Book Now?

This book is about the two meanings of the phrase "learning from the student's perspective." It is about how students experience learning—how learning is experienced, described, and analyzed from the student's perspective—and it is about adults learning from student descriptions and analyses of their learning. It is intended to be a practical guide to enacting effective teaching practices at the secondary level while at the same time challenging prospective and practicing teachers, school leaders, and teacher educators to analyze critically and begin to transform the cultural, institutional, and classroom structures within which teaching and learning unfold and that are not, at present, as conducive as they might be to either teacher or student engagement and success.

In an era of high-stakes testing and increasing pressure placed on schools, teachers, and students to perform well according to standardized measures, a book that argues for learning from the student's perspective might seem incongruous. But as Bains has suggested, while current educational leaders are formulating increasingly technical solutions to the distrust that permeates public schooling, "trying to solve the problems of public schools through more vituperative, technical decrees is absurd."[1] Furthermore, as Nieto remarked more than a decade and a half ago, "Reforming school structures alone will not lead to differences in student achievement . . . if such changes are not accompanied by profound changes in how we as educators think about our students." Nieto argues that one way to begin the process of changing school policies is to listen to students' views about them.[2]

1

This book offers—to prospective and practicing teachers, school leaders, teacher educators, and others—students' perspectives expressed in their own words. It argues that attending to students' perspectives on teaching, learning, and schooling as well as to other assessments of teaching practices must be an ongoing and never-ending process. And it provides strategies for and examples of how to act on those commitments. With this text, I join the growing number of researchers who argue that it will only be through learning from the student perspective that schools, teachers, and students will succeed not only according to standardized measures but, more importantly, in terms of their own commitment and capacity to become critical thinkers, engaged human beings, and responsible participants in the world.

I encourage readers to take up this book as a source of inspiration and guidance. The student voices included here, as well as the voices of teachers, school leaders, and researchers who have worked collaboratively with students, offer deeply felt, carefully conceptualized, and mobilizing suggestions for how to access and act on student perspectives and to work in partnership with students to create meaningful and enduring learning experiences.

Why Is It Important to Listen to Students' Voices?

Consider the following two statements:

> Students sometimes feel like their voices aren't being heard, but being asked to give advice to prospective teachers who want to learn from us was a nice change from the norm. It was nice to be able to express our concerns about teachers in a constructive way that would (hopefully) prevent some of the problems we see in our teachers from developing in future teachers. (Belinda, personal communication, 2007)

> Student voice is most successful when it enables students to feel that they are members of a learning community, that they matter, and that they have something valuable to offer. (Jean Rudduck, 2007, p. 587)

Belinda is a student who attends an urban, public high school in the northeastern United States. Jean Rudduck was one of the pioneering researchers in the student voice movement in England. From different positions within the educational system and from different sides of the Atlantic, they both articulate the basic rationale for learning from the student's perspective: that students have insights that can help improve teaching and learning and build community in schools.

For the past twenty years, I have worked as a teacher, a teacher educator, and an educational researcher to create opportunities and support structures for students to assume active and critical roles in analyses and revisions of educational practice.[3] This sourcebook draws on findings from the Teaching and Learning Together (TLT) project (ongoing since

1995, discussed in Chapter 13) through which high school students are positioned as teacher educators; it also draws on the research of colleagues in Australia, Canada, England, and the United States who have consulted students and documented their perspectives.

Why Should Students' Perspectives and Participation Matter?

As those who spend the majority of their days in classrooms and indeed have spent the majority of their lives in school, students have unique perspectives on teaching, learning, and schooling.[4] Many educators elicit and act on student feedback every day in their classrooms, and there is a growing body of research that argues for and substantiates the importance of consulting students about their learning strengths and needs.[5] And yet, not a single textbook foregrounds the student perspective in conceptualizing, enacting, and assessing effective teaching practices, and very few methods texts written for prospective or practicing secondary teachers include or refer to students' perspectives.[6] This book, however, is premised on the conviction that listening to what students have to say is essential to making classrooms and schools places where students want to be and can learn. Like other advocates of student voice, I do not argue that students' perspectives should replace all other perspectives on good teaching or be the sole impetus for revision of educational practices. Rather, I contend that students' perspectives should be included alongside those of teachers and researchers in conversations about effective teaching. Without that angle of vision and without those voices in dialogue with our own, we have an incomplete picture and insufficiently informed conversation regarding what happens and what could happen in classrooms and schools.

The Story of How I Came to Integrate Students' Perspectives in Effective Teaching Practices

In my first year as director of the Bryn Mawr/Haverford Education Program,[7] I had many conversations with a high school teacher friend and colleague. As she talked about her high school students' needs and interests and I talked about my preservice teachers' preparation to teach, it struck us that prospective teachers were learning to teach without much direct interaction with high school students. Specifically, we realized that no opportunities existed for interaction through which the high school students could tell the preservice teachers about their experiences and needs as learners. In response to this concern, we designed Teaching and Learning Together, a project that has become an integral component of the general secondary methods course I teach, Curriculum and Pedagogy, the penultimate course required for certification to teach at the secondary level through the Bryn Mawr/Haverford Education Program. This course is offered in the semester prior to practice teaching.

Through Teaching and Learning Together, high school students are positioned as teacher educators, each of whom maintains a weekly e-mail correspondence with one of the prospective teachers enrolled in my course and all of whom share their perspectives with prospective teachers through weekly school-based meetings among the participating high school students and a school-based teacher-facilitator. The project attempts to address basic needs of both partners—prospective teachers and high school students. It has immediate as well as long-term philosophical and practical use for prospective teachers, and it puts diverse, differently positioned high school students into dialogue with one another and with prospective teachers. These dialogues benefit both the prospective teachers and the students.

Like Belinda, a recent student participant in Teaching and Learning Together, many students are keenly aware both that they have important perspectives on teaching and that there are very few opportunities to share those. During one conversation among high school students who participated in Teaching and Learning Together in 1995, a student said: "Sometimes I wish I could sit down with one of my teachers and just tell them what I exactly think about their class. It might be good, it might be bad, it's just that you don't have the opportunity to do it."[8] Ten years later, another student who participated in Teaching and Learning Together said: "We don't often get the chance to give the constructive criticism that so many of us have thoughts on."[9] Every year the secondary students with whom I work reiterate a version of this statement. More educators need to give students the chance to share their perspectives and to have those perspectives matter.

Beyond Individual Educators' Convictions, What About Students' Rights?

While many teachers do, in fact, listen to their students and work collaboratively with them to make their classrooms productive learning environments, the mainstream educational system in the United States does not, in any systematic way, take student perspectives into consideration and invite active student participation when developing and reforming educational practices. This fact makes education the only provider of essential social services that does not consult its user population about their needs. As McIntyre and his colleagues point out: "It cannot tenably be claimed that schooling is primarily intended to benefit students if students' own views about what is beneficial to them are not actively sought and attended to."[10]

Although scholars offer various explanations for why students have been excluded from most conversations about teaching,[11] they all sound the same note that I have sounded regarding this elision: "There is something fundamentally amiss about building and rebuilding an entire system without consulting at any point those it is ostensibly designed to serve."[12] For a long time professionals in the medical and legal fields assumed, like educators, that they knew best how to conceptualize and deliver service. Since the late 1980s, however, the provider-client relationship and client satisfaction with services delivered have become foci for research and practice in these fields. As I have argued previously, it is time for the educational system to join medical practitioners, who recognize that understanding patients' concerns, expectations, and requests is essential for health care practitioners, policymakers, and researchers.[13] It is time to join lawyers, some of whom have been promoting a "client-centered" legal approach since the mid-1970s. They have learned that heavy client involvement and control lead not only to higher client satisfaction but can also, especially for disadvantaged clients, act as a mechanism of empowerment.[14] And, most basically, as Helen Demetriou points out in Chapter 6 of this text, in keeping with Article 12 of the UN Convention on the Rights of the Child, we in the realm of education need to heed what those we serve have to tell us. To ignore the views of the child is not only ineffective but also unethical, and such a violation of civil rights should not be taken lightly.

This book provides resources to support not only a student-centered but also a student-coconstructed approach. It is a concrete step in pursuit of the commitment Rudduck and Flutter articulate: to "see [students] differently and to reassess their capabilities" so that we may "review and change aspects of school organization, relationships and practices to reflect what young people are capable of being and doing."[15] As Sarason points out, the history of educational reform in the United States demonstrates that adults—teachers, administrators, researchers, policymakers—undertake all kinds of efforts to "alter curricula, change power relationships, [and] raise standards."[16] But, as Sarason continues, "if these efforts are not powered by altered conceptions of what makes [students] tick and keeps them intellectually alive, willingly pursuing knowledge and growth, the result will be inconsequential."[17] Sarason's point about the importance of students "willingly pursuing knowledge and growth" is essential here not only in terms of efficacy but also in terms of principles; students must have an active role in their learning if that learning is going to be meaningful and lasting, and such an active role should include having input into how their learning is facilitated. This is the right of the students, and it is the responsibility of the adults to ensure that that right is guaranteed.

The Ongoing Process of Consulting Students: What Should You Expect?

Even if the arguments for consulting students presented in the previous sections are persuasive, it might seem a daunting prospect to some teachers to invite students to share their views on teaching. What students have to say can be discouraging; it can be hard to hear; it can be reductive, misguided, or lacking in perspective because students are so rarely asked for their input or taught how to offer it; and it can require revision rather than reproduction of "tried and true" approaches.[18] And yet, if we as teachers are seriously committed to making student learning both productive and engaging, we need to enter into dialogue with students about what works, what does not, and what could work for them. Below are some reassurances.

Student Feedback Is Generally Constructive

For those who worry about consulting students regarding pedagogical issues, researchers Rudduck and Flutter offer some encouragement. They suggest that, while it is understandable, particularly in the present judgmental climate, that teachers might worry that consulting students could unleash "a barrage of criticism of them and their teaching," they find that that is not usually the case. They explain, "In our experience most [students] criticize the task or the procedures rather than the teacher and their commentaries are often very constructive."[19]

Student Feedback Aligns with Much Educational Theory

Many educators might be surprised by the fact that what most students ask for aligns remarkably well with a substantial body of educational theory. Indeed, many of the strategies for which students argue in this book are consistent with effective teaching practices that have been identified by both teachers and educational researchers. But effective teaching practices take on a different aspect and significance when explored from the learner's perspective—they sound different when articulated in students' words. Looking across student recommendations for approaches to classroom management, pedagogical strategies, and other areas central to teaching, one sees not only versions of some of the principles of constructivist, critical, feminist, and equity approaches but also recurrent themes that get to the heart of what students want and need in school: meaningful relationships, respect, and an opportunity to take responsibility for their learning and their lives. The resonance here is significant in that all these approaches and principles are context-sensitive and committed to looking at difference and diversity—realities of U.S. schools—as resources, not as deficits.

Learning from the Student's Perspective Is an Ongoing Project

While this text offers examples of a cross section of students' perspectives as well as strategies for accessing all students' perspectives and stories of implementing such strategies, the book is also intended to highlight the fact that no teacher ever learns once and for all what *the* student perspective is and what works for learners. Rather, becoming an effective teacher is an ongoing process of learning how best to support each new individual student and group of learners within each particular educational context.

Far from being a daunting prospect, this fact should be reassuring— giving both inexperienced and experienced teachers permission and encouragement to continue to learn, just as we ask students to engage in ongoing learning. Extending the commitment of teacher researchers to use the sites of their own educational practice as subjects of inquiry with the goal of developing, assessing, and revising theories that inform practice—consulting students and working collaboratively with them to improve classroom practice—positions the classroom teacher as "practitioner-inquirer" dedicated to an ongoing process of inquiry rather than practitioner-technician looking for a quick fix.[20]

Listening and Embracing Processes of Change

This book makes clear that genuinely listening to students requires not only a retuning of our adult ears but also a reconsideration and revision of prevailing teacher-student relationships and pedagogical practices. One essential component of such revision is making space for and developing a commitment to inviting students to engage in more conscious, deliberate, and supported processes of learning about themselves. Like teachers, students are in an ongoing process of learning and changing, not only regarding the subject matter they are encountering but also in terms of learning who they are and who they might become. Although we are older, we as educators are also always becoming.

Is There Research Support for the Claims Made in This Sourcebook?

For those interested in the research support behind consulting students, I offer an appendix that includes an overview of international models for listening to students. I outline as well frameworks that researchers in Australia, Canada, England, and the United States have developed for consulting students, and I discuss in particular efforts that have been made within the realm of teacher education to create active roles for students. I also present several categories of research findings on listening to students. These include building relationships that promote engagement and learning, accessing the student experience of school—and making school more accessible, and addressing social inequities. In addition to that appendix, I encourage readers to consult the references in the list of sources in the back of the book.

The growing body of research on consulting students supports Rudduck and Flutter's claim that student commentaries on teaching and learning in school "provide a practical agenda for change that can help fine tune or, more fundamentally, identify and shape improvement strategies."[21] Inviting students to be partners[22] in developing, enacting, and assessing educational approaches is the best—perhaps the only—way to create learning opportunities that students want to take up and truly benefit from embracing. For their part, as addressed in Chapter 5, students need to meet their adult educational partners halfway, taking up the responsibilities such consultation affords while also progressing on their own individual and shared learning trajectories. To be empowered in the ways explored in this text is not to sacrifice traditional success; rather, a collaborative approach can further individual achievement while also striving toward collective empowerment.

How Is This Work Related to Student-Centered and Constructivist Learning?

Learning from students is related to student-centered and constructivist approaches to learning in that it puts students at the center of the educational endeavor. It is different in that it consults students about the process as well as the content of teaching and learning: it asks students about their views regarding which of their teachers' practices are helpful or unhelpful and why, and about what characterizes the classroom activities or choices that they find motivating or productive.[23]

Student-centered approaches to learning shift the student role from one of passive reception to one of active engagement in deciding what to study; the student role shifts from learning by listening to learning by doing. A form of student-centered learning, "constructivism" means different things to different people,[24] but constructivist approaches have in common the belief that students actively construe and construct their own understandings.[25] This belief leads to a commitment to "the continual and sympathetic observation" of students' interests[26] and the development of pedagogical approaches that give students "the opportunity to explore their ideas and to try to make more sense of them."[27] Constructivists position students as active creators of their knowledge rather than recipients of others' knowledge.

When students have the opportunity to develop a metacognitive awareness of their learning, both in order to engage and as a result of engaging in serious dialogue with adults about their learning experiences and needs, they not only construct their understanding of subject matter content, as constructivist approaches to learning advocate and aim to facilitate, they also construct themselves anew—they become new versions of themselves.[28] The approach I discuss here is an extension of student-centered learning and constructivism but one with a focus on the self that develops when learners are active participants not only in knowledge construction but also in the construction of identities and relationships. In considering constructivism and its extension—listening to students' analyses of how they not only construe and construct knowledge but also how they construe and construct themselves—it is important to keep in mind that learning neither occurs nor is completed in a single event. Learning and understanding of that learning take place over time, and "learning changes not just what the learner knows . . . but also who the learner is."[29]

Thus, while listening to and learning from the student perspective is in part premised on student-centered and constructivist approaches to learning, it is an extension of those into a more political as well as differently practical realm. It requires taking on the power inequities structured into schools and society, taking on and affording others new responsibilities in teaching and learning.

Which Student Perspectives Are Included in This Text?

The students whose perspectives are featured in this sourcebook are located at various socioeconomic levels, are placed in different tracks within their school systems, and claim various racial and cultural identities. While I mention in the list below both the contexts in which these students attend school and some aspects of the various dimensions of diversity claimed by and assigned to them, I do not throughout the book identify each student I quote in terms of his or her school context, race, class, gender, or other dimensions of diversity. The reason for this choice is that the students articulate a strikingly similar set of perspectives regardless of their contexts and identities. Each time I quote a student, unless the source is from my own data, I indicate the source of the quotation with an endnote, and if readers want to further investigate the individual students or particular contexts, they can do so by consulting the source.[30]

The following groups of students are featured in this sourcebook:

1. 200 primarily white and middle- to upper-middle-class students who attended one of two suburban high schools outside a major city in the northeastern United States between 1995 and 2007.[31]
2. 280 African American and Hispanic middle school students who attended one of five urban schools in low-income neighborhoods in a major city in the northeastern United States between 2000 and 2002.[32]
3. 40 high school students of color who attended high schools in four cities in the northeastern and western United States in 2002.[33]
4. 200 students randomly selected across grade, gender, race, home language, track placement, and grade point average who attended one of 13 public urban schools in a district in southern California in 2001–2002.[34]
5. 209 students designated dropouts from Australian schools from 1997 to 1999.[35]
6. Students from various schools in England between 2000 and 2007.[36]
7. 36 students from five schools in England from 2000 to 2001.[37]
8. 29 student authors of various racial, ethnic, class backgrounds.[38]
9. Low-achieving students who experienced, participated in, or analyzed reform efforts in their schools.[39]
10. Five students from a suburban California high school.[40]
11. 182 secondary students representing 14 different underfunded to affluent magnet, inner-city, suburban, and rural schools.[41]

While a representative sampling of students' perspectives is included here, it is important to keep in mind that learners' needs and preferences are always individual- and context-specific, and while there are remarkable similarities across these learners' perspectives, I urge all teachers and researchers to take this text as a starting point, not an ending point, and to continue to consult students across contexts regarding their strengths, needs, and preferences.

Furthermore, as I discuss in the next section of this introduction, the student perspectives presented here are necessarily partial, and they need to be attended to not in isolation from but rather in relation to teachers', other educators', and other students' perspectives. My goal is to bring their words into an arena in which they might be heard, but it is the responsibility of those reading their words to bring them into further dialogue—with other students' and with variously positioned educators' words.

Guidelines, Cautions, and Reminders

Rudduck and McIntyre emphasize that, in order for the consultation of students to be effective, there must be reciprocal trust, respect, and recognition among teachers and students participating in the consultation process.[42] Students must feel that their perspectives and participation in school change are taken seriously.[43] As one student put it, "If you talk and people don't listen, you don't want to talk anymore."[44]

The chapters in this text illustrate the guiding principles for planning strategies for consulting students that Rudduck and McIntyre derived from findings of research projects in England and New Zealand.[45]

Guiding Principles for Consulting Students

Be Committed to Listening and Responding

Teachers should embark on student consultation only if they have a genuine desire to hear what students have to say and a firm commitment to try to use what students say to improve teaching and learning in their classrooms.

Be Prepared to Explain Your Purpose and Focus

Teachers should explain clearly to students the purpose and focus of their consultation, making clear how, and why, if appropriate, they were selected for consultation and what will happen to what they say, including the teacher's own willingness to be influenced by what students say as well as by other necessary considerations.

Create Conditions for Dialogue

For the consultation process to be productive, teachers need to create conditions of dialogue in which teachers and students listen to and learn from each other in new ways (i.e., not in ways that try to fit into existing assumptions and practices).

Choose Methods That Focus on Deepening Understanding

The methods of consultation used should be chosen to deepen teachers' understanding of students' experiences of teaching and learning in their classrooms. Examples of such methods are discussed in detail in Chapters 6 and 7.

Give Students Feedback

After consultation, students need feedback on how what they have said has been understood and on how it will influence or has influenced teacher planning and actions.

Be Realistic

Student consultation needs to be planned realistically from the beginning, with particular attention to the time and energy needed for all phases of it.

Following these guidelines will help make consultation a responsible process. But in addition to following these guidelines, it is essential to keep in mind, and work to avoid, some of the dangers of consulting students.

Potential Dangers of Listening to Student Voices

Listen to Students but Do Not Indulge or Exploit Them

There is danger in careless approaches to consulting students. Indulging students ultimately leads to dismissing their input, a result of an idealized view of young people. The "aren't they sweet" attitude "reflects the patronage of adults, but it does not contribute to understanding or analysis of the issues and concerns which are of importance to pupils."[46] An equally demeaning form of attention to student voices is seeing them as embellishments. Some educational researchers find that their e-mail in-boxes are "a virtual catalogue of invitations [from researchers, publishers, and policymakers] to 'gather student voices' as if they were Christmas tree decorations on an already predetermined reform 'for their own good.'"[47] Even well-intentioned efforts to increase student voice and participation can "reinforce a hierarchy of power and privilege among students and undermine attempted reforms"[48] when student voice is not genuinely attended to and when students are not, or do not feel, part of the change process.

There Is No Single or Unified Student Voice

Like feminists who warn against "claims to universal truths and . . . assumptions of a collective experience of oppression,"[49] those who conceptualize and pursue student voice as a uniform and united entity run the risk of overlooking differences among students, their perspectives, and their needs. Those committed to productive listening to and learning from the student perspective must work hard not to reduce students' comments and insights to any "single, uniform and invariable experience"[50] and to avoid making the mistake of "uncritically 'essentialising' [student] experiences by assuming that they are free to represent their own interests transparently."[51] Student perspectives are always both incomplete and complex, and they always need to be understood in context.

The Rhetoric of Student Voice Work Must Match the Reality

A concern among some advocates of student voice work regards the possibility that the oversimplification of the issues involved in changing school culture to make it more responsive to students will lead to tokenism, manipulation, and practices not matching rhetoric.[52] There is the potential, some theorists warn, for efforts that are "benign but condescending" or "cynical and manipulative,"[53] which keep students passive, their voices "only audible through the products of past performance."[54]

Reminders Regarding Listening to the Learner's Perspective

As the title of this sourcebook indicates, this is a book written about and, to some extent, from the learner's perspective. Therefore, the final reminder has to do with the importance of this different perspective and how to engage it.

Be Open to Students' Perspectives and Students' Meanings

This sourcebook foregrounds students' perspectives and students' words. It offers insights from students' angles of vision, and it presents their perspectives using their vocabulary. It is essential to keep in mind that students see from a different angle than adults and that they might mean different things by the words they use than what adults might mean by or associate with the same words. For example, in Chapter 1 a student uses the word "lenient" to describe a classroom where she feels safe and understood. Educators may have pejorative associations with that term: *lenient* as not sufficiently strict or demanding, as too easygoing or even indulgent. This student, however, seems to be highlighting the meanings of the term that emphasize compassion, tolerance, ease of being. Another important example is the term "friend," which many students use to signal the role they want teachers to assume in a respectful, trusting relationship, but to adults the term might signal an uncomfortable movement outside of the professional nature of the student-teacher relationship. There are many other examples of terms that signal different things to differently positioned people. I urge readers, therefore, to pay attention to what the students say and try to imagine what they might mean, rather than adhere to adult meanings and associations, and, further, to be prepared to explore such terms with students—to ask students what they mean by such terms both to learn and to extend what they might mean to students and to us as educators.

Respond Constructively to Your Doubts, Disagreements, and Defensiveness

Because some of what students say will challenge some of your beliefs, and because some of what they say may conflict with your perspectives, it is essential to pay close attention to your responses to what students have to say and, rather than becoming defensive or dismissive, ask yourself what you could do to better understand students' perspectives and help them better understand yours. The challenge often lies in overcoming our own feelings as teachers to recognize, understand, and accept the true feelings of our students in order to work collaboratively to build a more meaningful learning environment. No matter what students feel, and whether or not we agree, it is a real feeling to them, and our job is to work with them to move beyond their—and our own—limited perspectives. The perspectives students offer should not be seen as prescriptions but rather as input. As Bernadette Youens points out in Chapter 14, guidance offered by the student mentors who work with student teachers at the University of Nottingham "is just one perspective and it will not necessarily be one that they [student teachers] will, or should, agree with." Youens suggests that, "in practice, student teachers responded often to the spirit rather than the detail of the advice proffered, sometimes reinterpreting it in the light of their own developing understanding of the teacher's role." In reading the student perspectives presented here and in eliciting your own students' perspectives, think with students about what your responsibility is as a teacher and what their responsibility is as students. The ultimate goal is more frequent and effective dialogue between educators and students about what works, what does not, and what could work for learners, so I urge you to turn doubt and disagreement to opportunity for further learning.

Help Students Gain Insight into Teachers' Experiences

One of the most inspiring findings of Teaching and Learning Together (discussed in detail in Chapter 13) is that, when students are consulted about their learning needs, and when that process of consultation is a genuine dialogue, students gain insight into and deeper understanding of the challenges facing teachers. One student explained that hearing about what prospective teachers struggle with "made me realize the teacher's point of view, like, I never really realized what they go through, that they even care about this." Echoing this sentiment, another student said: "It made me realize how much the teachers have to think about what they're doing and that they don't just get up there every day and do their thing. That they actually think about ways that they can improve themselves and they work really hard to do what they do." These insights and understandings make students more empathetic and more willing to work with teachers to make schools places where both teachers and students can work to the best of their ability.

Collaborate with Students to Identify Larger Systemic Changes

The student perspectives presented here reveal both the capacity students have to identify and articulate the struggles they experience and the hopes they have for their education. They also reveal the limitations of the student perspective, particularly regarding the larger systemic structures and strictures within which educators labor. The excerpts of students' perspectives in Part I of this sourcebook are provided in isolation and with little context in order to include as many student voices as possible. However, such decontextualized statements do not illustrate the ongoing dialogue essential to this process of consultation and collaborative revision of educational approaches. The role of the educator is to continue to work with students to allow their voices to create a meaningful and constructive change well beyond the initial interaction—work that is represented vividly in the case studies at the conclusion of Chapters 1–5 in Part I and in the stories of teachers, school leaders, and teacher educators in Part III. Thus a final challenge this text presents is how to collaborate with students to identify their needs and hopes, to help them see the larger system within which both they and their teachers work, and to imagine together more effective ways to structure teaching and learning opportunities.

I offer these guidelines, words of caution, and reminders to highlight the fact that consulting students is a complex activity requiring a high degree of awareness and responsibility, and I encourage you to return to this section when you feel dismayed or discouraged by what you are reading.

Organization and Authorship of the Book

Following this introduction, the book is divided into three parts, followed by conclusions and an appendix. Each part has chapters that are authored or coauthored by various people, and each part has introductory or framing sections provided by me. With this authorial structure I aim to create space not only for student voices to speak for themselves but also for prospective and practicing teachers and professional educators who have worked to learn from the students' perspectives to tell their stories of that work. In this sense, every voice in this book is the voice of a learner. The statements offered by high school students, the guidelines for how to access student perspectives, and the narratives offered by practitioners are all stories told of learning by learners. I chose this structure to make visible the process of learning as it is taken up by learners at various points in their careers. The structure of the text thus strives to mirror its purpose: to model and inform learning in the classroom at all stages of one's educational lifespan. I offer a brief overview of each section's contents and authors below, which I expand upon in the introductions to each section.

Part I: Students' Perspectives on Effective Classroom Practice

This section presents students' perspectives on effective teaching practices, highlighting the underlying principles that inform those practices. Although student perspectives are presented throughout the book, this section features high school students' voices and perspectives most prominently.

The first three chapters address the following pedagogical challenges: (1) knowing students, (2) creating and maintaining a positive classroom environment, and (3) designing engaging lessons. Within each chapter are subsections that address particular components of each of these three areas of effective educational practice. The next two chapters look across students' advice on these three areas and discuss themes or recurrent assertions that thread their way throughout those three arenas of pedagogical challenge. These themes—respect and responsibility—surfaced regardless of the specific topic (classroom management, testing, etc.) being explored by students.

This part of the sourcebook is coauthored—or, more accurately, coframed and coarranged—by me, Jossi Fritz-Mauer, and Jessica Mitra Mausner. At the time that we organized these chapters, Jossi and Jessica were seniors at and subsequently graduates of Haverford College, and they both completed a minor in educational studies as well as their disciplinary majors. Their perspectives, as learners analyzing other learners' perspectives, are highlighted in the structure and content of these chapters. The high school student perspectives presented in this part reflect both what students already know and the fact that they are engaged in the ongoing process of learning.

Part II: Strategies for Learning from Students' Perspectives

This part of the sourcebook offers strategies—activities, questionnaires, discussion questions—for eliciting and acting on students' views and for including students as partners in creating meaningful educational experiences. Chapter 6 is written by Helen Demetriou, coauthor of *Consulting Pupils: A Toolkit for Teachers* (2003), and Chapter 7 is written by Kathleen Cushman, author of *Fires in the Bathroom: Advice for Teachers from High School Students* (2003). Here are lessons learned by adults committed to listening to students and offering frameworks and guidelines for others who share that commitment. The conceptual frameworks, questionnaires, activities, and other specific strategies for accessing student perspectives can be adapted to any context. The concrete strategies included in this section offer some guidelines for working to support, in an ongoing way, both student and teacher learning that embraces the cross-cutting themes and the complexities of the learning in which students are engaged.

Part III: Listening in Action:
Educators Learning from Student Perspectives

This part includes stories of how prospective and experienced teachers, school leaders, and teacher educators make learning from the student's perspective central to their educational practice by putting the kinds of strategies discussed in Part II into practice. These narratives reveal the process of coming to listen to students, the various approaches these educators have taken to doing so, and some of the challenges and possibilities of their efforts.

This section includes two chapters written by prospective teachers—educators at the very beginning of their careers—and one chapter written by an experienced educator who recently retired from a thirty-four-year career teaching in urban public schools. Chapter 8 focuses on how Darla Himeles developed an awareness of the importance of learning from students as a student herself, as a tutor, and finally as a student teacher. Chapter 9 highlights a realization that Brandon Clarke had: that he considered himself a teacher who listened to students but learned that he was not what he had thought he was. In Chapter 10, Marsha Rosenzweig Pincus provides a case study of a particularly challenging class she taught in the last year of her three and a half decades of teaching in an urban, public school in which she acted on a commitment to learning from the student's perspective that she had developed over the course of her teaching career. These narratives illustrate how beginning and experienced teachers put into practice their commitment to listening and responding to students and to having students' perspectives inform, in ongoing ways, the work of teaching.

Chapters 11 and 12 offer glimpses of how school leaders, one principal and one recently retired director of a school-based professional development center and a colleague still engaged in work at the school, build their educational contexts around the premises of listening to students and supporting active student participation in shaping their educational contexts. In Chapter 11, Peter Evans discusses how he developed Montpelier High School in Vermont around attention to student perspectives and forums for student voices to be heard. In Chapter 12, Lois Easton and Dan Condon describe how the Eagle Rock School in Colorado is built around student voice and prepares teachers through the Professional Development Center at Eagle Rock. In these chapters, readers can find discussions of school leaders' perspectives and examples of how listening to student voices and perspectives can be implemented on a schoolwide basis.

Moving from stories of classroom and school practices to stories of how teachers can be prepared to teach in ways that attend and respond to student perspectives, in Chapter 13, I discuss how I position secondary students as teacher educators through Teaching and Learning Together, a four-part project based in the semester prior to student teaching in the

Bryn Mawr/Haverford College Education Program in Bryn Mawr, Pennsylvania. In Chapter 14, Bernadette Youens discusses a program at the University of Nottingham in England in which secondary students serve as mentors during the teaching practicum of initial teacher preparation. These chapters offer teacher educators examples of how student perspectives and participation can be central to the preparation of prospective teachers.

Part IV: Conclusions

The last part of the sourcebook includes two chapters, one that summarizes some of the main points of the book and offers some action steps that educators can take, and one that introduces a metaphor for those who wish to explore the issues raised in this text within another conceptual framework. Chapter 15 revisits the notion of "perspective," a central term in the title and the guiding principle of the book, according to which the chapters and their contents are presented. This chapter includes some general recommendations regarding perspective, stance, and interaction for those interested in learning from the student's perspective and proposes action steps for high school teachers, school leaders, and teacher educators. Chapter 16 presents the metaphor of translation as a conceptual framework for thinking about how schools and education might change in order to learn and evolve through learning from the student's perspective.

Appendix

The appendix includes an overview of international models for listening to students, particular efforts that have been made within the realm of teacher education to create active roles for students, and research findings on listening to students.

As you turn the following pages and enter a world informed by student perspectives, I invite you to discover how much those perspectives have to teach us. A student sees, as one educator put it, what "I cannot from my vantage point, not only figuratively but also literally, as she has a line of sight into the space of the classroom which I do not have from where I stand." I hope others will, like this teacher, be inspired by the ways that student perspectives help, as this same teacher put it, "to open up for me the space in the classroom in ways which I have not seen before."[55]

Notes

1. *Teachers College Record*, February 14, 2008.
2. Nieto, 1994, pp. 395–396.
3. For other discussions of this commitment and the practices that follow from it, see the following books, articles, and book chapters I have published (complete

reference information is included in the bibliography): "Translating Researchers: Re-imagining the Work of Investigating Students' Experiences in School" (*International Handbook of Student Experience in Elementary and Secondary Schools*); *Education Is Translation: A Metaphor for Change in Learning and Teaching*; "Re(in)forming the Conversations: Student Position, Power, and Voice in Teacher Education" (*Radical Teacher*); "Teachers-to-Be Learning from Students-Who-Are: Reconfiguring Undergraduate Teacher Preparation" (*Stories of the Courage to Teach: Honoring the Teacher's Heart*); "Direct Links: Using Email to Connect Pre-Service Teachers, Classroom-Based Teachers, and High School Students within an Undergraduate Teacher Preparation Program" (*Journal of Technology and Teacher Education*); "The 'Constant Changing of Myself': Revising Roles in Undergraduate Teacher Preparation" (*The Teacher Educator*); "Listening to Students about Learning Differences" (*Teaching Exceptional Children*); "'A Teacher Should Be . . . ': When the Answer Is the Question" (*Knowledge Quest*); *In Our Own Words: Students' Perspectives on School.*

4. For examples of arguments for the uniqueness and importance of student perspectives, see Thiessen and Cook-Sather, 2007; Cook-Sather and Shultz, 2001; Nieto, 1994; Oldfather, 1995; Rudduck, Chaplain, and Wallace, 1996; Weis and Fine, 1993; Willis, 1977.

5. For examples of arguments for attending to student perspectives, see Cook-Sather, 2002b; Fine et al., 2007; Holdsworth, 2000; Levin, 1994, 2000; Mitra, 2007, 2004, 2001; Rodgers, 2006; Rudduck and Flutter, 2004; Silva and Rubin, 2003; Smyth, 2007; Smyth et al., 2004; Thiessen, 2007; Wilson and Corbett, 2007, 2001; Yonezawa and Jones, 2007.

6. For some exceptions, see Cooper and McIntyre, 1996/2000; Moje, 2000; and Stern, 1995.

7. The Bryn Mawr/Haverford Education Program is an undergraduate, secondary teacher preparation program at two selective, liberal arts colleges—Bryn Mawr College and Haverford College—located in the northeastern United States.

8. Shultz and Cook-Sather, 2001, p. xii.

9. Cook-Sather, 2006a, p. 352.

10. 2005, p. 150.

11. See in particular the very insightful and interesting discussion of constructions of children and childhood in Rudduck and Flutter, 2004.

12. Cook-Sather, 2002a, p. 3.

13. Kravitz, 2001. An increasing number of doctors elicit patients' perspectives both while care is being given (Barr and Vergun, 2000) and subsequent to delivery. There are even some nascent movements toward including patients' assessments of care in the training of medical practitioners (Greco, Brownlea, McGovern, and Cavanaugh, 2000). Because research finds that positive patient-provider relationships and patient satisfaction are positively associated with quality care (Meredith et al., 2001), many medical researchers advocate not only attending to what their patients want (Mann and Chambers, 2001) but also promoting patient autonomy built on kindness and respect for the patient as a person (Bruhn, 2001). There is, in fact, an international movement toward "patient-centered" medicine (Stewart, 2001), and research indicates that when patients perceive their care to be patient-centered, the health care provided is more efficient (i.e., there are fewer diagnostic texts and fewer referrals necessary) (Stewart et al., 1995).

14. Buss, 1999; Rosenthal, 1974.

15. Rudduck and Flutter, 2004, p. 2.

16. Sarason, 1991, p. 163.

17. Ibid.
18. Bragg, 2001; Johnston and Nicholls, 1995.
19. Rudduck and Flutter, 2004, p. 75.
20. Calkins, 1994; Burnaford, 2001, p. 235; Berlin, 1990; Cochran-Smith and Lytle, 1993; Martin, 1987.
21. Rudduck and Flutter, 2004, p. 29.
22. This text focuses on inviting students to be partners within their classrooms. An important related activity not taken up in this text is students as researchers. For more information, please consult the growing literature on students as researchers, including Fielding and Bragg, 2003; Fine et al., 2007; SooHoo, 1993; Thiessen and Cook-Sather, 2007.
23. Rudduck and McIntyre, 2007, p. 27.
24. Davis and Sumara, 2002; Phillips, 1995; Shapiro, 2002, 2003.
25. Davis and Sumara, 2002.
26. Dewey, 1964, p. 436.
27. Duckworth, 1987, p. 65.
28. Cook-Sather, 2006.
29. Dreier, 2003, in Wortham, 2004, p. 716; see also Packer, 2001, and Cook-Sather, 2006.
30. For sources other than my own data, there is also after each quotation an endnote with source information.
31. These students participated in a project I have facilitated through the Education Program at Bryn Mawr and Haverford colleges since 1995. Through this project, the students have been paired with preservice teachers prior to practice teaching and these high school students offer the preservice teachers their perspectives on best teaching practices through weekly e-mail exchanges and weekly conversations among the students held at the high school.
32. These students' perspectives are drawn from Wilson and Corbett (2007), "Students' Perspectives on Good Teaching: Implications for Adult Reform Behavior" (*International Handbook of Student Experiences in Elementary and Secondary Schools*).
33. These students' perspectives are drawn from Cushman (2003), *Fires in the Bathroom*.
34. These students' perspectives are drawn from Yonezawa and Jones (2007), "Using Students' Voices to Inform and Evaluate Secondary School Reform" (*International Handbook of Student Experiences in Elementary and Secondary Schools*).
35. These students' perspectives are drawn from Smyth (2007), "Toward the Pedagogically Engaged School: Listening to Student Voice as a Positive Response to Disengagement and 'Dropping Out'?" (*International Handbook of Student Experiences in Elementary and Secondary Schools*). Smyth and Hattam (2004), *"Dropping Out," Drifting Off, Being Excluded: Becoming Somebody without School*.
36. These students' perspectives are drawn from Rudduck (2007), "Student Voice, Student Engagement, and School Reform" (*International Handbook of Student Experiences in Elementary and Secondary Schools*) and Rudduck and Flutter (2004), *How to Improve Your School*.
37. These students' perspectives are drawn from Madeleine Arnot, Donald McIntyre, David Pedder, and Diane Reay (2003), *Consultation in the Classroom: Developing Dialogue about Teaching and Learning*.
38. These students' perspectives are drawn from Jeffrey Shultz and Alison Cook-Sather (eds.) (2001), *In Our Own Words: Students' Perspectives on School*.
39. These students' perspectives are drawn from Beth C. Rubin and Elena M. Silva (eds.) (2003), *Critical Voices in School Reform: Students Living through Change*.

40. These students' perspectives are drawn from Denise Clark Pope (2001), *Doing School: How We Are Creating a Generation of Stressed Out, Materialistic, and Miseducated Students.*

41. These students' perspectives are drawn from Donetta J. Cothran, Pamela Hodges Kulinna, Deborah A. Garahhy (2003), "'This Is Kind of Giving the Secret Away': Students' Perspectives on Effective Classroom Management," *Teaching and Teacher Education* 19, 435–444.

42. Rudduck and McIntyre, 2007.

43. Lodge, 2005; Fielding, 2004; Silva, 2001.

44. Mitra, 2001, p. 92.

45. The researcher projects were conducted by MacBeath et al. (2003); Fielding and Bragg (2003); and Kane and Maw (2005). For a fuller discussion, see Rudduck and McIntyre, 2007, pp. 35–38.

46. Pollard, Thiessen, and Filer, 1997, p. 2.

47. Fine et al., 2007, pp. 805–806.

48. Silva, 2001, p. 98.

49. Weiler, 1991, p. 450.

50. Silva and Rubin, 2003, p. 2.

51. Spivak, 1988, quoted in Cruddas, 2001, p. 63; Raider-Roth, 2005.

52. Atweh and Burton, 1995; Fielding, 2004a and 2004b; Holdsworth, 2000, 1986; Lodge, 2005; Thomson and Gunter, 2005.

53. Fielding, 2004b, p. 200.

54. Fielding, 2004b, p. 201.

55. Cook-Sather, 2008, p. 477.

Part I

Students' Perspectives on Effective Classroom Practice

This section features the voices and perspectives of students. Many of the statements come from conversations among high school students who have participated in Teaching and Learning Together, the project based in my secondary general methods course, which I discuss in detail in Chapter 13. Since 1995, Teaching and Learning Together has put high school students in partnership with prospective teachers and positioned them as teacher educators: asking them, both in weekly meetings facilitated by a teacher at their school and in weekly e-mail exchanges with preservice teachers enrolled in my course, to talk about what works for them in terms of pedagogical style, classroom management, and other dimensions of classroom practice, what does not work, and why. Their statements are complemented by student statements drawn from ten other sources—texts in which researchers, teachers, and other authors have consulted students about their experiences of school.[1]

Taken together, these statements are a generally representative sampling of students' perspectives, but as indicated in the introduction to this book, they are not intended to describe or reflect all learners or their needs. While students' statements over the years that I have maintained Teaching and Learning Together have been strikingly consistent across grade level, assigned track in school, and even school itself, it might well be the case that other educators would find that some of these issues resonate more deeply than others for them and their students depending on such factors as age, specific populations, and world events. These students' statements reveal patterns and tendencies that I therefore encourage educators to explore in relation to their own students' experiences and perspectives.

In keeping with the premise of this book, I invited two students, Jessica Mitra Mausner and Jossi Fritz-Mauer, seniors at Haverford College when I began writing this book, to assume the primary responsibility for reading through all the data I had gathered—both published and unpublished—and for identifying, selecting, organizing, and framing the chapters and their subsections. They began by reading a variety of methods texts, looking for student voice and the way the texts framed students' input. They then read the transcripts of all meetings of high school students through Teaching and Learning Together, read the transcripts a second time, pulled out every quote from students, and coded them all, initially separating the students' words into meta-categories (e.g., classroom management, relationships). They then assigned different statements to different sections and then read other texts focused on student perspectives to see if their categories remained valid. Drawing on all these data, they read through, coded, and assigned quotes from both my data and the other ten sources to different chapters and sections. Jessica Mitra Mausner, Jossi Fritz-Mauer, and I met regularly to discuss issues, patterns, themes, and organizational questions, but I felt strongly that their perspectives as students should significantly influence the shape of this section of the book.

Each chapter in this part opens with and is punctuated by short framing statements written by Jessica, Jossi, and me. These sections are intended as frames to support the main text, which is composed of high school students' own words. Our goal in writing these was to orient readers to the issues addressed within the chapter, and in particular we highlight words that recur across student statements. We hope readers will pay special attention to these words, as they not only signal what matters most to students, they highlight meanings of terms that might have different associations for adults and for young people or among differently positioned young people.

Chapters 1 through 3 focus on some of the most basic practices upon which students feel teachers should focus: getting to know students, creating and maintaining a positive classroom environment, and designing engaging lessons. The final two chapters in this section (Chapters 4 and 5) focus on less tangible issues that students nonetheless feel are critical to—indeed, underlie—good teaching: respect and responsibility.

Each chapter concludes with a case study that focuses on the theme of the chapter and that draws on a preservice teacher's analysis of what he or she learned from participating in Teaching and Learning Together. Thus each chapter ends with a student's perspective—in this case a prospective teacher's perspective—on learning from the student's perspective. With these case studies we hope to illustrate the dynamic exchanges out of which many of these student perspectives emerged.

Note

1. See the Introduction for a complete list of these sources.

1

Knowing Students

with Jossi Fritz-Mauer and Jessica Mitra Mausner

You always learn in school. . . . But [what] you're going to remember is going to be all the relationships.

—Student[1]

Chapter Overview

Focus of this chapter: The importance of knowing students as individuals and as people with a range of both shared and different experiences
Discussed in this chapter:

- Personal connections
  - Equality
  - Relating as human beings
  - Flexibility
  - Recognizing individuals
- Learning styles
- Case study: Knowing students and their learning needs

When students argue that teachers need to know their students, they do so within the general frames of personal connections and learning styles. In other words, their comments tend to address their needs as social (not isolated) beings and as diverse (not uniform or monolithic) learners. Recognizing young people's multiple identities—student, nonstudent, and others—can help teachers more successfully meet the profound challenge to know their students.

Within the general frame of personal connections, students address issues of equality, relating as fellow humans, flexibility, and being recognized as individuals. When they experience these qualities in their relationships with teachers, students build their self-esteem, which is essential to their

23

engagement and success in school. For these students, caring equals high expectations and encouragement.

———————————

When we think of schools, we think of cinderblock hallways, classrooms full of rows or rings of desks, regulated curricula and hardbound textbooks, days divided by buzzers and bells. When we asked students to write about school, they rarely discussed these traditional features. Rather, their focus was on their relationships with the people who share and shape their schooling . . . Within the overarching theme of students' relationships with others:

- Students want to have more human and humane interactions in school. They are looking for care, respect, and support from their teachers, peers, and others who influence their educational experiences.
- Students want to be their whole selves; they do not want to be fragmented, categorized, compared to and judged against one another, treated differently or discriminated against.
- Students want school to be engaging. Countering the stereotype of apathetic, disaffected, or otherwise recalcitrant teenagers, these student authors describe the ways that they want their teachers to make school interesting and relevant and invite students to actively participate in their learning.[2]

Personal Connections

Students suggest that personal connections can only be developed by fostering actual relationships (not simply by understanding that humans are relational). Students' juxtaposition of "person" and "teacher," the notion of an "encourager," and the teacher's demonstration of an obvious desire "to help" are all indicators, from these students' perspectives, of teachers' efforts to build personal connections.

[What] you're going to remember is . . . [all] the different people you worked with and how to work with those people. You're going to carry that a lot longer than you are how to find the area of a triangle or something.[3]

If you have a relationship with your students, they're gonna trust you more and they're gonna respect you more and then they'll be nicer to you.[4]

It doesn't work when a teacher tries to force the connection or try too hard to relate to us. When they say, "I understand what you're going through," we know they don't.[5]

We've got some teachers we can walk up to, see them in the hallway, and start a little conversation with them. They tell us how we are doing in school, how we are doing in classes. I like that because it shows that the teachers really care about us—not just in the class but outside the class, too. They are leading me toward the right direction, making me want to go to class, and making me want to get those extra grades that I know I'm capable of.[6]

In my experience I found that a teacher who uses her position to be an encourager is most effective. 'Cause when a teacher goes out of her way to give you direction, or just to let you know that they really appreciate what you've been doing, even if you're not the highest student in your class, even if you're the lowest, if the teacher comes to you and says, "I really admire you for what you're doing, you're sticking with this," or even if you're doing great and the teacher comes to you and says, "This is great, I'm just really proud of you for what you've done." Just having that extra boost of encouragement makes the difference.[7]

A lot of what the teachers do is become our friends and mentors and that helps us a lot . . . just listening to you and knowing a little bit about you, which helps you feel comfortable with them . . . you know that the teachers respect you so you kind of assume that students will also, just for that. And it really helps to have teachers as friends, I guess.[8]

There are teachers who give you the work and say, "Do it" and then those who will show you how. If you feel a teacher really wants to help you like after school then I make time for them and it will be an amazing outcome.

One of my teachers really push kids to do work. She is the most caring teacher. She really want you to do work. Sometimes that make me mad but I still try to do the work. It nice to know you got a teacher who cares.[9]

Equality

High schoolers necessarily negotiate their identities as students with respect to their relationships with teachers. Although high school students have different perspectives on the nature of the student-teacher relationship, they all speak to forming closer connections that also allow them to be contributors both to the relationship and to their learning that is supported by that relationship (or not). They use terms like "friendship" and "communicate," regarding teachers who are "learning from" students as well as being "open to answering questions," and being on the "same" personal "level."

> If you don't have a friendship relationship with your teacher, or at least feel that you can talk to them or anything, then it's not going to be like a good learning environment because you're not able to communicate or think that you're friends with your teacher. I don't mean best friends. Like a friend you can talk to. Some people don't feel like they can do that, then that could hinder their learning.

> I want the teacher to be like a student, too. I mean, to not only be an instructor but also to be a peer and maybe a guide. You will spend most of your time with her and they can influence you.

> I like a teacher who is not doing all the teaching. They realize that they're learning from their students too.

> When the teacher can get on a more personal level with the student, then the student has more respect for the teacher and feels more comfortable in the teacher's presence.

Relating as Human Beings

Students recognize the multiple roles that teachers play and ask to be seen as similarly complex people. Personal connections are founded on the ability of both students and teachers to recognize the humanity in one another and relate through that humanity. The words "human" and "interest," as well as "respect," show up a good deal in these statements.

> A teacher should be human. I remember my calculus teacher and I went to her and I started getting very upset in her office, and she handed me a tissue and she was like, "I'm a human first and a teacher second." I think a lot of times teachers sort of need to remember that.

> [Teachers who were] easy to talk to . . . [would] actually sit down with me and help me with my work. . . . [They] talk to you politely when you are not in lessons . . . someone you can turn to when you're struggling with your work.[10]

> [Teachers] should put themselves on our level and realize that we are human and relate to us and realize our problems and things that we have to, all the things that are going on in our lives.

> I'm not really comfortable asking for help from the teacher. I don't know why. But it's because they don't listen to you. I just prefer to talk to my mum and dad and my brother.[11]

> I think the one thing that most teachers lack is showing interest in the kids, like asking . . . say you're in there for help or something, they can ask what you're doing outside of school if it comes up in conversation, those teachers tend to be the most well liked and popular, because you feel like they're relating to the kids. If more teachers did that, I think they would find a lot more respect from the students.

> Having a relationship with a teacher, having one-on-one talks and stuff about my academic records, just having the teachers be on top of things with myself.[12]

> Just [talk to students every day during] free time like a few minutes before class or something when [students] first meet the teacher or whenever you [teachers] talk to them. [As a teacher] you're just better off getting to know them a little bit, get them to like you.[13]

> I want to tell the teachers reading this that you are important too, or you could be. The psychology teacher who made me finally see that school learning could actually be meaningful and personally relevant, interesting. The writing teacher who forced shy girls like me to read aloud and bring our voices and our work into a room full of the most intimidating critics . . . other students. Or the language arts teacher who shed a real tear while reciting a poem about war. A *real* tear. One moment of realism and it sticks forever. Be vulnerable. Be real.[14]

Flexibility

Recognizing the impact of schooling on the lives of students is an important aspect of personal relationships. Getting to know students and remembering that they are human beings allow for nuanced flexibility in the classroom that reinforces personal connections and creates a positive learning environment. Words like "realistic" and "lenient" show up here alongside "approachable" and, once again, "human." These words appear to have different resonances for students than they might for teachers, who are responsible for challenging as well as empathizing with students.

> I think that people, like teachers, you need to realize that we could be having a really bad day, and just like the fact that maybe we could say, you know I am having a bad day today, could you not like pick on me or whatever, um, that's helpful. My French teacher did that last year and it was really good, if we were having a bad day we would just tell her, and she would lay off a little bit. And you knew that you couldn't do it every day, she was like, "I don't want you to do this all the time," and she was strict and everything. But the fact that she was open to that was really relieving.

> The other thing is, I think you should set realistic expectations, and should keep in mind our schedules and things like that, and not just think about what [you] want to get done in a certain amount of time, and think about what's realistic and how much time instead of cramming as many things as possible so we can get all the information because we're not going to get all the information if [you] did at once, it's not going to help at all.

> Teachers that have rules laid out that they're not so strict that they are constantly enforcing them on you and that they're so rigid that if you know, you make a mistake or something happens that they don't come down on you, but that you do understand that there are limitations that you have but they're not enforcing them constantly.

> I also think that if you have a lenient classroom then your students, if they don't understand something, are going to be willing to be coming to you and asking for help.

Recognizing Individuals

Students also ask teachers to recognize the impact of their out-of-school lives on their schooling. Teachers need to know "what their kids are going through" not only within classes but outside, in their social and family lives, because what happens outside the classroom affects what happens inside the classroom.

> It's really important the teachers know their students as individuals. You need to know, not to lower your expectations but to be realistic.[15]

> You need to provide the necessary information of that subject, but also to take into account the class's progress and pace and its capabilities. But also to move past that and get to know the students on an individual level, get to know their preferences, not to shape the curriculum around them but just to keep it in line and know what might work better and what might not work as well.

> A teacher should understand and be knowledgeable of what their kids are going through to some extent. Be aware of living situations or if someone's from a tough area, they should understand that this kid is walking by a crackhouse every day.

> You [the teacher] have to act like you really do care what's going on with the kid, not just in class, but outside of class.[16]

I think a lot of times teachers don't take into account like family, you know, like, they understand if like a family member dies but they don't really seem to understand when families are going through rough times, like, I don't know, economically or just anything like that. Teachers aren't that understanding of it, you know, and that sort of puts a, like it's a big problem for students who are struggling with things at home and then things at school aren't getting any easier, you know.

Sometimes a teacher don't understand what people go through. They need to have compassion. A teacher who can relate to students will know when something's going on with them.[17]

Learning Styles

Regarding the second aspect of knowing students—recognizing students as diverse learners and focusing on the person in an educational process—students emphasize the importance of discerning and responding to different learning styles. They suggest that understanding of students' diverse learning styles is a matter of recognizing each student as having unique strengths and needs that should be honored, not simply understanding in the abstract that everyone is different. Students speak not only about the reality of multiple learning styles but also to the difficulty of addressing different students' needs.

Well, I know there's a whole issue about how people learn different ways so maybe the teacher should get a variety of different evaluations, such as . . . sometimes you test and other times you give projects and then maybe have one-on-one meetings where you can discuss with students what's been going on in class. I think that's the best way to meet your students' needs . . . [because] people learn differently and express themselves differently, so that's the best way of knowing what you've learned.

Everyone has their own learning needs and in the true ideology of education everyone would get those needs addressed. It sort of saddens me that or I feel guilty or anxious about that fact and I think that is one of the major problems of this century, what kids to focus on and what kids to let alone.

The new [subject] teacher, she doesn't respect the way we learn [because] some of us learn at a slower pace than others and she has no respect for the slower ones.[18]

Try and use different teaching techniques so that students with different learning styles can understand what's going on.

In history the first day my teacher passed out a paper with a couple of questions about how you learn—like: what type of issues do you have with history, do you like it? That was the first time a teacher seemed to actually care about how a student learns, so she could meet their needs. It made me think about how I learn—I never thought about it before, because I'd never been asked.[19]

I have teachers this year, two teachers this year, that just teach the same way and it doesn't work for some people in the class, and one teacher especially when somebody doesn't understand something, she just assumes they were slacking off or something so she'll call their house and be like, "Oh, your son or daughter wasn't doing this," but it doesn't work. She only teaches one way, and it doesn't work for everybody. You have to realize that you're teaching a variety of people, and each person learns differently, some people learn visually, some people learn by repeating stuff, some people—it's just different in how a person teaches, and that's why a teacher should try as much as possible to teach in different ways if possible.

Case Study: Knowing Students and Their Learning Needs

A history major at Bryn Mawr College, Justine, a European American female, maintained a partnership with Arthur, a European American male assigned to the regular track in the eleventh grade of his school.[20] After causing her significant frustration, Justine's exchange with Arthur taught her about the importance of human connections and different learning styles.

Early on in the partnership, Justine struggled with how to communicate with Arthur about educational issues. She explains:

> When I first undertook the dialogue project with Arthur . . . I expected that I would share ideas about education with a person representing those whom I would eventually be teaching. However, his introductory letter listed the types of music he liked, some career possibilities, his after-school job. He did not mention any specific thoughts about education. By the third week, I realized that Arthur was not terribly interested in educational issues, at least not as I had presented them.

Like any enthusiastic teacher who expects her students to engage with the subject matter right away, Justine was disappointed to learn that Arthur did not appear to share her enthusiasm for the topic at hand. Her initial response was to "give up" on what she had hoped to get out of the project: a sophisticated dialogue about how to be a good teacher. So, instead of focusing on issues clearly connected to pedagogy, Justine "strayed from the texts and issues we were covering in 'Curriculum and Pedagogy' and discussed instead a wide range of topics based primarily on interests or thoughts that seemed pertinent at the time."

As their correspondence continued, Justine found that it was effective to share stories from her own experience as a way to invite Arthur to address important aspects of his educational experience. As she put it, "it was through examples from my personal life that I asked him about such topics as motivation, block scheduling, career choices, community service, and school policies regarding dress codes." Justine shared the same perspective in one discussion in Curriculum and Pedagogy: "My partner wrote a lot [this week because] he responded to a situation I gave him with my sister. I used

continues

Case Study Continued

that as a way in, saying, 'This happened to my sister. What do you think of this?' And he said, 'Oh, wow, that happened to me too.'" Justine found she could elicit responses from Arthur that "embedded his opinion within situations he had experienced or witnessed." As she put it: "His interests and needs came not through a discussion of Freire's pedagogy, but instead from his own personal experience."

While Justine initially felt that she would be learning directly from Arthur—from what he wrote and said—she found that she learned more from her interactions with him. She learned, in short, about the importance of building a more human relationship with Arthur. Reflecting on this realization at the end of the semester, Justine wrote: "I remained mildly frustrated until I realized that I was expecting [Arthur] to speak in my language. Amid our discussions of student voice and its value, I had neglected to realize that his learning, his method of articulation, was through experience and concrete examples. I had sought to give him voice while failing to hear the sound of his individual words." Justine connected this insight into her interactions with Arthur to her thinking about different learning styles and modes of expression. About the latter, she wrote:

> Although many students may be capable of thinking abstractly, they may not have practice doing so or be comfortable with it. Therefore, if I come into a classroom assuming they can, I may immediately alienate them. I must instead associate concrete examples with what I am teaching. Arthur offered quite a few insights, drawing on his own experience and projecting accompanying conclusions to global significance. Nonetheless, I failed to recognize them because I viewed them only as narratives of experience.

Justine realized that she could learn about Arthur's interests and needs not "through a discussion of Freire's pedagogy, but instead from his own personal experience," and, further, that by constructing "narratives of experience" Arthur might well be engaging in the kind of learning that is most effective for him. She thus gained important insights not only into Arthur's needs and preferences as a student but also into some of her own assumptions as a teacher and the importance of being aware of them.

Notes

1. Quoted in Rubin, 2003, p. 31.
2. Cook-Sather and Shultz, 2001, pp. 1, 3–4.
3. Rubin and Silva, 2003, p. 31.
4. Cothran et al., 2003, p. 439.
5. Cushman, 2003, p. 1.

6. Sanon et al., 2001, in Shultz and Cook-Sather, 2001, p. 82.

7. As I mentioned in the Introduction, quotations from my data do not carry an additional reference to source information.

8. Keiser and Stein, 2003, in Rubin and Silva, 2003, p. 183.

9. Wilson and Corbett, 2007, p. 289.

10. Smyth and Hattam, 2004, p. 180.

11. Arnot et al., 2004, p. 70.

12. Wing, 2003, in Rubin and Silva, 2003, p. 159.

13. Cothran et al., 2003, p. 439.

14. Strucker et al. 2001, quoted in Shultz and Cook-Sather, 2001, p. 155.

15. Cushman, 2003, p. 97.

16. Cothran et al., 2003, p. 439.

17. Wilson and Corbett, 2007, p. 292.

18. Arnot et al., 2004, p. 56.

19. Cushman, 2003, p. 5.

20. Drawn from the analysis paper that a prospective teacher enrolled in my methods seminar, Curriculum and Pedagogy, wrote as part of Teaching and Learning Together.

2

Creating and Maintaining a Positive Classroom Environment

with Jossi Fritz-Mauer and Jessica Mitra Mausner

If I'm not comfortable, then I'm not learning.
—Student

Chapter Overview

Focus of this chapter: The importance of creating and maintaining a positive classroom environment based on comfort, respect, and challenge
   Discussed in this chapter:

- Learning environment
  - Comfort
  - Respect
- Classroom practices
  - Atmosphere
  - Rules and discipline
  - Grading
  - Homework
  - Assessment
- Case study: Reflections on developing a classroom management style

Chapter 1 focused on relationships between students and teachers and the personal connections and attention to learning styles that students hope teachers develop with them. This chapter addresses the classroom environment, which is determined both by the establishment of those relationships and how they serve as contexts within which students learn subject matter. Classrooms, then, are places for both learning to relate to others and learning the curriculum. Students are acutely aware of the interaction of these two realms of learning within the classroom, as is apparent in advice to teachers.

Students identify two components of the positive classroom: learning environment and classroom practices. How teachers set up and maintain the classroom affects the comfort level of the students and by extension the quality of learning. Students ask to be treated as fellow humans, but they also ask teachers to affirm their student identities. The intertwining of multiple identities is played out in the descriptions and suggestions students offer.

Learning Environment

For quality teaching and learning, a balance is required in the classroom—a balance between positive social relationships, control and order with a sense of purpose, and wide ranging teaching skills for presenting, explaining and delivering learning activities.

—Morgan and Morris, 1999, p. 136

When discussing the learning environment, students emphasize how they feel in the classroom and how this affects their success. Their comments are often made in reference to their personal experiences, but it would be a mistake to focus only on the content of their words; instead, we need to acknowledge the feelings behind the words, which inform everything students experience within a classroom. Their frustrations and recommendations demonstrate a common desire to feel comfortable as they learn. In the creation of a positive classroom environment, students see comfort and respect as especially important.

Comfort

Students speak about how teachers affect the tone of the classroom. They frequently use words like "easygoing," "approachable," "relaxed," "understanding," and "lenient."

> When teachers are easygoing and approachable, you really feel like if there was something going on you could talk to them and they would understand what you are going through. I think that makes for a much more relaxing environment.

> I think it's important for students to feel comfortable with their teacher because if they can't get comfortable with their teacher, then they often times won't be able to feel comfortable asking questions, and it'll kind of hamper their learning experience. I think it's important for a teacher to set boundaries and guidelines, so that if a student steps out of line, they know they're stepping out of line, and

they know that they'll face repercussions. But at the same time don't make those boundaries too close so that it causes the students discomfort.

I should be able to walk into a classroom and feel comfortable and not be like, when's the bell gonna ring, not be counting the minutes—seriously, I do that in two of my classes: I sit there and count the minutes until the bell rings, because I just hate the classes, it's just like, I'm not comfortable in the classroom.

I think that the most effective way a teacher can teach is put their mind in the frame of the learner; rather than teaching like they're experts, teach like they don't know what they're doing either. That way they can get your questions, [because] usually they really won't.

The teachers are real at ease. They take the time, you know, go step by step. We learn it more. It seems like they got the time to explain it all. We don't have to leave anyone behind.[1]

There's not really discussion happening [in the class], because you don't feel comfortable, like, actually discussing things.[2]

I also think that if you have a lenient classroom then your students, if they don't understand something, are going to be willing to be coming to you and ask for help.

Respect

When speaking about all aspects of their schooling, students consistently ask to be treated with respect, which is manifest in different ways. In this section, they emphasize the feel of the classroom. Instead of "giving us a perception that we are below" the teacher, or acting "like we are nothing," students want to communicate "with words from the soul and mind connected to the heart."

I have a teacher that treats us all like five year olds, and that really doesn't help at all, you know, just like, talking to us like we're not on the same level as the teacher, which I mean, we're not exactly, but we're not five years old, so we don't really need that. It's almost like, it's not like she's just giving us an attitude, but she's giving us a perception that we're below her and that we don't know what we're doing when that's not necessarily true. So knowing your age group, knowing what age or like what maturity level the students are on, is a big part of managing the students and keeping a good atmosphere.

People say to respect your elders but they should respect us also. Teachers, they just act like we're nothing. They talk to us any kind of way and if we have something to say back, we're wrong.[3]

If you respond to someone's question with "You don't know that?" it doesn't really make you feel too good about asking questions, does it?

You can't have good communication without respect. If I don't respect you we can communicate. But what I am saying would not be what I am honestly thinking because I do not respect you. So respect and communication go together.[4]

If you think that a teacher doesn't like you, or is disrespecting you in a way, you're going to start disrespecting him or her.[5]

Reach me with more than words from textbooks—but words from the soul and the mind connected to the heart. What got you to teach me? Wasn't it to reach me? . . . Relate to me, debate with me, respect me. Stop neglecting me.[6]

Respect them [students] so they can respect you back.[7]

Classroom Practices

The classroom practices section continues the general discussion about relationships in the classroom while also focusing on descriptions of specific practices and student recommendations. This is not at all to downplay the significance of relationships, but to show how both components—relationships and specific practices—contribute to the overall positive classroom. Teachers are frequently concerned with rules and discipline, grading, homework, and assessment. Students' comments show the major role that these topics play in their school lives.

Atmosphere

Students provide various examples of positive classroom atmosphere. The variety in these comments speaks to the multifaceted nature of the classroom and reinforces the importance of getting to know students and their learning preferences. Students point out that particular modes of working, such as collaboration, create an atmosphere conducive to learning, and when teachers "have a set plan for the day," have "tools and resources available in the classroom," and invite students actively to engage with those, students "gain responsibility, gain trust, and gain independence."

> Being comfortable with people in your class is really important. That's one of the reasons that I'm into collaboration is because I feel more comfortable speaking in a circle when I am with the people that I am comfortable with. So I think that helps, and also, really small things, like the way the desks are arranged, I know it sounds kind of trivial, but [rows] seem kinda really formal and rigid, but if you're in a circle or all together, I think that that provides a more easygoing, positive environment for kids to learn in.

> It makes a big difference when teachers have a set plan for the day, like, I appreciate the fact that some of my teachers will take notes and then during class refer back to those notes as to where we're supposed to be, what we're supposed to be accomplishing, examples, you know, I think that shows that they've spent a lot of time thinking about what we're going to be learning in our education.

> It helps when a teacher is able to, like at the beginning of the class, you don't walk into class and then the teacher starts lecturing, but where the teacher actually kind of talks to you for about ten minutes of the class, then you do your work that you need to do for the day, do whatever you need to, and it's just like a relaxed atmosphere.

I think another thing about maintaining a good learning environment, and maintaining the students' attention, is having more tools and resources available in the classroom.

When possible, give us the choice to read or not, and our choice is going to benefit us. I know some kids who don't care and aren't going to read it, and are just going to go out and hope they don't have a quiz on it. But then, there are other kids who're going to be like, "Alright, she's given me some freedom, why don't I take this freedom and prove to her that I'm going to use it to benefit myself?" Kids say this to parents all the time: "Give me the room and you'll see what I do with it." That's how you gain responsibility, gain trust and gain independence. You do it with guidelines.

I think sometimes it helps if you can choose where you sit, and if, I mean, people say that it's not going to work out because, yeah, people are going to sit with their friends, and that might not work, but then like, we'll try it first, and then if it doesn't work, you can always move people.

Rules and Discipline

Students have varied opinions about rules and discipline. Some believe teachers are solely responsible for both, and others view them as a give-and-take process. Students use words like "control," "balance," "boundaries," "authority," "realistic," and again "comfort" to describe these practices.

Schools don't focus on your mental capability, they just focus on your behavior.[8]

I think [discipline] is part the student's responsibility and part the teacher's responsibility. . . . You need to be comfortable. To help decide the comfort level . . . they should make the rules together.

I think maybe if you talk with the students—*with* them I mean—like, "If someone talks out in class, what are we going to do?" then they won't want to break their own rules.

Don't make false threats because nobody will ever trust you.[9]

To a certain extent you have to have a personality that students respond to. But that doesn't mean you have to be our best friend, because that will cause our education to suffer. I hate to admit it, but respect and authority are part of the job. Kids expect adults to give us directions and boundaries, but it's a balance.[10]

This is kind of giving the secret away, but you've gotta lay down the rules on the very first day. . . . Don't let us break the rules and then try the rules later 'cause no one will pay attention.[11]

If they don't keep after you, you'll slide and never do the work. You just won't learn nothing if they don't stay on you.[12]

If you're one of these goody goodies getting straight A's and stuff you can pretty much wear what you want, but if you're one of these people that tries to stand out a bit and you wear the slightest thing wrong, that's it, "Go to the detention," "Go and get expelled" and stuff. I mean I think they've taken it too far to a point where you're not allowed to learn any more, you're there to be disciplined, you're there for the teachers to make themselves look good.[13]

I think [teachers] have to make it known that they are in control, and that they have the last word in everything. And they have to make sure that the students understand that, like, they have to be somewhat disciplined, and that they have to follow the rules. But then they also should realize that, they should put themselves on our level and realize that we are human and relate to us and realize our problems and things that we have to, all the things that are going on in our lives, so it's definitely a balance between those.

Grading

Students speak both about specific grading practices they have experienced and about the impact of grading on their learning. Although grades are largely an evaluation of an individual, the students' comments express an understanding of grading's link to grouping, ranking, and labeling students and how these are read by different audiences (peers, parents, college admissions officers, etc.). Students are at different places in their thinking about what grades mean, how grading is helpful or relevant to them. Words like "learning" and "progress" are juxtaposed with "pressure," "achieving," "succeed," "overloading," and "money," showing the complexity of the interactions among these and around grading as a practice.

I think it would be so much easier if the teacher confronted the class about this before. . . . I mean at the beginning of the year have the teachers present themselves and for the first marking period they give you a [handout] about this is what I'm gonna grade on.

Last year in Ms. M's class, for grading, tiny bits of homework were necessary for a good grade but I got a lot out of the class because it gave me the chance to do a lot of writing. So it was a de-emphasis of grades and just more active learning. She would assess you just by seeing how your progress came along and making sure that you were at least making an attempt of improving your writing.

Like, if I turned in something, if I wasn't here, you know, and I like turned something in late, she'll still accept it and give me extra, you know, just a little bit of points to help me out. You know? I mean, most teachers wouldn't do that. You know, "If it's late, I—I won't take it," you know.[14]

That's where this argument of grades vs. learning comes in because if you're someone who knows everything, does all the tests and you want the grades then you do the homework because it really would be simple for you if you know it that well. So that's where the grade and learning comes in. You want the grade, you do the homework. If you don't want the grade, but you just want the learning, you have the learning, and the grade doesn't matter to you so you take the B or the C or whatever. If you wanted that A really badly you could go ahead and do your homework and then you can get the A.

I was really sick of this school because of all the pressure, and I mean you get a couple of letters home saying "Oh, congratulations, you're a 4.0 student blah, blah, blah. . . ." And then that just got me stuck on the whole achieving process.[15]

If I know there's no chance I'm going to get graded for it, I'm not going to do it.

I think that before talking about grades, we should make sure that we know whether grades are being given to evaluate how much you know, the knowledge of that one person, against opening doorways for your future.

You feel like oh if you don't get good grades, you won't go to college and all this bad stuff will happen to you—you're bad, you're stupid, that type of stuff. It just feels like if you don't get the good grades then you won't succeed in society. And . . . being a perfectionist, I could not allow myself to get anything lower than A's, 'cause I knew I was an A potential person. . . . I just, I was always like oh I got to get an A, I have to get an A on this test, have to do all my homework, have to do everything, and I just got so overloaded.[16]

People study to get the grade they want, not the education.

People don't go to school to learn. They go to get good grades, which brings them to college, which brings them the high-paying job, which brings them to happiness, so they think. But basically, grades is where it's at.[17]

Most people don't think this is at all feasible, but I don't think we should have grades at all, because I think that they create boundaries between students and teachers; the teachers have this power, they have grades. And grades determine what you get on your report card, what your parents do to you for what you get on your report card, whether or not you get a diploma and are ready to go on after that, and whether you graduate at all.

Homework

The connection between grades and homework becomes apparent in the students' comments. They ask for homework to link to their learning in the classroom, using words like "boring" when it doesn't and "interesting" and "meaningful" when it does. They speak about and question its purpose and necessity, some suggesting that if it is well conceptualized it can help them learn, and others feeling that it does not contribute to their learning. The bottom line is that homework needs to be compelling and meaningful enough to warrant doing.

For homework, whether you get credit or not, I think that if you don't have credit there's no point in anyone doing it. If you're giving homework for a reason, obviously for kids to learn and try and do stuff on their own.

Well, I think that homework is very meaningful. I think that it helps to boost your grade a lot of times in some difficult classes.

This year I've been doing my work a lot more because it's so much stricter and it's like it actually matters a little bit more than it did last year.[18]

I think that it is a good idea to give homework, but homework every night that's pretty much the same stuff is boring, and nobody wants to do it. And you're going to find that a lot less people will do it consistently. But, if you really change it up and give them creative assignments rather than just worksheet, worksheet,

worksheet, if you throw in a few projects, not really hard ones, or you just don't give it to them every night, and just say, due tomorrow, due tomorrow, due tomorrow. Or you can say, Here's all your assignments for the week, you can turn them in whenever you want, this week. I've never actually had a teacher do that exactly but I've had a similar situation and I think that would be a good idea.

Homework, if it's given right, can help you learn more. But, depending on the class, it's not always necessary.[19]

I think that in a number of classes homework really doesn't do anything for the way that students learn. . . . It's got to be something that actually is like . . . it's got to be something interesting, something theoretical or that students want to learn about.

In math and science classes I really need homework because sometimes in class we're going so fast that I'm not really comprehending, I'm just copying down notes. So that my grade homework is a chance to sit down and really understand it and review the notes while I'm doing homework. But, I don't think that teachers should be obligated to check it every day because there are some kids who understand during class and they don't really need to do it . . . so I feel like unless it's a really big assignment, they don't need to check it every day.

I think my most effective teacher that I've had in high school is my history teacher last year, 'cause he, even though it was an honors class and it's supposed to be hard and you're supposed to be challenged and everything, but I actually felt like I was learning something, and the homework I was doing, it wasn't useless homework, it wasn't just a worksheet just because you're supposed to have homework, it was, like, work, like, you would do the work, you would talk about it in class, and you would understand it, honestly. After this year looking back on it, I appreciate the way the teacher taught because it was like, everything was useful, he didn't give useless homework. And so teachers should teach like that: make sure everything you do is useful and pertains to the subject.

Also, they should make sure it [homework] has a purpose and that it's meaningful because a lot of times teachers will just assign homework because they feel it's necessary to, like, to fill up the spot in your day that you're allotted for this subject, but, and it's really only a waste of time, so they should make sure there's a purpose to the homework that you're doing.

Assessment

There is a natural link among grading, homework, and assessment. Students recognize this, and also make connections between assessment and its effect on other classroom practices as well as its effect on their overall experience of their education. Words and phrases such as "game," "studying to pass," "effort," "subjective," and "individuality" are used by students to signal the complex relationship between assessment practices, students' interpretations of and interactions with those, and the match between assessment and learning. Also present are students' expressions of how they experience all of these things—words and phrases like "hurt" and "puts me down" or, in contrast, "learn to enjoy" reflect the emotional power of assessment.

I think teachers should give more practice tests so that students sort of see what the teacher's getting at, like an exact model of what to expect . . . yeah, review packet, very important.

I don't think it's wise to give all these practice tests and stuff because it turns the education system into almost a game. Like, you know, you have to find out what the teacher wants, and then you study to find out and pass those teachers' tests, and it's all just about studying to pass instead of studying to learn.

I hurt when I get a bad grade! You feel like you're doing all that hard work for nothing. Then you don't want to work more, if you're just going to get bad grades. Whenever my grades get low I feel like dropping out of school.[20]

I understand it as much as everybody understands it, but the point, the thing is, why, why did I get a B, you know, and this person got an A if we both know the same material and it's my fault that, that I could blank out on a test and do so poorly? . . . When it comes to the test, it's like oh my God I just don't, you know, I just forget. . . . it just puts me down more.[21]

He gave us a study guide and you could use the paper notes. But the stuff that he told us to study didn't seem like none of it was on the test. I was like "Oh well." [cynical and resigned] [I used] his notes and I did the study stuff he told me to do, but I couldn't deal with it.[22]

I think by having a student tell you what they learned instead of having the teacher test what the student should have learned, it allows for more effective assessment.

I really want to learn, but I want to show that I have learned, not just listen all the time. Like show that I've learned by doing things myself.[23]

You want to know that when you work hard it will be rewarded or acknowledged. If teachers don't pay enough attention to know when a student has really put in some extra effort, then I don't think that students will try hard—because what difference does it make.[24]

If you have a nonstandard kind of test, and you do it on an individual basis. You say to every student, find a way to show me you understand what we've been teaching, and it's subjective.

The biggest problem is the lack of individuality. They've got a middle ground and if you don't fit into that, then the high school is going to fail you. . . . If you're not capable of sitting there with a pad and a pen and copying and doing what you've been told, then you're not, in their eyes, you're not learning. . . . you're going to fail.[25]

Well, I think as far as getting the students interested, I think that's one of the most important roles that teachers play. Not just actually doing the teaching of the information, but making the students see why that information is important and why they should bother to learn it in the first place. And even, sometimes go as far as having the students learn to enjoy, understanding learning that information. And, I think as for the set curricula, often it comes from the need to standardize a test. You have to be able to see what the students actually know, and if you have those varied curricula that would almost negate the test.

Case Study: Reflections on Developing a Classroom Management Style

Arlene, a European American female and a mathematics major, struggled with the various, and sometimes contradictory, student perspectives she heard through Teaching and Learning Together.[26] In reflecting on what she heard, she brought those perspectives into dialogue:

> The teacher needs to be strict, yet not strict enough to put a bad taste in the students' mouths where it would turn them off from liking the teacher. . . . The teacher needs to be liked by the class, the best teachers are ones who can be viewed as "friends" outside of class, but as superiors within the classroom or else they will lose the class. Another student says: "no rules = procrastination, but all rules = rule breakers."

In response to the latter student's formula, Arlene wrote:

> We discussed how students do need some structure and rules to create a healthy and safe learning environment. However, if a teacher creates too much structure or discipline, students will rebel or feel trapped or restricted. Similarly, if a teacher does not clearly state her rules, students will always be testing [her] and the class will lose structure. [One student] said the "touchy part" for the teacher "is finding that medium zone where you can have enough structure to build on but not so much that you become a tyrant."

Figuring out how to "find that medium zone" is further complicated by the fact that students' desire for certain kinds of strictness comes as a surprise. Arlene quoted Dave, her high school student partner in Teaching and Learning Together: "I believe that [teachers] should set down the rules they want, and under no circumstances make any exceptions to them. If you say that this will not happen in the class, and if it does, you come down and come down hard because if you make idle threats then the students aren't going to respect you." Reflecting on this statement, Arlene wrote: "It is surprising to me that a student would actually value a teacher coming down hard on rules being broken. In my mind, the 'nice' teacher is the one who is lenient and relaxed, but what Dave tells me is revealing: the 'nice' teacher isn't necessarily the teacher that is most respected; it's the teacher who does what she says she'll do that will earn the student's respect."

Prompted by the perspective of the particular student with whom she corresponded to rethink her assumptions about classroom management, Arlene found support for her student partner's perspective elsewhere:

continues

Case Study Continued

Dave is not alone in his desire for a teacher who is strict. In *Listening to Urban Kids*, an anonymous student talks about the kinds of teachers s/he prefers: "I like the ones that don't allow excuses. It's my turn to get an education. I need to have someone to tell me when I'm tired and don't feel like doing the work, that I should do it anyway."[27]

Arlene recognized also that she is not alone in her misperception. She mused: "There is a common misconception that if students had the choice, they would choose a teacher who didn't force them to do anything—someone who allowed them to be as motivated or wild as they wanted. Several students in *Listening to Urban Kids* claim to prefer some form of strictness or perseverance in their teachers' approaches to teaching, and clearly so does Dave." Listening to these various student voices helped Arlene rethink her assumptions about classroom management and, in turn, her plans for practice.

Anticipating her student teaching experience, Arlene wrote:

When I imagine myself as a teacher trying to enforce rules, I worry that I will be seen as mean, and it makes me hesitate to be too much of an enforcer. Then I remember that students' liking me right away is not as important as students' learning to respect me and to learn effectively in my classes. I also remember that having rules doesn't have to mean having a list of thirty unbendable rules, but maybe three to five rules that remain firm. Furthermore, some rules can be broken in life, and I should be sympathetic to unique circumstances that require a rule to bend, but when such outstanding circumstances are missing, I must be stern in my rules or I can't hope to maintain a productive learning space. No cheating means no cheating ever. No disrespecting anyone in the classroom means calling someone "gay" or some other common pejorative name is strictly prohibited. I might seem harsh at first to students, but with their respect, with time, will also hopefully come their affection. Some of my favorite teachers growing up were also some of the hardest and strictest—not because they were mean (they weren't), but because they took their jobs and their students seriously and expected us to take our studies and classroom experience seriously as well. Dave's words encourage me to worry less about enforcing rules as a teacher.

Notes

1. Wilson and Corbett, 2007, p. 291.
2. Rodriguez, 2003, in Rubin and Silva, 2003, p. 59.
3. Cothran et al., 2003, p. 440.
4. Sanon et al., 2001, in Shultz and Cook-Sather, 2001, p. 86.
5. Sanon et al., 2001, p. 87.
6. Strucker et al., 2001, p. 162.
7. Cothran et al., 2003, p. 440.
8. Smyth and Hattam, 2004, pp. 63–64.

9. Cothran et al., 2003, p. 438.
10. Cushman, 2003, p. 19.
11. Cothran et al., 2003, p. 437.
12. Wilson and Corbett, 2007, p. 288.
13. Smyth and Hattam, 2004, p. 7.
14. Horn, 2003, in Rubin and Silva, p. 99.
15. Pope, 2003, p. 115.
16. Pope, 2003, pp. 82–83.
17. Smyth and Hattam, 2004, p. 6.
18. Rubin, 2003, in Rubin and Silva, p. 194.
19. Cushman, 2003, p. 113.
20. Cushman, 2003, p. 78.
21. Pope, 2003, p. 130.
22. Rubin, 2003, in Rubin and Silva, p. 39.
23. Arnot et al., 2004, p. 18.
24. Cushman, 2003, p. 80.
25. Smyth, 2007, p. 649.
26. Drawn from the analysis paper that a prospective teacher enrolled in my methods seminar, Curriculum and Pedagogy, wrote as part of Teaching and Learning Together.
27. Wilson and Corbett, 2001, p. 71.

3

Designing
Engaging Lessons

*with Jossi Fritz-Mauer
and Jessica Mitra Mausner*

We were talking about teachers being enthusiastic, because it's so obvious when a teacher walks in and they don't want to be there . . . and that just starts it off and you don't want to be there.

—Student

[Education is] that reconstruction or reorganization of experience which adds to the meaning of experience, and which increases [one's] ability to direct the course of subsequent experience.

—Dewey, 1916, p. 76

Chapter Overview

Focus of this chapter: The importance of designing lessons that are engaging and meaningful to students

Discussed in this chapter:

- Enthusiasm
- Variety in components of a lesson
- Pedagogical styles
  - Making lectures engaging
  - Hands-on activities
  - Peer instruction
  - Discussion
  - Student choice

- Relevance
  - Relevance to themselves as individuals
  - Relevance to life beyond school
- Case study: Responding to students' diverse learning needs

Chapters 1 and 2 focused on the relationships that students feel should underlie classroom interactions and the kind of environment and practices that build on those relationships and facilitate learning. In this chapter, student comments focus on designing engaging lessons. Within this larger frame, they discuss the importance of teachers feeling and demonstrating enthusiasm for what they are teaching, having variety in components of a lesson, using a range of pedagogical styles, and making their lessons relevant to students.

Enthusiasm

As in the previous chapters, an essential underlying theme here is teachers' engagement with and enthusiasm about what they are doing. Whereas in the first chapters students focused on students as people, here students emphasize the subject matter. Terms and phrases such as "fun," "like what they are teaching," and "enthusiastic" show that students are attuned to the emotional engagement of their teachers with the subject matter.

If they seem like they're having fun, they seem like they love what they do.

You gotta have fun with your lessons. I think that if you have a little fun with your lessons you will get a lot of respect from it and people will pay attention and give you the full attention.[1]

I think the teacher should really like what they're teaching, and if they don't like something in the curriculum, a student can sense that.

I think it's important for the students to know that the teacher wants to be there, and enjoys teaching the students as much as the students should enjoy learning.

If you're enthusiastic about what you're teaching, the kids are going to be more inclined to be enthusiastic too.

A teacher's job is not just to teach but they should inspire their students to learn.

Variety in Components of a Lesson

Students emphasize the importance of differentiation, engaging presentation, and just basically changing things up in a regular way. They recognize that "everyone learns differently" and, therefore, that teachers need to teach to those differences.

Sticking 30 people in a class . . . and then try[ing] to teach them all the same way . . . when everyone learns differently . . . that's just not fair.[2]

I've been in classes where the information the teacher's giving might be perfectly correct but it's so hard to pay attention, it's just the same, because it's a lecture, every day the same kind of thing. You need some variety; it makes it a little more interesting.

I like the different things that she did in class. Like, with a stick [pointer] and with doing it on the board and we were telling her and so it's just lots of different ways of showing you and trying to get it across. . . . So some people might understand when she shows us with the pole [pointer] and other people might not get that at all. And other people might understand it when she does it on the board so it's for the whole class to make sure that everyone understands.[3]

I think in some subjects there's a lot of variety and you can do a lot of different things and it's really good and the teaching is very . . . very . . . a high standard. But with others, it's terrible. . . . It's the same thing every lesson and you just want to, like, kill someone and it's just . . . God! . . . yeah, it's awful.[4]

Last year in one of my classes, the teacher would write out handouts for us, we would use the overhead, we would listen to tapes, we would watch videos, we would make up our own skits, it was varied, and you actually walked into the classroom and felt comfortable, you know, and you're ready to learn, and this year it's like a higher level class, this year it's sit in your desk, don't move, I'm standing up here, you learn, if you don't learn, I'm gonna call your parents, you know? It's like, it's one thing . . . the teacher just gets out sheets, there's no listening, there's no video, and if there's listening, she does it, and that's it.

A lot of teachers just focus on the chalk board, but having a chalkboard, and a projector, and a TV with a VCR, and a computer so that you can show movies and kids do occasionally write on the blackboards sometimes, so it's not just every day, write on the blackboard, you know, us taking notes, variety.

Pedagogical Styles

Just as students emphasize the importance of teachers recognizing various learning styles among their students, students also emphasize the importance of teachers employing a range of pedagogical styles to address those different learning styles. Specific issues they identify include making lectures engaging, using hands-on activities, peer instruction, discussion, and affording students choices. Across this variety, students identify not only what works for them but also why.

Making Lectures Engaging

Students point out what can be problematic in lecturing and also what works well for them. Affirming the place of lecture among the array of pedagogical approaches a teacher takes, students also point to the benefits of role-playing, talking as a group, and worksheets. These efforts and others, such as maintaining "eye contact," can help students "be active" and not "lose concentration."

> She rambles on a bit and that makes us lose concentration. . . . She talks and talks and talks and talks and she doesn't stop. And that goes on for ages. We just get so bored that we lose concentration and start talking to our friends.[5]

> Like Maths. Instead of teaching the class he would actually, like, write up on the board and as he was writing he would be talking to the board and teaching the board and we'd be sitting there like, yeah okay, and you'll go through it and the next thing you know you're lost and . . . too late, he keeps going so you just, oh. So that's when you start talking to your friends because he's actually like talking to the board. He's got no eye contact with you so you just lose him and then if you don't understand a problem you put your hand up and he can't see you so he just keeps going so you miss that part, miss that part, you just give up. You just don't worry about it.[6]

> Students do not like to sit in the class, get lectured throughout the whole class. Kids want to be active in class. Kids like to talk. Kids don't like it when the teacher says, "Be quiet. I'm talking to the whole class."[7]

> Teachers can use reenactments and role-playing to bring the material to life and to help the students get into the material.

> Small groups should discuss what they already know about a subject and then share with the class. This is followed by a lecture and group discussion. It is also good to have a review game, notes, and dittos. Class should end by going over the worksheets. (Worksheets are good because you can't "discuss" certain topics, and they allow for individual work.)

Hands-on Activities

Students point out that it is often very difficult to learn something simply by listening to their teachers talk about it, which can lead to their feeling "totally lost." They need, instead, hands-on opportunities to engage with the material.

> I remember in biology. We were working on atoms. I was totally lost in that class. Then the teacher pulled out these little things, like tinker toys, and told us how they fused together, and stuff like that. And all of a sudden, I was like all right, now I'm understanding it.[8]

> Use computers and/or hands on activities.

Peer Instruction

Many students find that they can learn as well or better from a peer—someone "on [their] level"—than from a teacher. They encourage teachers to create opportunities for such peer-to-peer interaction.

I learn a lot better when a person on my level learns something and then teaches it to me as opposed to the teacher who does everything.

Sometimes a student can explain it better to another student.[9]

If there's a problem, somebody can go up and, if they know how to do it, they can explain it. Sometimes you might not get the way the teacher does it. If the teacher understands that and doesn't mind if somebody else might be able to explain it better, letting anyone who can explain it best just kinda go up and do it.

Discussion

Not only do students want to engage interactively in activities, they also want to talk to one another and the teacher about the subject. They suggest that students need opportunities to share with one another how they feel about what they are studying, "how it affected them."

> It's really important to get the whole class to talk in class discussion. Everybody loves to tell their story. If you can get all the students to talk about the same thing . . . not studying, give the student a chance to talk about what they think, how they feel about it, how it affected them. Class discussion.

> I like it when everyone joins in and it's not just the teacher talking and pupils listening, like when the whole class gets involved and everyone's like giving their point of view. . . . It's more like teaching each other than the teacher just teaching us.[10]

> If you were able to do like maybe once a week or once every two weeks where you had a class period where you just talk about the stuff you're learning and see the students' opinions on it, and stuff like that. I personally know I'd enjoy the class better, but if it's all like, facts facts facts, you have to know this for the test but like, blah blah blah, then I'm just gonna be like, whatever, you know?

Student Choice

In addition to choices teachers might make about how to engage students in various ways, students want to have choice. Such choice can correspond to "the interests of the students," allow them "freedom of thought," and let them "focus on things that [they] are actually interested in."

> There should be a balance between what the teachers *have* to teach and the interests of the students.

> I felt like school was keeping me from learning. I wanted to read books I chose and do my own art, but you didn't have time.[11]

> I think it's important for the teacher to find balance between giving the student the ability to be free-thinking, have freedom of thought, but also that and with the balance of having something that you want to teach the students. Like hav-

ing your curriculum, or also things they want to teach the students in exchange, like different kinds of writing. Not to limit the students by saying, "You have to write it in this form" or something.

[Years 11 and 12 should be organized] on the individual student. Not have like, a set; like, you have to do this, you have to do that. I think it should be styled to the individual student. I mean not all students are gonna be good at Maths. Not all students are gonna be good at Science, or Art . . . your education should be styled to you. OK, yes, you have to do Maths, but make sure that the whole— all of the whole is, of your education—is styled to you.[12]

I know we're not experts on, like, what we need to know and science and every-thing, but I am thinking, you get to a point in your education where after that it's just kinda like extra that you don't really need to know, so maybe if we could still have, like, history, but you could have different types of things so that you could focus on things that you are actually interested in instead of just like, U.S. history, or you know certain things that everybody has to do, [because] I know that as you get older as seniors and juniors you can do Environmental Science, or you know, Organic Chemistry, or something else instead, so you have more choices, maybe? You can choose what you're interested in?

I think all kids have things they want to learn. Because there is something somewhere you want to learn. Like you might see something and say, "Yeah, that's kind of cool." And I mean it might not happen at school. I mean seeing something. You might be out with friends or on the job and discover something cool like related to physics and then say, "I want to learn more" and then come to school and somewhere be able to do that. Not now we can't.

Students don't like to be told what they have to learn. So you know a lot of peo-ple want to be able to choose what to learn because you may already have an idea about what you want to learn or be.

Relevance

The final category students emphasize in terms of designing engaging les-sons is relevance. They stress the importance of relevance in catching and keeping their attention, getting and keeping them engaged, and allowing them not only to learn the material at hand but also to pursue other learning opportunities. But on a deeper level, they talk about relevance to them as people, as human beings, as growing and changing beings who need to experience and make meaning.

Relevance to Themselves as Individuals

Students argue that when schoolwork lacks relevance to themselves, to them as people in the world, it is sometimes hard to connect with that work. This point speaks directly to the issue of equity and how consult-ing students can lead to more equitable approaches: if students do not feel addressed by what they are studying, they have trouble opening themselves to it or, conversely, seeing ways that they could be more central to their own learning. They want what they learn to "relate back to [their] own life," and they want school to help them find out who they are.

> My school work fits into the gaps in my life, not the other way round. I figure that if I'm not enjoying my life I might as well be dead so I'll enjoy it as much as I can and school work is something to do in my spare time.[13]

> So what they tell you will become part of what you're thinking. Same as when they told black people they were meant to be slaves or entertainers, and that's what they grew up thinking. I hate school when the information that I'm learning doesn't reflect the person that I am.[14]

> But whenever I start doing good, I feel like there's only this little part of me that's really getting her life together. The other part, the real me, is just sort of standing in the shadows, the me that thinks real thoughts and feels real things.[15]

> [I want] to find out what it is in life that I actually want to do . . . and to find out who I am and then I'll know what I want to do about it [and I] definitely wasn't finding that at school.[16]

> It really does help when you're trying to learn something when you can relate it back to your own life. If you are trying to learn something and it just seems so irrelevant to you and your life, it's gonna be difficult to want to learn about it if it just seems like it has nothing to do with you or everyone.

Relevance to Life beyond School

Not only do students want what they learn to reflect and connect to them in some way, they want to see how it connects to "real" life—life outside of and beyond school. Students want what they study to relate to their daily lives, and, they suggest, "kids have to know why they are learning something." A challenge facing teachers, then, is to make what they teach relevant and, equally important, to ensure that students perceive and experience the significance.

> I think that until a kid has a reason or will to learn, they won't. They won't [because] they don't see why they should. . . . Somewhere in the curriculum the kids have to know why they are learning something. Like in geometry. Like somewhere they have to see real life in it. Like what it means.

> A lot of math teachers fail to make anything that they're teaching seem like it's going to help you ever again, and I think that's a really big problem.

> Some students don't understand what they are working for. So in a way you have to see and understand what you are working for and what it is you are trying to do. School should be something productive. Like for the future.[17]

I think a lot of the time it helps to know the meaning of why we're reading a book or watching a movie because we're so busy worrying about getting the homework done and getting that grade that we don't even understand.

The majority of stuff that you learn . . . you don't need it and you know you're learning all this stuff and it's like, OK, I'm learning this, OK, I have an understanding of it, but where am I going to use this in real life, you know, everyday life?[18]

I also think it's important to make that material more interesting, to relate it to today, or to relate it to our daily lives, because a lot of times students are asking themselves, "When am I ever going to need to use this?"

[Teachers] spend so much time trying to teach things that they think [students are] going to need, like in order to get a job, or go to uni[versity] or something, whereas they should be teaching [students] more about life and about . . . things that you actually really need to know to be able to be successful in life as a person.[19]

Case Study: Responding to Students' Diverse Learning Needs

Jessye, a European American woman and a history major at Bryn Mawr College, corresponded with Anub, an Indian student in the gifted track of the eleventh grade in his suburban public school.[20] Reflecting on her discussions with Anub, Jessye was struck by "the depth and breadth of our dialogue," but found the most valuable lesson concerned "the wide array of learning preferences in a classroom and the importance of including as many as possible in my teaching." Her analysis of her exchange with Anub illustrates how the dialogue afforded Jessye the opportunity to think through—with a student—both the possibilities for classroom practice and the benefits and drawbacks of those possibilities.

In one of her messages to Anub, Jessye posed this question: "What is your favorite learning style: independent work, group work, lecture, discussion, or hands-on? Are there any other methods that work well for you?" He replied to Jessye: "I actually like a mixture of all the ones you mentioned. I get bored of doing the same thing all the time (no matter what)." Elsewhere, though, Anub, like some of the students quoted in this chapter, "expressed a strong preference for whole-class discussions," Jessye explained. She continued: "He felt it was the best way to get everyone involved and make the material meaningful. He wrote: 'even the quiet kids seem to like listening to peers more than listening to a teacher.'" She explained: "He also likes 'hands-on stuff' and 'games that have education (but not lame) links.'" Reading Anub's response,

continues

Case Study Continued

Jessye reflected to herself: "This presents a challenge to the teacher: to include all of the above without seeming 'lame.'" Jessye suggests that she was prepared for this challenge but found Anub's reiteration of it useful: "In [our Curriculum and Pedagogy class] we had read many studies stating the same thing. What made Anub's response interesting was both that it reinforced what I had been taught and that it showed some students actually consciously agree with those studies."

Anub was also clear about what did not work for him. Describing a class in which the teacher showed a video about slavery and then discussed it, Anub "thought the class seemed dead and that their assignments were 'pointless busywork.'" When Jessye asked Anub to elaborate, he explained that the teacher's attempts at discussion "became preachy lectures" and the video, in Anub's assessment, "did nothing to spark ideas, imagination, creativity, and independent thought." He advocated instead "small group structured debates or discussions."

Jessye and Anub also discussed classroom activities that were sometimes beneficial and sometimes problematic. Jessye explains: "Anub told me about his tenth-grade geometry class. Students were in groups of four, taught each other, and decided when to take each test. He said that he

> learned the material from the first semester much better (when the teacher was "teaching") but I have to admit that it was a good basic idea. I did resent not being able to work at my own pace (which was faster than the group of four) because I felt that if I am going to have to teach myself, I should at least have the right to proceed at my desired pace.

Jessye wrote: "What does a teacher do in this situation? I plan on using group work in my classroom, so this is a dilemma I must face. The point is not to finish quickly; it is to gain a richer understanding of the subject and each other." Her exchange with Anub helped her see the pitfalls of group work and clarify for herself her pedagogical goal in using it.

Anub's favorite class was physics, which, according to him, "'involved learning to think for oneself, with little stress on memorization.' Students did not turn in homework or receive a grade for it, which, Anub explained, 'allowed me to do what I needed and skip the easy stuff. Of course, many students chose not to do the homework but theirgrades suffered indirectly.'" Jessye felt that this approach presented a different set of complexities:

continues

Case Study Continued

Here was a teacher who tried to challenge his students, to make them think and behave in ways other than those to which they were accustomed. His motto of teaching is Einstein's saying, "Through confusion comes understanding." It is an example of what the students called "controlled floundering." The problem is that what is controlled for one might be "complete floundering" for another. Anub admitted that it was very difficult for many students, that people dropped out after the first test, but that he thrived on the challenge. All students need to be challenged, true, but the fact that some became so frustrated as to drop the class leads me to believe that something wasn't working properly. I could never gain full insight without taking the class, so I will just have to keep these thoughts in mind for my own teaching.

Jessye's willingness to question, to ponder, and to keep thinking about these issues bodes well for her future as a teacher. Such a process requires ongoing listening and learning, even after one has begun teaching. In the conclusion of her reflection on her exchange with Anub, Jessye wrote:

As a teacher, I must remember that students will not all like to learn the way I do. I enjoy discussions, but not as much as Anub does. I certainly like a good video now and then, to break up the routine and give everyone (the teacher included) a break. Group work is invaluable, but only with the proper setting, instruction, and practice. Anub has given me a lot to consider; hopefully, this experience will make me more attentive to my students' needs and preferences.

Notes

1. Cothran et al., 2003, p. 439.
2. Pope, 2003, p. 101.
3. Arnot et al., 2004, p. 11.
4. Rudduck and Flutter, 2004, p. 81.
5. Arnot et al., 2004, p. 11.
6. Smyth and Hattam, 2004, p. 178.
7. Sanon et al. 2001, quoted in Shultz and Cook-Sather, 2001, p. 77.
8. Marzan et al. quoted in Shultz and Cook-Sather, 2001, p. 100.
9. Cushman, 2003, p. 92.
10. Rudduck and Flutter, 2004, pp. 80, 83.
11. Cushman, 2003, p. 100.
12. Smyth and Hattam, 2004, p. 146.
13. Rudduck et al., 1996, p. 136, quoted in Rudduck and Flutter, 2004, p. 93.
14. Cushman, 2003, p. 103.
15. Judon et al. in Shultz and Cook-Sather, 2001, p. 47.
16. Smyth and Hattam, 2003, p. 93.

17. Sanon et al., 2001, in Shultz and Cook-Sather, 2001, p. 78.
18. Smyth and Hattam, 2003, p. 148.
19. Smyth and Hattam, 2003, p. 94.
20. Drawn from the analysis paper that a prospective teacher enrolled in my methods seminar, Curriculum and Pedagogy, wrote as part of Teaching and Learning Together.

4

Respect

with Jossi Fritz-Mauer and Jessica Mitra Mausner

Reach me with more than words from textbooks—but words from the soul and the mind connected to the heart. What got you to teach me? Wasn't it to reach me? . . . Relate to me, debate with me, respect me. Stop neglecting me. I get nothing but tired empty wordswordswords . . . make them real.

—Student[1]

Chapter Overview

Focus of this chapter: Respect as central to students' experiences of school

Discussed in this chapter:

- Respect
  - Respectful treatment
  - Receptivity, openness, and trust as forms of respect
  - A reciprocal dynamic
- Power dynamics
  - Within the classroom
  - Across the school
- Case study: Respect

Throughout their discussions about knowing students, creating and maintaining a positive classroom environment, and designing engaging lessons, students sound an underlying note: the importance of respect. We return to this issue here and devote a separate chapter to it, because, as one student asserts, "If you don't have respect, what do you have?"[2] We hope that reading students' own statements regarding the importance of respect will make this point clearly.

The root of the word "respect" is to look back—to return the gaze of someone looking at you—but given that literal looking back can mean different things in different cultures, it is important to consider such a return more metaphorically. Definitions of respect include the terms "regard" and "esteem"; they have to do with attending and taking seriously. They also have to do with reciprocity.

Respect

Teacher-pupil relationships have to be respectful, and the respect must be in both directions.

—Rudduck and McIntyre, 2007, p. 53

In their statements about the importance of respect, students discuss the effect disrespect has on their engagement and interest and, alternatively, how much of a difference it makes when teachers show they care and are interested in their students as people.

Respectful Treatment

One of the most powerful recurring themes across student statements is the potential of teachers' treatment either to support or undermine students. If teachers treat them "like a child instead of a person," it sends one kind of message; if they "encourage each individual," it sends another.

> Teachers sometimes treat you like a child instead of a person. They just make you feel dumb. . . . No, not necessarily dumb, just like it doesn't matter what you think. And you don't care, you stop trying.[3]

> We are all human, you know, you don't need to act like you're so above us and everything and not listen to anything we say.

> Yeah, like they think you're dumb. . . . We don't expect them to treat us like their own children. We're not. But we are still kids. I'd say to them, "You've got kids. You treat them with love but you don't need to love us. All you need to do is treat us like humans."[4]

> The best teacher I suppose is someone who knows what they are teaching so they do have a certain authority, but someone who respects the students. Because if they treat us like idiots, then I can't respect them. How would they show respect? If they acknowledge the sort of work I'm doing and they tell me what is good and what is not good and then I know what they're talking about and I know that they're trying to help me along. And they encourage each individual to learn in their own way. Some students work better if they are taught straight from the textbook, or from a teacher handing out sheets, but some don't learn that way.[5]

> I have one teacher that if she gets like, if we ask her too many questions, she acts like you're stupid, and she like, actually like gives you attitude though, she'll like, I mean, she'll keep being like, "You don't know that?" and you'll be like, "Well," and she'll actually be like mad because we don't understand some-

thing or because we're asking a question, and it's just I'm like why do you have to give us attitude, it's like totally immature.

They know how to have a good time with us—how to talk to us—how to find out what we're thinking but at the same time not really act childish. They still know their—have a good time and let the student know they are older and they do have a certain respect.[6]

They care about the students. Basically, they treat you like friends. You can call them by their first name, just like they call you by your first name. It mainly has to do with respect. They're caring.[7]

I don't think I'll ever go back to school. I mean, the teachers have got to learn to treat you fairly. If you're going to respect them, they've got to respect you. Like they need to speak to you properly like you're not dirt or trash. They need to let you give your opinions on the work. They need to understand you and not turn their backs on you.[8]

Receptivity, Openness, and Trust as Forms of Respect

Students talk about the importance of "mutual" engagement, about receptivity and openness, and about fairness. These, in students' minds, are all expressions of respect. They demonstrate that teachers are "showing interest in the kids."

I think the most effective teachers are ones who are always open to answering questions. . . . They have to be willing to treat the student at a very mutual level.

I like someone who puts themselves in our shoes. . . . I guess a teacher don't got to be nice, but they got to be respectful.[9]

I think that a teacher who expresses themselves toward everybody and not just toward one set of people [gets] more respect from everybody.[10]

I think the one thing that most teachers lack is showing interest in the kids. Those teachers tend to be the most well liked and popular, because you feel like they're relating to the kids. If more teachers did that, I think they would find a lot more respect from the students.

It's nice to have a teacher who trusts you to do something on your own.[11]

A Reciprocal Dynamic

Students offer repeated statements regarding the reciprocal nature of respect. Echoing Rudduck and McIntyre's statement earlier in this chapter, students offer variations on the theme "If you respect students, then they'll respect you."

A student will respect a teacher that respects them. They won't respect a teacher that doesn't respect them.

[On the issue of] respectful presence—I feel that is one of the most important things, because I hate it when teachers think you're so below them, they act like they're power, they're all mighty. I just can't stand it. That's the worst quality, to disrespect students. I think if you respect students, then they'll respect you.

I think that it's necessary to maintain the student/teacher thing but I think also that the teacher and student should cultivate respect for each other and sense of equality because students need . . . that [sense] to learn, definitely. A relationship, they would listen to each other, have respect for each other, and this means equality, because the students would then be more receptive to what is being taught.

Power Dynamics

Highlighted in the students' discussion of respect is their awareness of the power dynamics of the classroom, the educational system, and the larger society. Because teachers occupy the positions of greater power within the classroom and school, because of their age and role, they must take the initiative to treat students with respect. To demand respect from students first, rather than first modeling it, is to reinforce the power differential that already disadvantages students. Students discuss what happens when teachers do and when they do not make that choice.

Within the Classroom

Students discuss the challenges of encountering teachers who exercise power over them rather than share power with them. Words like "involved" are contrasted with terms like "control." Students want to feel "relaxed," not "scared."

We don't want teachers to be in control, we want to be more involved.[12]

The teachers . . . seem to think that because they are the teachers, that they have the right to tell the students what to do, and they don't really give the students any feeling or say in what, whether they think that's right or that's wrong.[13]

Of course, the teachers have the final say. Regardless of how self-governed we are, they are the final check.[14]

I don't know, it's basically "them and us" like there's teachers and there's students and a lot of the friction is the discipline they try to give us.[15]

The teacher has to have some kind of authority, but they shouldn't be so that the kids are kind of scared of them. It's kind of a balance you have to learn as a teacher.

Across the School

Students also indicate that they would like to be afforded more power to shape what happens in their schools. They want adults to "open up," to "give up some of the power," and receive "all this information that students are giving out." These students' comments speak to the ways in which students want to collaborate with educators to improve schools.

> Changes in the high school are mainly done by the administration. . . . I know we had one or two discussions but I don't think students really got involved because I think they were scared of facing the teachers and facing the administration. Both sides need to open up—students opening up to teachers and teachers need to open up and [receive] all this information that students are giving out.

> I think really what she [the principal] wanted to do was take everything that the school was and everything that people knew about the school and reverse it, like . . . trying to show them [the teachers] that if they could just give up some of the power, like over teaching and running the school and everything . . . if they could just give it up the students weren't going to make a mess of it, and that it was going to be dirty for a little while, and they were going to feel really anxious about it, but if they could just give up the power the students were going to benefit from it.[16]

Case Study: Respect

Jessica successfully completed both her B.A. and certification in physics at Bryn Mawr College.[17] A thoughtful, animated young woman of European American descent, she was paired in Teaching and Learning Together with Reggie, an African American student placed in the regular track of the eleventh grade at his high school. Jessica chose to focus her analysis of her dialogue with Reggie on the issue of respect. The following questions guided Jessica's analysis: "How do I respect my students and their differences and ensure that my classroom is a safe space for different types of students? Also, how do I foster that respect in my teacher-student relationships?"

In the early part of the semester, Jessica focused on Reggie's experience as an African American student and the ways that his school attempted to address racial and cultural differences. After a discussion of the Prejudice Awareness Union at Reggie's school and some of the activities they sponsor, Jessica wrote to Reggie:

> Do you think I could use any of these activities? I am a little bit nervous about trying to teach respect for other people's differences in my classroom. I am not really sure how to go about it, other than not letting people make fun of each other, or use derogatory language. Do you think a teacher even has the right to teach these things in a classroom?

Reggie wrote back:

> Should you teach these ideas in physics class? I say "Yes!" Students should learn about other students. I also say that teachers have a right and a responsibility to teach these kinds of attitudes towards students. My idea of what you should do is talk about how many ethnic groups have helped the progress of physics.

continues

Case Study Continued

Reggie connects teaching respect with using a multicultural approach. Jessica pursued this connection: "This emphatic statement really got me thinking. He was saying that I as a teacher have a *responsibility* to include multiculturalism and diversity in the curriculum." As she thought further about Reggie's assertion, Jessica realized that his belief

> influenced my own thinking about standard physics curriculum. I did not realize just how narrow the curriculum is, when analyzing it in terms of cultural representation, until he forced me to think about this issue. Reflecting on that, I think I will also like to discuss [in my future classroom] the lack of minorities in scientific history and the possible reasons for this. I think by keeping silent on this issue, I am teaching that only white students can become scientists. My responsibility, as Reggie puts it, is to teach attitudes towards students, and this includes exploring race in the context of history.

In addressing the issue of respect among students, Reggie led Jessica from thinking about the kinds of approaches his high school's Prejudice Awareness Union employs to the question of how curriculum can influence students' perceptions of themselves. This part of the exchange helped Jessica to consider what she as a teacher can do to inspire respect among students for themselves and one another.

Turning to the question of respect in teacher-student relationships, Jessica wrote to Reggie, "I know that a few weeks ago we talked about student respect—how to make students respect individual differences in terms of race, gender, etc. Now I am wondering about teacher-student respect. Could you tell me about some of the teachers you respect and why?"

Reggie responded:

> Respect is a hard thing to get from students. Some give everyone respect while others believe that a teacher should earn their respect. . . . I respect teachers who care for their students. Teachers who don't say anything when they notice a drop in [student's] grades or blame students for what another student does I don't have respect for. You are a teacher and it is your job. Not every student will like you, but that is their loss.

Prompted by Reggie's eloquent assertions, Jessica recognized and struggled with a reality of teaching that many preservice teachers find hard to accept: that, as Jessica put it, "not all of my students will like me, but they still should respect me." Facing this reality inspired Jessica to further reflect on her motives for wanting to be respected. She explains:

> Before I started this [exchange with Reggie], I equated teacher respect with academic productivity. I thought that respected teachers could motivate

continues

Case Study Continued

their students to do their homework, participate in class, listen to each other. After reading and rereading [Reggie's] letter, I came up with a different definition of respect. . . . This new definition involves a more holistic approach to learning and assumes that respect needs to originate with the teacher *and* the students.

Jessica attended closely to Reggie's assertion that "a teacher must care about her students in order to be respected, but more importantly, he advises me to listen to the student 'and then go from there.' In other words, respect starts with listening to and valuing students' voices."

In thinking about her future as a teacher, Jessica stated: "I need to remember to treat all of my students like I treated Reggie: by listening to their feelings and experiences and respecting their viewpoints. I need to find a comfort level in my interactions with the students that is comfortable for both parties. Most importantly, I need to remember to keep the dialogue open and ongoing so that I can continue to learn from my students."

At the end of the semester, Jessica reflected on what she had learned from corresponding with Reggie:

What this project taught me was that students at the high school level think about these issues just as much as we do, except we've been studying them in textbooks so we have all these names for the things, but Reggie would say something in one way, and I would say it in another way, and we would be saying the exact same thing. Reggie validated a lot of what I had been studying and that was really good.

Notes

1. Strucker et al. in Shultz and Cook-Sather, 2001, p. 162.
2. Judon et al. in Shultz and Cook-Sather, 2001, p. 45.
3. Yonezawa and Jones, 2007, p. 694.
4. Arnot et al., 2004, p. 47.
5. Smyth et al., 2004, p. 113.
6. de Jesus, 2003, in Rubin and Silva, 2003, p. 140.
7. de Jesus, 2003, in Rubin and Silva, 2003, p. 138.
8. Smyth et al., 2004, p. 184.
9. Wilson and Corbett, 2007, p. 288.
10. Bates et al., 2001, in Shultz and Cook-Sather, 2001, p. 145.
11. Arnot et al., 2004, p. 15.
12. Cushman, 2003, p. 106.
13. Smyth and Hattam, 2003, p. 77.
14. Keiser and Stein, 2003, in Rubin and Silva, 2003, p. 175.
15. Smyth et al., 2004, p. 5.
16. Smyth, 2007, p. 649.
17. Drawn from the analysis paper that a prospective teacher enrolled in my methods seminar, Curriculum and Pedagogy, wrote as part of Teaching and Learning Together.

5

Responsibility

with Jossi Fritz-Mauer and
Jessica Mitra Mausner

I think it's the teacher's responsibility to keep order but also the students have to be mature, and that is not up to the teacher. You're old enough to know that you're responsible for your own actions.

—Student

Chapter Overview

Focus of this chapter: Teacher and student responsibility as essential to positive classroom experiences for students

Discussed in this chapter:

- Teacher responsibility
  - Having high expectations
  - Treating students equally
  - Believing in, challenging, and supporting students
- Student responsibility
- Case study: Taking responsibility for engaging students in dialogue

The second theme that cuts across the points that students emphasize in previous chapters is responsibility. "Responsible" means answerable or accountable, as for something within one's power, control, or management.[1] "Responsibility" refers to the social force that binds you to the courses of action demanded by that force, the proper sphere or extent of your activities, and a form of trustworthiness.[2] Responsibility can also be about taking the initiative to act, as in adults demonstrating respect to students as part of an effort to create a reciprocally respectful dynamic. The theme of responsibility takes us full circle, back to relationships: dynamics between and among people and the actions required or expected given those relationships. Responsibility is about one's ability (or inability) to respond within the parameters of any given context and relationship, and it is about the action one takes based on one's sense of accountability to others.

Some students are at a point in their development at which they understand that not only are teachers responsible but students, too, must take responsibility for creating positive relationships with teachers, developing a productive learning environment, and participating in lessons. Other students have yet to achieve this perspective, and it is in part the teacher's and in part the student's responsibility to work toward that. Students describe those structures and practices that they feel prevent them from taking responsibility, they identify the kinds of responsibility they would like teachers to take, and they discuss the kinds of responsibility they would like to take.

Teacher Responsibility

Among the "conditions of learning" in school that students identify [i.e., conditions they need in order to learn] are respect, responsibility, challenge, and support.
—Rudduck, 2002, p. 123

The teacher should initiate respect in the teacher-student relationship.
—Cothran et al., 2003, p. 441

Teacher responsibilities, according to students, include having high expectations, treating students equally, and believing in, challenging, and supporting students. These responsibilities underlie the critical issues addressed in Chapters 1–3: knowing students, creating a productive learning environment, and designing engaging lessons. Like respect, teacher responsibility and how it intersects with student responsibility are, from the student perspective, at the root of effective teaching.

Having High Expectations

Students' comments show that there is a complex relationship between high expectations for learning and standard measures of achievement. Believing that students can learn and achieve is essential to their doing so, according to students. But beyond that, students want high expectations to be keyed to genuine engagement and learning, not simply high grades.

Whenever a teacher tells me I can't do something, I actually start believing that. And that's the worst feeling.[3]

You shouldn't ever let kids think it's OK to fail. They will then. I know from my Special Ed. classes. That's why I hated them. "I'm stupid," so I was. Until I got out of Special Ed.

The teachers concentrate more on you in top [levels] and not the people who are below you.[4]

I take mostly honors classes but I take some standard classes and if I were in a standard class I sometimes don't do as well as you might think because I think that the classes aren't demanding enough and that the students aren't being challenged even though they have the ability. I don't know if I'm making sense but that's the way it is.

Treating Students Equally

The importance of being treated equally is apparent in many student comments. Playing favorites, holding and acting on prejudices, and showing differential levels of interest are all practices that students suggest are damaging. They see it as the teacher's responsibility to work against these, not only treating each student equally but also judging each student as an individual.

There are things I don't like about teachers and the main one is they have favorites and they let the clever girls do whatever they want.[5]

Teachers need to set a good example for their classroom. They can do that by watching what they say, recognizing their prejudices, acknowledging them, and keeping them in check.[6]

In [the higher] level the teacher was very outgoing and funny and lively. She was interested in the students like. She was happy to see us. In the [lower-track classes] "Who cares?" She isn't happy to see us. She doesn't care.

Right now I'm working with a kindergarten and Ms. R. just told me a couple of weeks ago that the kindergarten no longer compares a student against a student. They now compare how far the student is, and that's what I feel like they should do all the way from the beginning to end of your schooling.

Believing in, Challenging, and Supporting Students

Having high expectations and treating students equally are connected, in students' assessment, with believing in, challenging, and supporting students in their academic efforts and as people. The difference between teachers who state, or believe, "Those kids can't do nothing" and those who "push [students] to learn" is dramatic.

I heard teachers talking about people, saying "Those kids can't do nothing." Kids want teachers who believe in them.[7]

There's a difference between being a teacher and being an instructor. Especially a good teacher because they are going to be the ones who want to reach out and help these students and an instructor can [and will only] tell you the book and tell you to read the chapter and take a test.[8]

It's not that I'm lazy, but I like a teacher that push me to learn. I might not be that confident at first, but then I'll get it.[9]

She's the greatest teacher I've had because she's there to help. . . . Most teachers will give you a certain time to come in and help—be helpful. She'll be there. She says she'll be [here] fifth period, seventh period, eighth period, after school, and she won't leave until you're done, you have what you need.[10]

I like the ones that don't allow excuses. It's my turn to get an education. I need to have someone tell me, when I'm tired and don't feel like doing the work, that I should do it anyway.[11]

A good teacher takes time out to see if all the kids have what they're talking about and cares about how they're doing and will see if they need help.[12]

Student Responsibility

Because of the hierarchical nature of schooling and society, teachers must allow students to take responsibility; students cannot simply assume it. Therefore, student reflections on the kinds of responsibility they want to take rest on the premise of teachers affording them the opportunity to do so. Students emphasize the importance of having agency within the classroom and in larger decisionmaking processes. They hope to have agency in making choices about their engagement, in questioning what is presented to them, in struggling in productive ways with content, and in influencing school reform.

I think in some cases teachers make it boring. But in some cases students make it boring. Because if you know you are not getting good grades in that class and you know there is a chance you might fail then you're going to get bored because you don't want to do that work.[13]

We have to know more to be able to ask a question than to answer it and I think that's true. Kids will probably be more prepared if they could ask more questions and challenge more. And if kids are interested in like [the] question they ask, they're gonna remember it better.

I think another reason kids don't feel motivated is because it's like everything [teachers] teach is supposed to be true. You have to take it like it's true. I mean we have to believe it, right? There's no room for like . . . um . . . like to question. . . . I need to be able to question why we are learning and what we are learning. There's no challenge otherwise and no reason to use your brain.

With confusion comes understanding. This is Mr. Z's motto. He game plans all of his lessons for controlled floundering. He leads things to the next level to where you make your own point of view. You sort of come around to it on your own then. He gives you the basics. He's what I consider a very good teacher.

It's *my* education. . . . They [administrators] usually get the final say, but I am here to remind them that they are supposed to be watching out for *me*.[14]

Kids should be involved in decisions made by the school and concerning the school. Kids are the ones using what the school does. Sometimes the school puts money into ridiculous things that we don't like.[15]

Case Study: Taking Responsibility for Engaging Students in Dialogue

Julie, a French major at Haverford College seeking certification to teach French,[16] took seriously Freire's assertion that "without dialogue there is no communication, and without communication there can be no true education."[17] While she recognized that, as a teacher, her responsibility to engage in dialogue with students was the foundation for related responsibilities, as students discuss above, Julie realized that believing in engaging dialogue is not the same as doing it.

Framing her reflection on her e-mail exchange with her high school student partner through Teaching and Learning Together, Julie wrote:

> I have always held a high opinion of all forms of dialogue: between individuals in general, between myself and others, and between myself and my own thoughts. Dialogue, or rather an exchange of ideas and experiences between people, provides access to the lives of others as well as a more intimate passage into my own. In my experiences as a learner and teacher, I have seen how dialogue has enhanced my understanding of my students, myself, and the surrounding world. Open communication with others has taught me to become not only a healthy talker, in the questions I ask and the feedback I give, but also a good listener.

> In my former schooling and through the experiences that stemmed from it, I became familiar and comfortable with the idea of healthy communication and dialogue with my teachers and with other students. This kind of mutual exchange between individuals was an intrinsic part of my daily routine and was encouraged. As a student, I interacted with my teachers and with peers in varied contexts, not only in class, but on sports fields, in meetings, and at school functions. I felt that I could always approach my teachers with any issue and that I would be heard. I knew that my teachers wanted to learn more about me and my interests. In hindsight, I realize that these exchanges led to a more personalized and comfortable classroom environment where I felt a connection to the people surrounding me, and consequently, to the subject matter. This cohesive group was the perfect environment in which to engage in productive dialogue. It was through this kind of interaction with others that I developed an appreciation for, and an affinity to, such exchanges.

These reflections on her own experiences, *making explicit what she experienced and why it was significant,* helped Julie identify and articulate the importance of open communication as foundational to her educational philosophy. She built on this foundation at college.

> As I pursued my studies in education at the university level, I maintained such dialogue with others, both professors and students. . . . But in addition, as I prepared to be a teacher, I began to engage in more internal dialogue prompted, I believe, by this shift in role. As a student, I realized the importance of being heard as well as initiating dialogue as I talked through my interests and struggles with others. As I made the shift into the role of teacher, I started to look at such dialogue from a different perspective, valuing the listening skills of teachers and the feedback given to students, as well as the need to be heard.

continues

Case Study Continued

Teaching and Learning Together gave Julie an unusual opportunity to put into practice her basic philosophy:

> I believe that students should be able to connect to the subject learned by voicing their interests, beliefs, and opinions, and that this connection leads to meaningful learning. In addition to guiding the activities of the classroom, the teacher guides the opportunities for the student's voice to be heard. The strength of student voice can have a notable impact on the student's personal experience in the classroom: they can feel connected, separated, or indifferent all based on how much of a chance they are given to express themselves.

However, partway through her exchange with Nikki, her high school partner in Teaching and Learning Together, Julie realized that she was not acting on this philosophy:

> As I engaged in dialogue with my partner, I began to realize a discrepancy between the dynamic I wanted to create, and what was actually happening. Instead of listening and following the student's lead, I was directing the progress of our letters. I began to notice an obvious trend in whose voice was being heard. I felt that [Nikki] and I were falling into a question-answer cycle that was characterized by my questions and her answers.

Recognizing that something was amiss, Julie stepped back from the exchange to reevaluate.

> In light of my philosophy of education, the path that our conversations were following did not coincide with what I believed about student voice, in both the letters and in the classroom. In order to stand by my beliefs, I wanted to reframe the letters, ask more open questions that would leave room for her voice, and explicitly address the format that I noticed to see what she would say.

Looking back on her experience with her high school student partner, Julie analyzed not only the immediate exchange with a single student but also what implications it had for her future classroom: "By reevaluating my philosophy regarding student and teacher voice, I had to ask myself two primary questions as a developing teacher: whose voice do I want to be heard and how can I set up an environment that makes this possible?"

Through her analysis, Julie gained a new depth of understanding regarding what it takes to foster dialogue between her students and herself. She learned that embracing a philosophy is not enough; you need to take responsibility to create a classroom environment that makes it possible to put the philosophy into practice. She wrote:

continues

Case Study Continued

Upon starting my student teaching in the spring of my senior year, I wanted to establish an environment where the student voice could be heard and taken into consideration as I shaped my own teaching style. I wanted to get to know my students and give them a space in which to voice their opinions. I wanted to achieve this goal for myself, but it had to be done within the limits of the context created for me: my student teaching site. By working in my cooperating teacher's classroom and by participating in the community of the school as a whole, I had to make an attempt to achieve my goal within the boundaries created for me.

Julie realized that within Teaching and Learning Together, dialogue with students had been not only supported but also required. In her own classroom, in a new role, she would need to create that kind of space for herself and for the students, as it would not be provided. "With my responsibilities changing, I would develop a newly formed philosophy of education, including a revised philosophy of student voice. This would focus more on the integration of student voice into my thinking on education and into the decisions I would make regarding my classes."

Challenged by her student teaching context, which did not value student input, Julie struggled to put her philosophy into practice.

In a setting such as student teaching, I needed to negotiate the discrepancy between my beliefs and my actions in practice in a realistic way. I needed to put my ideals into perspective, and make decisions that were grounded and suitable for the environment in which I found myself. I decided to use my class time more wisely, talking to my students at the beginning and end of class, as well as asking questions during class time that would encourage my students to connect their lives to their learning. I created a note-writing system between my students and myself, where they would each write me a weekly note and I would respond, giving them space to voice their opinions on the class and their progress. I also profited from my role as a student-teacher by observing as many classes as possible, seeing how my students engaged themselves in other courses. All of these changes allowed me to reshape my role and my philosophy on student voice, given the teaching circumstances.

My new role, new limitations, and new context caused me to reflect on my new perspective on the . . . issue of student voice. But this reflection seemed to arise only as the result of a conflict between theory and practice in varied circumstances. I was forced to revisit my already established theory, challenge my beliefs, and reshape them to fit the reality of my teaching environment. I have learned that if I revisit my beliefs, I can shape them in a way that supports my actions.

Balancing one's ideals with reality, while still striving to take the responsibility one knows one needs to take to support dialogue with students, is a career-long challenge.

continues

Case Study Continued

As I look to my future in teaching, I recognize the healthy nature of conflict regarding my teaching and the decisions I will make as an educator. It isn't the conflict that changes my teaching, but the reflecting on this conflict that leads to a more profound understanding of myself and my views on education. Each time I interact with a student or a group of students, I revisit why I want to hear my students' voices and how I can integrate their voices into my thinking. So the combination of my students' voices through my dialogues with them, and my own voice through dialogue with myself, aid me in my ongoing need to reshape my beliefs to withstand the reality of the situations I face. With each experience, I make firm the ground on which I build my beliefs and my identity as an educator.

Notes

1. "Responsible" retrieved from Dictionary.com Unabridged (v. 1.1): http://dictionary.reference.com/browse/responsible.

2. "Responsibility" retrieved from Dictionary.com Unabridged (v. 1.1): http://dictionary.reference.com/browse/responsibility.

3. Wilson and Corbett, 2007, p. 694.

4. Rudduck and Flutter, 2004, p. 58.

5. Arnot et al., 2004, p. 54.

6. Dunderdale et al., 2001, in Shultz and Cook-Sather, 2001, p. 67.

7. Wilson and Corbett, 2007, p. 292.

8. Yonezawa and Jones, 2007, p. 696.

9. Wilson and Corbett, 2007, p. 289.

10. Wing, 2003, in Rubin and Silva, 2003, p. 161.

11. Wilson and Corbett, 2007, p. 289.

12. Wilson and Corbett, 2007, p. 291.

13. Sanon et al., 2001, in Shultz and Cook-Sather, 2001, p. 76.

14. Pope, 2003, p. 44.

15. Sanon et al., 2001, in Shultz and Cook-Sather, 2001, p. 83.

16. Drawn from the analysis paper that a prospective teacher enrolled in my methods seminar, Curriculum and Pedagogy, wrote as part of Teaching and Learning Together.

17. Freire, 1990, p. 81.

Part II

Strategies for Learning from Students' Perspectives

The student perspectives offered in Part I show the striking consistency with which students experience schooling and the equally striking consistency of their hopes for school experiences. There are also, of course, within these broader categories that cross lines of diversity, variations among student hopes that individual teachers must access. Thus, to reiterate a theme I stress throughout this sourcebook, becoming an effective teacher is an ongoing process of learning how best to support each new individual and group of learners within each particular educational context. That means asking each new group of students to enter a collaborative relationship through which they work with teachers to make the educational experience for themselves and for others in their classroom the best it can be.

Choosing to embark on a process of consulting students requires a genuine willingness to take on explorations of the messiest aspects of teaching. This section of this sourcebook contains two chapters that offer concrete guidelines for eliciting student perspectives in that process. Chapter 6 is a revised version of MacBeath, Demetriou, Rudduck, and Myers, *Consulting Pupils: A Toolkit for Teachers* (2003). In this chapter, Helen Demetriou presents three categories of consultation that she and her colleagues have developed and includes specific examples of approaches within each category. Chapter 7 presents the guidelines that Kathleen Cushman and her colleagues used to gather student perspectives for *Fires in the Bathroom: Advice for Teachers from High School Students* (2003). In this chapter, Kathleen Cushman focuses on facilitating discussions with students, offering tips for structuring dialogues as well as question sets and exercises to prompt discussions. Thus, Chapter 6 offers a wide range of consultation approaches, and Chapter 7 offers an in-depth set of guidelines for one particular consultation approach. These guidelines can be used in different ways at different points in one's career, as educators need to consult students over time, not once and for all.

To steer the use of the approaches Demetriou and Cushman present, I reiterate here the set of guidelines for consultation offered by Rudduck and McIntyre (2007):

- Be sure you are committed not only to listening but also to responding. Teachers should embark on student consultation only if they have a genuine desire to hear what students have to say and a firm commitment to try to use what students say to improve teaching and learning in their classrooms.
- Be prepared to explain your purpose and focus. Teachers should explain clearly to students the purpose and focus of their consultation, making clear how, and why, if appropriate, they were selected for consultation and what will happen to what they say, including the teacher's own willingness to be influenced by what students say as well as by other necessary considerations.
- Create conditions for dialogue. For the consultation process to be productive, teachers need to create conditions of dialogue in which teachers and students listen to and learn from each other in new ways (i.e., not in ways that try to fit into existing assumptions and practices).
- Choose methods that focus on deepening understanding. The methods of consultation used should be chosen to deepen teachers' understanding of students' experiences of teaching and learning in their classrooms.
- Give students feedback. After consultation, students need feedback on how what they have said has been understood and on how it will influence or has influenced teacher planning and actions.
- Be realistic. Student consultation needs to be planned realistically from the beginning, with particular attention to the time and energy needed for all phases of it.

The strategies for consultation, tips for structuring dialogues, and question sets and exercises included in this section of the sourcebook offer teachers concrete approaches for consulting students, but individual teachers must take responsibility for following the recommended guidelines, heeding the cautions and revisiting the reminders regarding consultation that I list in the Introduction. As I discuss in the Introduction, student consultation can do more harm than good when those guidelines, cautions, and reminders are not heeded.

6

Accessing Students' Perspectives through Three Forms of Consultation

Helen Demetriou

Pupil consultation can lead to a transformation of teacher-pupil relationships, to significant improvements in teachers' practices, and to pupils having a sense of themselves as members of a community of learners.

—Rudduck and McIntyre, 2007

Chapter Overview

Focus of this chapter: Forms of consultation developed by researchers in the United Kingdom for use by classroom teachers
   Discussed in this chapter:

- Introduction: Historical, policy, and research context
- The emergence of the toolbox: Developing an inventory
- The toolbox
- Ways of consulting students
  - Direct consultation
  - Prompted consultation
  - Mediated consultation
- The toolbox
  - Questionnaire-based approaches
  - Approaches using more open forms of writing
  - Approaches requiring a minimum of writing
  - Talk-based approaches
  - Creative approaches
- What can be gained by consulting students?

73

- What students say they gain from being consulted
- What teachers say about the impact of consultation
- Conclusion

Introduction: Historical, Policy, and Research Context

Rudduck and McIntyre's research that investigated the importance of consulting students[1] regarding teaching and learning was published in 2004. Since then their findings have been disseminated widely, and the need for schools to consult their students has escalated ever since. Indeed, in England, young people's views have recently found a place on the government agenda. This may be ascribed to political expediency, an instrumental view about improving standards, or a growing recognition that young people have a right to be heard and have something worthwhile to say about their school experience. There is a changing social context, a slow swell of opinion about the place of children and young people in today's and tomorrow's world, a climate in which young people are less willing to be taken for granted and in which they are physically becoming adults while still in their middle years of schooling.

The UN Convention on the Rights of the Child sets out four basic principles that include children's right to be heard: nondiscrimination (article 2); best interest of the child (article 3); the right to life, survival, and development (article 6); and the views of the child (article 12). The growing prominence of citizenship education in the school curriculum is another source of support for student voice. There is an extensive and growing literature on student voice, which is not entirely disconnected from its ascendancy on the policy agenda. Several strands run through that literature:

- A historic neglect of students as a source of evidence[2]
- The limitations of seeing students simply as sources of data[3]
- The role of students in school self-evaluation[4]
- The potential contribution of students to school improvement[5]
- The role of students as partners in their own learning[6]

Underlying this development is a premise clearly articulated by SooHoo: "Somehow educators have forgotten the important connection between teachers and students. We listen to outside experts to inform us, and, consequently, overlook the treasure in our very own backyards, the students."[7] While there is comparatively little in the literature on tools with which to dig for the buried treasure, there is evidence of a growing acceptance of the idea that students should have a say about learning (and, even more challengingly, about teaching) and that such tools would be welcomed by teachers. This chapter aims to communicate the importance and power embedded in consulting students in the classroom. Once unlocked, this power has the potential to enhance the quality of teaching and learning and transform the dynamics in the classroom for the benefit of all concerned, not least the students.

Consulting students can take a variety of forms. This chapter illustrates the means of consultation with the concept of a "toolbox" containing a variety of "tools" that represent the means by which students can be consulted. We will illustrate the effectiveness of such a device through schools that have used the tools themselves.[8]

The Emergence of the Toolbox: Developing an Inventory

Instead of placing the tools haphazardly into the toolbox, we felt the need to classify them into sections, so that, like an actual toolbox, when we need a particular tool, we would know where to find it. The following section describes each section of the toolbox with examples of tools that belong in each section.

We identified three forms of consultation, each with its own set of "tools":

- Direct consultation
- Prompted consultation
- Mediated consultation

Direct Consultation

This approach asks students directly about their experiences or views of teaching and learning, usually through questions posed in interviews or group discussion, questionnaires, or checklists. Students respond in words, whether spoken or written, or they tick boxes or smiley faces to mark a view that is similar to theirs or to indicate the extent to which they agree or disagree with the view offered.

The questions that lend themselves to direct consultation are ones where students are likely to have something to say and want to say it: for instance, the things that help them learn and that get in the way of their learning, how they might improve teaching and learning, or support for teaching and learning.

Prompted Consultation

These methods approach the students' thinking and feelings by a more oblique route. Where students are not used to expressing an opinion or where the topic to be explored is one that they might feel uneasy about or not know where to start, it can be helpful to encourage—and legitimate— their comments by starting with things that other students have said about the topic. For instance, a card with a statement by a student from another school or another country can be an effective way of stimulating a response, and so can a video clip or photograph of a differently organized classroom.

Feeding back the results of a questionnaire that the whole class has completed can also be a useful prompt for discussion and can lead to shared recommendations for the improvement of practice.

Mediated Consultation

With this approach, students' comments are, initially, invited in a form that does not rely on words, whether spoken or written. Instead, they communicate feelings or summarize experiences through drawings, taking photographs, making a videotape, or creating and performing a role-play. They may loop back to words but they often find it easier to talk about something they have created themselves and is full of meaning for them, rather than having to respond to someone else's questions.

For instance, students have photographed places, in and out of school, where they feel most comfortable working and role-played different classroom events where they feel that their concentration is undermined by the behaviors of others.

The Toolbox

A toolbox is a virtual container with many instruments designed for a range of users that may be selected for use in different contexts. Despite a wealth of tried and tested approaches to consultation, in our present research we recognized the need for varied and fine-grained tools. Our concern was to enhance the confidence of teachers in engaging with students while consulting them about teaching and learning. Having researched the various approaches for consultation, drawing on recent work with schools as well as the existing literature, we accumulated a variety of tools. Below is a list of these tools. Some are more familiar and more commonly used than others, and some are easier to administer. Our aim is to provide a list of ways in which students can be consulted about their teaching and learning. Such tools included:

Questionnaire-based approaches
- tick-box
- yes/no
- number scales
- symbols
- two-dimension questionnaire
- sentence completion

Approaches using more open forms of writing
- logs and diaries
- writing a note to drop in a suggestion box

Approaches requiring a minimum of writing
- checklist
- spot check
- force field

Talk-based approaches
- conversations
- discussions
- interviews including picture-stories
- reviewing video footage
- evaluation of work

Creative approaches
- drawings
- posters
- photographs
- role-play

Figure 6.1 The Toolbox

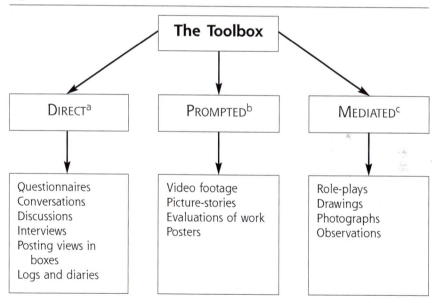

Notes: a. Students are asked directly for their views.
b. A stimulus is used to prompt students to express their views in talk or writing.
c. Students express their views through art or drama and then talk about what they wanted to communicate.

In the pages that follow there are examples of different ways of consulting students and involving them in reflecting on their learning that teachers have used; in some cases the outcomes are summarized. But unlike tools in a household toolbox, these need to be adapted to suit the task and the context, including the age of the students consulted. There are, therefore, no full-length questionnaires or interview schedules but, rather, brief samples. We hope that teachers can decide what kind of approach would fit their purpose and see how they might adapt it for their context. This is therefore a selection of approaches that schools have found useful and that do not make demands that cannot be met in the time and with the resources generally available.

Questionnaire-Based Approaches

Questionnaires have been one of the main tools in the researcher's toolbox and are now commonplace in virtually every walk of life. Schools increasingly use questionnaires internally whether for parents, teachers, or students. The result is that questionnaires have become overused and sometimes abused.

Questionnaires come in all shapes and sizes. Some are based on number scales of 1 to 5, some require yes/no responses, and others depict smiley faces. These and other variations of the questionnaire are explained more fully below as are actual examples from schools that administered their own questionnaires.

Yes/No Questionnaires

Frequently, questionnaires have worded questions for yes or no responses with opportunities to comment further. Examples follow:

> *Do you feel that you have been supported and given opportunities to achieve?*
> *Do you feel that you have been given opportunities to participate in the life of the school?*
> *What improvements have you seen in the following areas? E.g., environment/facilities/study support . . .*
> *Are there any developments you would like to see to benefit younger students in the school?*

Questionnaires Using Number Scales

Questionnaires could include a list of items and require students to rate the degree to which each helps them learn on a scale of 1 to 3. Such items might include *listening to instructions, not doing homework, being polite, being allowed to work on my own, being allowed to work in groups, forgetting equipment, having a short break from my work every period, using my homework diary, being allowed to talk to my friends in class, volunteering to read or to answer questions.* Such questionnaires can lead to students elaborating on their ideas under headings of things that help them learn compared with those that hinder their learning. Students can then be asked to focus on the list of items that help them learn and asked for their ideas to make them happen as well as the things that hinder their learning and asked for their ideas about dealing with these.

In order to ascertain students' thoughts about a subject, questionnaires could be constructed on a 1 to 5 point scale, with 1 as "strongly agree" and 5 as "strongly disagree."

Statements might include:

- *My teacher explains clearly what the lesson is going to be about.*
- *I like it when I am asked to read aloud to my teacher.*
- *When I do very well in class, I feel pleased.*
- *At the end of the lesson I feel that I've learned something.*
- *The teacher is available during the lesson if I want help.*
- *The atmosphere in the lesson is helpful to learning.*
- *I am satisfied with my overall level of performance.*
- *My teacher ignores me.*
- *I work hard in lessons.*
- *Tests are boring.*
- *I find learning difficult.*
- *My parents help me with my schoolwork.*

The questionnaire can then ask students to elaborate by listing reasons for not being satisfied with progress and asking them to mark the ones relevant to them. Moreover, students could be asked to think of other reasons why they are not making satisfactory progress and also if they can think of other ways in which the lessons could be improved.

Wade and Moore developed a questionnaire with a series of statements to which students were asked to circle one response ranging on a five-point scale from "always" to "never."[9] Students were asked to be honest in their responses and assured that no one would know how they responded as they need not write their name unless desired. Statements included were similar to those above.

In the schools where we worked, questionnaires came to be seen more as a starting point: the data they generated raised questions and suggested leads to be followed up—demonstrating the limitations of the questionnaire as a single tool for consulting students about their learning. They play an important role as "tin openers," leading teachers and students more deeply into further inquiry and stimulating different and more sophisticated strategies. Here are three examples used in different contexts:

Questionnaires Using Symbols

Particularly easy to complete and to analyze are questionnaires that use scales where students mark the number, word, or picture that best represents how they feel. In addition, sometimes there are spaces where students can explain their responses. If teachers want to ensure that students avoid the middle position on a three- or a five-point scale, they construct questionnaires with a four-point scale or opt for yes/no responses. Questionnaires that depict smiley faces are particularly useful for students whose reading and writing skills are limited. They may feature faces ranging from sad to happy or pictures of cartoon characters expressing three different emotions: euphoric, indifferent, distressed. Statements might include those shown in Table 6.1.

The Two-Dimension Questionnaire

A useful tool, and one that can generate a lot of discussion, is the questionnaire that asks students to give two responses: first about how true they think a statement is for the school, class, or teaching/learning, and second how important that statement is in their view (see Table 6.2).

Sample questions include:

- If you get stuck, teachers help.
- Students help each other with their learning.
- Students have a say in making decisions.

Table 6.1 Sample Questionnaire Using Symbols

I know how well I'm doing in class.		
1	2	3
Agree	Not sure	Disagree

I work best when I am sitting with my friends.				
1	2	3	4	5
Agree		Not sure		Disagree

I look forward to math lessons.		
Often	Sometimes	Never

I like my classroom.		
☺	☺	☹
All of the time	Some of the time	Never

Table 6.2 Tick Box Sample: Teachers Explain Things Well

This happens in your school now		*Its importance for you*	
True	☐	Very, very important	☐
Mostly true	☐	Very important	☐
Rarely true	☐	Important	☐
Not true	☐	Not important	☐

- I am encouraged to think for myself.
- I am given responsibility at school.
- Nobody minds if you make a mistake.
- The school recognizes all the things I am good at.
- Teachers are fair to everyone.

Another example appears in Figure 6.2.

Alternatively, the questionnaire might ask for students to discriminate between the importance of an item in the teacher's view and the students' perspective (see Table 6.3).

Again, while the "raw" outcomes of the initial questionnaire—how many students thought this and how many thought that—will be of interest to teachers, there can be added value in sharing and discussing the data with students. The focus of discussion and what emerges can sometimes be unpredictable.

Figure 6.2   Responses to "What works in teaching and learning?"

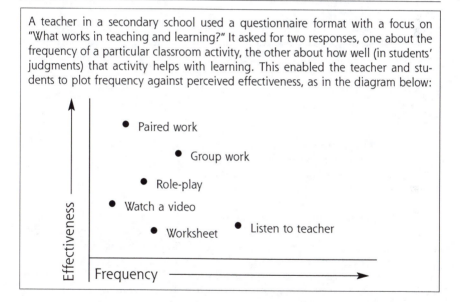

A teacher in a secondary school used a questionnaire format with a focus on "What works in teaching and learning?" It asked for two responses, one about the frequency of a particular classroom activity, the other about how well (in students' judgments) that activity helps with learning. This enabled the teacher and students to plot frequency against perceived effectiveness, as in the diagram below:

Table 6.3   Tick Box Sample: Written Pieces of Work Are Neatly Presented

This is important to teachers		This is important for me	
True	☐	Very, very important	☐
Mostly true	☐	Very important	☐
Rarely true	☐	Important	☐
Not true	☐	Not important	☐

In some settings, it can be useful to invite a group of students to analyze the data and present a summary to the rest of the group. And, of course, the questionnaire may have been designed by a group of student-researchers, with support from the teacher.

Sentence Completion

This questionnaire enables students to elaborate on statements. Schools have presented statements such as the following for students to complete:
    In lessons . . .

- I wish teachers would . . .
- I wish teachers wouldn't . . .
- I wish I could . . .
- It would be great if . . .
- Why do we have to do . . .
- I don't like it when . . .
- The best thing is . . .

Such questionnaires could be given to students to complete individually or in groups, in which case the "I" at the beginning of each statement would be replaced by a "We." Responses can be categorized into positive points, negative points, no response, or more specific categories.

The incomplete sentences below are other examples of those given to students to finish. Students are given instructions to complete them in any way they like.

- When I'm having a test I feel . . .
- I like my favorite subject because . . .
- Some people don't like me because . . .
- Teachers are helpful when they . . .

Questions that referred to the classroom, for example, were then displayed in boxes as shown in Figure 6.3. Students may be asked to write a paragraph or a sentence at the end of a lesson about what they enjoyed, what they found hard, what they learned, or what they didn't learn. Thirty such comments handed in anonymously (or "mailed" to the teacher in a special mailbox) can provide a rich resource for very little investment of time and effort.

Approaches Using Open Forms of Writing

Logs and Diaries

Logs and diaries allow a greater degree of freedom for students to adopt their own style than sentence-completion questionnaires. Diaries offer commentaries on aspects of learning over a limited period, perhaps for a

Figure 6.3 Questions Referring to the Classroom

> 1. What do you think of your classroom as a place to work?

> 2. What could *students* do to make it a better place to learn?

> 3. What could the *teacher* do to make it a better place to learn?

week or even a day. If they are to be shared with teachers or peers, students need to know this in advance. Overall, diaries can be an effective way of eliciting students' ideas about teaching and learning.

Diaries proved particularly useful in an early exploration of students' engagement in Year 8 (equivalent to the seventh grade in a U.S. school), for example.[10] (See Box 6.1.) Entries in special booklets given to students to write about lessons they enjoyed gave the researchers and teachers involved in the project invaluable insights into what the students—who

---

Box 6.1   Sample Diaries

Sample female 1
Spanish—today I learnt the numbers, they were hard at first but then it got easier, it was really fun because we have got scared just in case you did them wrong, but I was all right in the end.

PE—was good today because we did netball and it was excellent. We played dodging and a game, we won two and drew one.

History—In history we did good things and bad things about the churches, it was good because it made us learn more about churches.

My best lesson was PE because we played netball and it was really good.

Sample female 2 (November)
Today in science it was good because you had to experiment with liquid.

French—today we made some posters it was excellent because we were so busy with them that you forgot you were in school.

Technology—Today it was good because I made a chilli and I hadn't made it before, so it has learnt me how to make it.

My best lesson today was technology because it learnt me a lot about cooking.

---

often had difficulties with their work—found engaging. The diary entries also indicated that students had a rather limited vocabulary for talking about learning. (On the occasion when we observed this approach, the outcomes were not shared with the students.)

Students might keep diaries for one or two weeks (as the novelty might wear off sooner for some students), after which the teacher could analyze each diary and report back to students. The range of skills could then be collated and entered in the back of the diaries for reference in lessons. Teachers could also analyze the diaries and note the main issues that arise, such as those that students value in helping them to learn. For example:

- ambience
- teachers
- range of teaching and learning styles
- preferred ways of learning
- enjoyable aspects of lessons
- challenges
- hindrances
- what students feel they have learned
- other factors

The teacher may then interview a small sample of students in groups on the issues raised in the diaries and track one student from the interview sample in order to gain that student's view of the issues raised. Alternatively, teachers could track a student for a day to gain some idea of how much crossover of skills from lesson to lesson is apparent and then interview a number of students to pursue significant issues in greater depth. It is important where diaries are concerned to emphasize the issue of confidentiality to students and also to ensure that students are given feedback. (See Box 6.2 for an example.)

Box 6.2 Talk Diary

The Talk Diary was used to great effect in one school. Students were asked to indicate their thoughts about paired, group, or individual work. This consisted of giving themselves a rating from 1 to 4 (where 1 was the highest) for items such as listening to other people, responding to other people's ideas, helping to organize the talk, helping others in their group, explaining their ideas clearly, understanding the ideas, and enjoying the discussion. Students were then asked to elaborate on their thoughts about the day's discussion and their intentions for the following discussion sessions. Room was made available at the bottom of each page for teachers to add their comments.

Posting Perspectives in "Mailboxes"

Another method of obtaining students' views is to set up "mailboxes" throughout the school into which students may drop a note about their views of different aspects of school (see Box 6.3). This approach has the advantage of making fewer demands on students, as they are able to write notes voluntarily, as well as allowing anonymity. For example, one school set up such "listening posts" where students would post their views about school issues anonymously if they wished and these would be addressed. Some of the suggestions made by students are shown in Box 6.3.

Approaches Requiring a Minimum of Writing

Some tools require a minimum of written commentary by individuals or small groups of students and yet are capable of stimulating discussion. Examples of these are the checklist, the spot check, and the force field.

The Checklist

This approach is useful for students to evaluate the extent to which they feel a given activity contributes to their own learning, using two four-point scales: from "very often" to "rarely or never," and "really learn a lot" to "learn nothing."

These may comprise a blank schedule (as shown in Table 6.4) requiring completion of various activities, or in order to give a greater sense of ownership, it may be used as a class exercise to get students to generate the items themselves (see Table 6.5). The results of using this instrument may be plotted in Figure 6.4.

The Spot Check

An example of a tool requiring a minimum of writing is the spot check. It consists of a form that takes a minute or less to fill out at a given moment in the class. It gives a snapshot view at a given moment of a student's motivation and emotional and intellectual engagement with the lesson.

The spot check provides the teacher with useful, and often challenging, information on the efficacy of teaching and its relationship to learning.

Box 6.3   Examples of Student Comments

I would like it if teachers spent less time talking and more time *listening* to us.

Science lessons are too noisy.

I would like to go on more school trips.

Table 6.4 Sample Checklist

Very often	Quite often	Only sometimes	Rarely or never		Really learn a lot	Learn quite a lot	Learn a little	Learn nothing
				Listening to the teacher				
				Answering the teacher's questions				
				Doing experiments				
				Working on the computer				
				Watching a video				
				Listening to a tape				
				Acting out or doing a role-play				
				Working in pairs				
				Working in a group				
				Taking notes while the teacher talks				
				Taking notes from a book or worksheet				
				Making things (like models)				

Table 6.5 Sample Blank Checklist

Very often	Quite often	Only sometimes	Rarely or never		Really learn a lot	Learn quite a lot	Learn a little	Learn nothing

Figure 6.4   Results of Sample Checklist

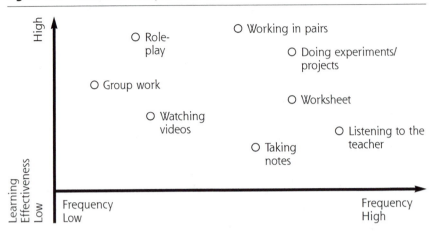

However, if the data are simply scrutinized by the teacher, the value of the tool will be limited. Rather, if it is used as a basis for dialogue, the spot check can be a rich resource. Alternatively, or in addition, the data could be given to a group of student-researchers to analyze and to provide a summary for their peers and teacher.

See Table 6.6 for some useful items to include in the spot check; more could be added. The two columns offer alternative states at any particular moment during the lesson, and students indicate on the three-point scale which end they think they are nearer to. This tool has yielded useful cross-validation information on, for example, students' judgments that teacher talk is the least engaging form of learning for students as compared to when they are active, role-playing, using drama, experimenting, creating, discussing, or discovering.

Table 6.6   Sample Spot Check Form

Concentrating	1	2	3	Thinking about other things
Relaxed	1	2	3	Anxious
Energetic	1	2	3	Tired
Happy with being here	1	2	3	Wishing to be somewhere else
Excited	1	2	3	Bored
Pleased with work	1	2	3	Disappointed with work
Active	1	2	3	Passive
Cheerful	1	2	3	Irritable

The Force Field

Taken from physics, the model is one of opposing forces, pushing forward and backward. If the conditions for learning are looked at in this way, students and teachers together can begin to think about what inhibits and promotes learning and then about what can be done jointly to create the best conditions for learning.

Individual students are given a sheet with the force field diagram as shown in Figure 6.5 and are asked to write down three things that help and three things that hinder their learning. In a class of thirty this task can generate 180 separate items, 90 pluses and 90 minuses, many very similar but some unique to individuals. The summaries can be extended until a list of the most common features emerges—but a parallel list of minority views needs to be kept. Figure 6.6 is an example of a summary from one group of students in a secondary school.

A limitation of this approach is its artificiality: equal numbers of positive and negative features are required. While this pattern may not match the actual balance of feeling of individual students, it is designed to encourage students to think positively as well as negatively. The symmetry is, of course, not sacrosanct, and students can break the rule and may even be encouraged to do so by the teacher. The strength of such approaches is that students become aware of similarities and differences within a class, as do teachers, who are often surprised by aspects of the feedback. As with other tools, it is when these data are explored together that useful pointers emerge.

Figure 6.5   Force Field Diagram

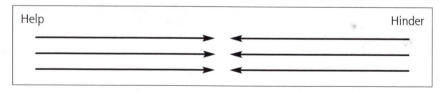

Figure 6.6   Summary List from Force Field Exercise

Things That Help	Things That Hinder
Teachers explaining things when you don't understand Working with someone else Mind maps Using computers Doing a variety of different things	Students who disrupt the class Not getting help when you need it Not being allowed to go to the toilet when you have to Having to just listen all the time Teachers going mental if you forget your pencil

Talk-Based Approaches

The three most common forms of talk-based consultation are conversations, discussions, and interviews. While each approach differs in the degree of formality it offers, all three approaches are able to build into a habit of constructive dialogue about learning and help to establish and sustain an open relationship between teachers and students. Where these three forms of consultation usually rely on direct questions, teachers might also use a variety of prompts to encourage students to talk about the things that matter to them. Toward the end of this section we look briefly at different kinds of prompts: statements made in other contexts by students of a similar age, pictures of young people in identifiable and familiar classroom situations, remarks on pieces of work that students had completed, comments on lessons that students had observed.

Conversations

Informal conversations are a way of tuning in to students' concerns. They take place in a variety of situations but very often away from the classroom: in after-school clubs, on field trips, or in residential settings. Freed from the imperatives of curriculum coverage and classroom control, they allow a spontaneous interchange, especially when they are not initiated by teachers. Moreover, conversations in a relaxed environment are a powerful strategy for honest talking and deep listening. While they do not yield systematic data, they do help to convey the message that teachers are interested in what students have to say. As conversations tend to be informal, students may not consider whether the exchange is confidential—and students may offer greater frankness than in a more formal setting. Outside a research framework, conversations may represent the informal "ideal" of consultation, but it is important to be sure that *all* students feel able to initiate and engage in conversations with the teacher; conversations should not be dependent always on the authority of the teacher to start them or to choose whom to talk to.

Discussions

In contrast to the informal nature of conversations, discussions tend to be more structured and examine a particular topic through argument. Teachers question, elicit questions, and seek feedback from their students as a part of their regular professional practice. For example, they frequently ask in lessons, "Is there anything you don't understand?" "Do you want me to go over that again?" "What do you think?" This form of consultation focuses primarily on individuals and on the *what* of learning. But discussion can focus more on the process, on the *how* of learning, involving groups of students and teachers in a more sustained dialogue about ways of improving learning and teaching.

Discussions about learning are not confined to the classroom but can take place in other forums such as the school council or a research focus group. These occasions usually involve a small group of students, a topic that they are concerned about, a chairperson or interviewer, and a means of recording or summarizing the exchanges. Practical issues include the maximum size of the group and its composition, and whether a self-selecting friendship group or a specially constructed group of students. For example, studies of discussions between ten-year-old friends and non-friends found that friends are more likely to:[11]

- engage in more mutually oriented and less individualistic utterances
- agree with one another more often
- repeat their own and the others' assertions more readily
- pose alternatives and provide elaborations more frequently
- spend less time engaged in "off-task" talk

Boxes 6.4 and 6.5 contain some questions that might be used to stimulate discussion and an example of how a discussion group worked.

Here, the discussions led to a regular student briefing for the senior management team: when this happens, attention needs to be given to the

---

Box 6.4   Discussion Questions

How do you think you learn best?
Can you remember a time when you felt you learned something well or you were particularly successful with something you did at school?
What do you think made you successful?

Can you remember trying to learn something that was really difficult?
What helps you to learn when it is a struggle?
Can you tell me about something you struggled to learn, either in school or outside, and what helped you to overcome the problem?

Are there things that stop your learning sometimes?
Do you find yourself distracted from learning sometimes? Why?
Are there other things that get in the way of your learning at school or at home?

What makes some things harder to learn?
Are some subjects or some ways of working more difficult? Why is that?
What do you think teachers could do to make it easier for you to learn in these subjects or in these activities?

What encourages you to work hard and to achieve?
Do you feel that learning is important? If so, why?
What do you want to achieve?
Are there things that encourage you to try harder?

How do you know if you have been successful in your learning?
How do you know when you have done a good piece of work?
Whose comments do you value most in assessing your work?
Are there things that could improve lessons?

Box 6.5   Discussion Group on Learning

A secondary school invited volunteers (who included some disaffected students) from Year 8 (equivalent to sixth or seventh grade) to take part in a series of discussions about learning. The group met for an hour a week at lunchtime. With the group's permission, the sessions were video-recorded.

The agenda for the first meeting was set by teachers and included items of current policy debate in the school. In later sessions students set their own agenda. Extracts from the videotapes were played back to the whole staff; feedback on what the staff meeting found interesting in the student comments was given to the students. The students' views had an immediate impact on practice—for example, they succeeded in banishing the teacher's red pen for marking. A longer-term outcome was that the senior management team decided to invite students on a regular basis to talk to them about issues in the school that needed reviewing.

---

identities of members of the key informant group and whether they do, in fact, represent a range of student opinion.

Sometimes it is best to approach students' thinking and feeling by a more oblique route. In one form of discussion, a teacher may present a stimulus for students to respond to—statements made by students in another school or country, a video clip or photograph of a differently organized classroom. Feeding back the results of a questionnaire for students to discuss is an example of a prompt; another is lesson observation where the student observers' reports provide the stimulus for discussion.

Observing learners at work can be a powerful source of insight for the observers, and the observation reports can generate lively discussion within the student group. However, student observation does require support and guidance from teachers in what is a sophisticated art (see Box 6.6).

Interviews

Interviews are the most formal way of finding out about what students think. They might be conducted by a teacher, a researcher, or a student. They differ from conversations in that they are much less spontaneous and differ from discussion in that one person asks the questions and the other person (or people) responds. While interviews are often tightly structured, requiring short answers to a number of questions—and more like an oral questionnaire—they can also be open-ended, inviting longer, more reflective responses. Interviews are often one-to-one, but students can feel more relaxed in the company of their peers. It is helpful to record responses on tape or by taking notes, although both may inhibit students' being completely open unless there is a clear explanation of purpose, a high level of trust, or the promise of anonymity. Box 6.7 demonstrates an example of students interviewing other students.

Box 6.6   Student Observations Generate Discussion

Working with their tutor, Year 7 (equivalent to U.S. fifth or sixth grade) students brainstormed about different ways of learning, discussing pros and cons of each: Were some methods more effective than others? Did this depend on the subject or the topic being studied or the teacher? Did it depend on the individual learner? They then decided to try to observe some methods in action. Some subject teachers agreed that they could observe their lessons. The class devised an observation schedule where they rated, in their judgment, students' level of engagement in different teaching strategies: three ticks indicated high engagement. Each student observer focused on one student. A student observer commented on the dilemmas of judging engagement:

> I gave him [the student being observed] three ticks all the way through the test. This was because he was focused all the way through. I think that when you say that you have an important test people try to do their best even though it may be boring. Some people are afraid that if they do not do their best the results will be really bad. Also if the teacher is going to read out the results in front of the class and yours is the worst you'll feel embarrassed. Then again when I saw him thinking about the test I could have been mistaken because he could have been thinking about anything with his mind somewhere else. For me I know the word "test" makes an important effect on my brain.

In the follow-up discussion, issues of procedure were raised and these allowed questions of pedagogy and learning to surface as well.

Box 6.7   Interviews

Year 10 (U.S. eighth or ninth grade) students interviewed groups of four or five younger Year 8 (U.S. sixth or seventh grade) students regarding the impact of friendships on their learning. This interview approach was successful as students are often more willing to talk freely with other students than with teachers.

Ways of Prompting Responses by Using a Variety of Stimuli

Here, we look at ways of prompting a response. We mentioned above the use of statements made by other students, pictures of familiar classroom incidents or contexts, or the use of a particular piece of work that a student has completed. A more unusual approach might include the use of students' comments after they have conducted an observation of a lesson in their own year group or school—or an observation after visiting another school.

The picture-story. The picture-story is another example of a prompted approach that elicits responses while not making students feel that they are being targeted personally. So, for example: "Here is a picture of a boy in his classroom. He has not done very well on his test. How is he feeling? How would you feel?" The two questions often surprisingly reveal discrepancies between how the boy feels and how the student being interviewed would feel. So students may respond: "He feels sad" and "I would feel happy," or "He feels happy" and "I would feel sad."

It is equally important to ask for reasons behind students' responses, as these will validate their answers. An advantage of this approach is that well-planned and -executed picture-stories often provide effective stimuli for the arousal of emotion; however, it is important to consider that emotions may be suppressed when reporting to a "stranger" or someone with whom the student does not feel comfortable.

Reviewing video footage. Students may be filmed during group discussion or lessons and this film played back to them. This has the potential of capturing some of the thoughtful body language of teachers and students and gives an opportunity for reflection and retrospective analysis on the discussion or lesson. Prompting questions might include:

- And what were you thinking of there?
- What might an alternative question have been?
- Did you learn a lot in that lesson?
- What would have helped you to concentrate more?

Evaluation of work. "What do you think makes a good piece of work?" In one school, the teacher-researcher asked each student in the sample to bring a piece of work that he or she was really pleased with and to talk about it. The students answered questions such as these:

- Why were they pleased with it? What was good about it? Was the topic one that they particularly enjoyed? Was the process one they particularly enjoyed? Did it involve doing some research out of school? Did they usually do less well in this subject?
- Did it take a long time—longer than usual?
- Did the teacher think it was a good piece of work? What do they think the teacher liked about it?
- Have they shown it to their parents (or whoever looks after them)?

Creative Approaches to Consultation

In social research pictures have the capacity to short circuit the insulation between action and interpretation, between practice and theory, perhaps because they provide a somewhat less sharply sensitive instrument than words and certainly because we treat them less defensively.

—Schratz and Walker, 1995, p. 76

Drawing or painting does not rely on words at all. An advantage of drawing as a way of communicating is that it is not associated with "success" or "failure," "right" or "wrong," in the same way that writing is. This can mean that students are less concerned about producing the answer they think the teacher wants. Making posters provides another opportunity for nonwritten communication: students can convey their views through symbols and colors with no—or minimal—writing. (See Box 6.8.)

Drawings

Image-based techniques may be very effective ways of generating information. In an attempt to explore the visual image of a research question, students may draw images to convey some aspect of the issue and explain in detail how the pictures relate to their experience. However, it is important to appreciate the limitations that drawings alone may display. Drawings should therefore sometimes be used as prompts in discussions, rather than as data in themselves.

Burnard's "Rivers of Experience" approach has also proved to be successful.[12] The technique allows students to investigate their thoughts through contemplation and reflection on experience. Unlike an interview, this approach encourages reflective conversation, and like rivers, words in reply to a question flow with few constraints. Moreover, students are invited to visualize their lives as a winding snake or winding river in which each twist in its body or bend in the river represents a change in direction of, or intention for, gaining friends, achieving, and so on. The events are then located on different bends along the length of a winding river or snake. Once students are asked to reflect on the whole picture, patterns begin to emerge.

Box 6.8　Posters

In a secondary school, groups of Year 8 (U.S. sixth or seventh grade) students created posters on the topic "How we like learning in Geography." The teacher started the session with a general discussion about learning and the group brainstormed "different ways we learn" to remind them of a range of possibilities. Some students split their posters into likes and dislikes. The posters included drawings of, for example, graph work and maps (least liked), computers and videos (most liked). Some included text, for example:

"We never stop learning but there are always things we do and don't enjoy about learning. My least favorite ways of learning are end of module tests, working from worksheets and textbooks, and homework. However, I like to draw, watch videos, have class discussions, tell stories, work on projects, taste food, find information on the net and put myself in the picture."

Photographs

Photographs are quite often used as tools for evaluating aspects of teaching and learning; they allow students to identify key features of learning environments. Students are given disposable cameras with which to take photographs of people and places around the school or home related to specific issues. The photos can then be used as a way of encouraging students to explain their findings by discussing the contents of the photographs (see Box 6.9).

Some teachers have used photographs in a counselling approach with students with behavioral problems. In one instance this tool was used with a girl who could speak but had difficulty expressing emotions. The photographs successfully gave her an extra way to show how she felt.

Role-Play

Schools have asked students (especially those who are more outgoing and enjoy drama) to enact a typical classroom scene with a student acting as the teacher and the others as students, in order to ascertain their perceptions of the classroom as a learning environment. The students would then discuss their roles with the class as a whole in order to, for example, enhance learning in the classroom.

In a secondary school, students enacted a geography classroom scene where the class learned about volcanoes. A student was chosen to act as the teacher and other students acted as themselves. The "teacher" then taught the class about volcanoes using a blackboard, in the way she had previously seen her teacher doing. At the end of the improvisation, all the students discussed what they had learned, what aspects helped with their learning, and which things got in the way of their learning.

What Can Be Gained by Consulting Students?

How can we gauge the impact of consulting students? It is not easy to find reliable evidence of impact: students are exposed to so many sources of influence that it is difficult to be sure what exactly is creating a particular effect. However, here are some ways of judging impact; they would all be enriched through personal testimony from the students themselves as well as the observations of their teachers.

You might look for evidence of:

- raised attainment of students in a subject linked to the consultation;
- the achievement of a group of students more broadly defined who have been involved in consultation;
- students' attitudes toward learning or toward school.

Box 6.9   Photographs Used in Homework Research

A secondary school used photographs to research homework and home study. Selected student volunteers were given a disposable camera and allowed to take up to five photos in one evening or weekend. The camera was then passed to another student. Over the course of a week one camera was shared by five students and generated up to twenty-five photos. These were then brought into class and made into a display. Students then circulated around the "art gallery" and questioned one another about their photos. These were some of the things students said or wrote about their photos (in captions) as things that helped them work at home:

> my chair and my computer
> music, which helps me concentrate
> my radio and good music
> TV, which helps me relax when I'm doing HW
> my mum who's clever
> friends

The teacher commented that photo evaluations helped students to reflect on their learning; they liked being able to communicate their thoughts in this different way, and the photos were a good stimulus for discussion within the whole class. Students at the school had previously taken photographs of places in school where they felt safe.

*   *   *

In a secondary school, Year 8 (U.S. sixth or seventh grade) students took photographs of things that indicated the good and bad things about doing schoolwork at home. When the photographs were developed, each class divided into groups to discuss the evidence and then produced a composite poster of good and bad points.

Good points:

- No distractions; no one to hinder you or break your concentration
- Unrestricted use of a computer
- You can listen to music at the same time
- You can take a break when you like
- There's no rush—you can take your time
- You learn how to organize yourself
- You can phone a friend!
- You can choose when, where, and how to work

Bad points:

- Too many temptations not to work—television, music
- No teacher to help you

continues

> ### Box 6.9 Continued
>
> - Miss out on seeing your friends
> - No one to talk things over with
> - It takes too much time
> - Temptation to rush things because you are going out
> - Not enough time on your own to relax
> - Sometimes you wonder if what you are doing is really worthwhile
>
> After the class discussion the photos were mounted and displayed in a corridor with questions asking passersby to consider their own experiences of homework. The school then used the findings for a more in-depth discussion on how homework helps learning.

Or you could look for evidence of a different kind, such as

- students thinking more critically and reflectively about their learning;
- students using tools to evaluate their own learning.

Such approaches clearly require some baseline data before the consultation starts so that you can judge impact. Alternatively, or additionally, you might rely on the testimony, or self-report, of students and their teachers.

The focus of evaluation is often the academic progress or attitudes to learning of a group of students, sometimes in a particular subject, who have been involved in consultations about teaching and learning. But the focus can be broader, such as the longer-term capacity of the school to sustain effective consultation as a basis for self-improvement and knowledge creation. More ambitious measures of impact—provided that the consultation has been sustained over time—would be:

- a growth in teacher awareness of how and when to consult students most effectively;
- the embedding of consultation approaches in the daily practice of classrooms as well as in home learning, field trips, and other learning experiences and occasions;
- a formal commitment by the school to the continuing development of opportunities for consultation and to using the outcomes openly and constructively.

What Students Say about Being Consulted

We can only offer some general indications of the kinds of things that students identify as the benefits of consultation. These include:

- feeling that you are respected and that you are listened to and taken seriously;

- knowing that your views are having an impact on how things are done in the school and classroom;
- feeling that you have greater control over the pace or style of teaching and learning;
- feeling that you are able to talk about your own learning and are more confident about how to improve it;
- feeling more positive about learning and about school because you feel more involved with its purposes.

The negative things students say about being consulted tend to focus on:

- lack of feedback or follow-up action;
- teachers making the important decisions themselves;
- teachers not really interested in what students have to say ("like when they give out the evaluation forms in the last 30 seconds of the lesson and we don't have time to reflect")

What Teachers Say about the Impact of Consultation

Teachers tend to echo the things that students identify as positive outcomes of consultation. For example:

- students are more able to talk about their learning and are more aware and accepting of their learning needs after consultation;
- students are more confident about telling their teacher if they don't understand something;
- students have a greater sense of why they are doing a particular task and a stronger sense of ownership;
- students are more ready to become involved and to take initiative.

Here are some verbatim comments from secondary school teachers:

> We've learnt a lot . . . about how students rapidly improve in their learning and their self-esteem and their motivation through dialogue with staff, through feeling important, feeling cared for, feeling their views matter. I think it's had a really, really significant effect.

> We've had some very clear pointers from students about how they like to learn and I think it's given quite an encouragement to different ways of teaching. . . . The information . . . certainly has had an impact on the syllabus that I deliver. We've modified things or developed things further—and had the courage of our convictions.

Teachers also say how their perceptions of students' capabilities have changed as a result of talking with them about some of the taken-for-granted aspects of teaching and learning. They report a much more positive view of students' capacities for observation and constructive analysis:

> I know I shouldn't be [but] I'm still astounded at the depth of their honesty. And about how much if we listen we can learn and influence what's happening with them and be part of what's happening with them.

Staff that you thought wouldn't ever listen who'd see this going on and think, "Fine, yes, but that's not for me"—once they see the students reacting and hear what they're saying (and they may be saying in a lesson, "Well, would you mind if I did that a slightly different way, would that be all right?") they're suddenly thinking, "Well, maybe they do know what they're talking about." And that brings more staff in.

Conclusion

This chapter has aimed to show the wide array of tools that can be used to consult students about their teaching and learning. If we dig into the toolbox, it is important that we choose the appropriate tool for the job. In so doing we customize the consultation process and tailor it to the particular context. Only then can the consultation be effective and yield the optimal feedback and thereby contribute to our ongoing knowledge of teaching and learning in the classroom.

Notes

Continuing thanks go to all the students, parents, and teachers of all the primary and secondary schools who took part in this study and particularly for their enthusiasm and cooperation. This chapter is written in memory of Professor Jean Rudduck, who will always be remembered for her commitment, enthusiasm, contribution, and inspiration to educational research.

1. Although the term "pupil" is commonly used in England, throughout this chapter the term "student" is used to be consistent with usage throughout this book.

2. Fullan, 1991.

3. Fielding, 1999.

4. MacBeath, 1999.

5. Rudduck, 1995.

6. Groundwater-Smith, 1998.

7. SooHoo, 1993, p. 389.

8. I use "we" in acknowledgment of my coauthors of the publication upon which this chapter is based: J. MacBeath, H. Demetriou, J. Rudduck, and K. Myers (2003), *Consulting Pupils: A Toolkit for Teachers* (Cambridge, England: Pearson Publishing). Because the current sourcebook is a text for secondary teachers, those consultation methods appropriate to older students are highlighted, and some that appeared in the source text have been modified for a secondary school student population.

9. Wade and Moore, 1993.

10. In England, the primary school system typically ranges from reception class to Year 1 through Year 6—a total of seven classes with students ranging in age from four to eleven years old. The secondary school system ranges from Year 7 to Year 13—a total of seven year classes with students ranging in age from eleven to eighteen years old.

11. Hartup, 1995.

12. Burnard, 2002.

7

Accessing Students' Perspectives through Discussion Groups and Questionnaires

Kathleen Cushman and student researchers

Chapter Overview

Focus of this chapter: A collection of guidelines, question sets, and exercises developed by researchers in the United States to gather student perspectives on their schooling experiences[1]

Discussed in this chapter:

- Background on this resource
- Tips for structuring dialogues with students
- Reminders for respectful discussions
- Question sets and exercises to prompt discussions with students
- Theme 1: Personal connections to the teacher
- Theme 2: Expectations and motivation
- Theme 3: Learning inside the classroom and out
- Theme 4: Classroom climate and management

Background on This Resource

In the book *Fires in the Bathroom: Advice for Teachers from High School Students* (2003), urban teenagers across the country speak bluntly about their school experiences. Their comments, gathered during intensive discussions and writing sessions with researchers at the nonprofit group What Kids Can Do, Inc. (www.whatkidscando.org), met with immediate interest on publication. Many educators, even those seasoned by years in the classroom, found themselves struck by aspects of the student experience that had somehow slipped their notice. "This book is both painful and wonderful to read," commented Deborah Meier, whose career as an educational leader spans over forty years.

The insights in *Fires in the Bathroom* reflect a fundamental feature of adolescence that is curiously ignored by most current school reform efforts: the need for teenagers to enter into meaningful partnerships with adults. Increasingly, research suggests that addressing this developmental need within the school setting has significant positive effects on students' motivation, engagement, and academic achievement. If we seek those outcomes as an educational priority, improving communication between students and their teachers would be a good place to start.

Encouragingly, listening to students does not depend on any particular expertise. Anyone who likes young people and values their opinions can do this work. It takes time, persistence, and attention to organize, but it can easily take place in the context of a classroom or advisory group. It requires thoughtful analysis to sort out patterns and draw conclusions from a flood of material, but educators and students possess those talents in abundance.

This chapter, originally produced as a short manual for teachers, offers a starting place for those interested in finding out what students have to say. Using the same questions that prompted the discussions leading to *Fires in the Bathroom*, teachers can begin for themselves the honest dialogue from which both students and adults so richly benefit. Whether gathered through student writing or transcribed conversations, the responses will begin to build a base of mutual confidence that students have something valuable to contribute to their own education. As students encounter the teaching tools devised by the young coauthors of *Fires in the Bathroom*, they can critique and enlarge them based on their own experiences. And as teachers hear their own students speak their minds in a structured and respectful setting, they can begin to adapt their practice to meet students' learning needs more effectively.

Tips for Structuring Dialogues with Students

The steps below reflect the experiences of researchers for What Kids Can Do as we gathered students' opinions about school for publication in *Fires in the Bathroom*. Though your own process might easily vary, the basic principles remain important, reflecting our fundamental belief that adults must actively seek to understand what students think and why they think it.

Root the Process in Inquiry

Begin by developing questions that will yield what you're really interested in learning about. In our case, we needed to know what new teachers worried about most as they prepared to teach adolescents in diverse urban classrooms. So we began by querying several groups of beginning teachers: "If you could ask your students any question about what or how you teach, what would you ask?"

We shaped questions from their replies, sorting them into sets that seemed to go together. We tried to keep our questions concrete, basing them in students' experiences, not just their opinions. And we learned to recognize the questions that bombed, asking students during uncomfortable pauses: "Is this the right question? What do you think the real question is?" We constantly asked what we might be forgetting.

Steadily, students transformed our questions—that is, the questions of new teachers—into their own. For us, this was a crucial goal from the start: that the students be collaborators, not subjects, in the research.

Gather Students Willing to Express Their Thoughts

Unlike teachers who have ready access to young people, we had to locate the students who would collaborate with us for *Fires in the Bathroom.* Using every available professional connection, we sought out students who would talk openly about their school experiences. Whenever we found students willing to participate, we asked whether they could interest a friend in coming, too. Academic success was not a requirement; in fact, we most wanted students who struggled in school. We paid students for their time at an hourly rate comparable to that of an undergraduate research assistant. Though most teachers will not be able to offer stipends, they can seek other concrete ways (a quiet and comfortable environment, refreshments, help with transportation) to convey respect for students' time and energy.

Keep Groups Small

Typically, we gathered in small groups of three to five students—which clearly will not be possible for teachers if they use class time for their discussions. Advisory groups of around twelve students, or extracurricular teams or clubs, however, could provide smaller alternative settings.

Each of our groups met for at least three sessions of three to five hours, for the most part on weekends and during school vacations. Inevitably, given the press of their lives and their skepticism about this unusual enterprise, only half of those we expected actually showed up. Teachers may have an advantage in this regard, if they can schedule more frequent but shorter sessions during or after school.

Write Everything Down

Our sessions combined writing and discussion, in proportion to students' capacities and rhythms. We recorded on a notebook computer everything students said, and we later transcribed their handwritten responses to our question sets as well. That visible commitment to take account of everything students said created a climate of serious purpose. The facilitator often read back what people had said for accuracy, asking follow-up questions and giving them the chance to critique, amend, or amplify their comments. A conversation that spiraled into casual chitchat returned more quickly to the subject as students saw their words written down.

Video or audio tape recorders later proved good alternatives to writing down student comments, particularly when used in combination with notes on chart paper that everyone could see. Though recording conveys the desired tone of purpose and consequence to the discussion, transcribing the recordings is an important next step—one that makes analyzing and sharing student comments with others much easier.

Ask for Evidence

Because students are as ready as adults to rely on abstractions or generalizations, we continually sought supporting details and specific situations in their responses. If a student complained about a teacher, for instance, we tried to nail down the offending behavior, not merely record the student's annoyance. Kids got used to our saying, "Can you tell me more about that?" or "What was *that* like for you?" As students worked together, they grew more adept at supporting their own assertions and probing each other's experiences for nuance and contradictions.

Analyze the Material Together

Because the goal of our book was to offer advice, our discussions always ended with: "So what would you suggest to a teacher?" We weighed whether spontaneous advice ("We shouldn't have homework!") was merely frivolous or contained kernels of wisdom. Analyzing students' suggestions together, we created lists of Dos and Don'ts, calendars, questionnaires, and exercises to help teachers and students better understand each other. This chapter presents a few examples of the many that appear in *Fires in the Bathroom.* Students in different settings might alter or expand upon them or create their own from scratch.

Create a Written Product

The fact that we had to write something from students' responses lent a sense of purpose to our conversations. Teachers may likewise benefit from proposing a written product of some sort as a culmination to the discussions. Whether it takes the shape of classroom norms posted on the wall, an article in the school newspaper, or a presentation before the school board or PTA, having to create a written document adds seriousness to the endeavor.

In most cases, we chose not to publish the names of teachers when they came up in student comments, whether positive or negative. But encouragingly, students' suggestions often derived from the example of a particularly effective teacher in their school.

Reminders for Respectful Discussions

Though teachers and other professionals undoubtedly draw on their own norms for group discussions, we offer the following tips as reminders for keeping conversations respectful, positive, and productive.

1. If possible, limit the number of group participants to twelve.
2. Make sure only one person talks at a time. Write down a speaking order if necessary, and do not allow interruptions.
3. Make sure everyone has the opportunity to speak; one or two people should not dominate the conversation.
4. Ask neutral, open-ended questions. Avoid leading questions and those that can be answered with a simple "yes" or "no."
5. Opposing points of view should always focus on the idea or opinion, never the person expressing it.
6. Make sure to designate a note-taker. If appropriate, appoint a clock-watcher to keep track of the time.

Question Sets and Exercises to Prompt Discussions with Students

In the sections that follow, we provide examples of the question sets we used with our student coauthors of *Fires in the Bathroom*. So as to break up the material into smaller parts, we group the questions—and exercises that accompany them—into four themes.

- *Personal connections to the teacher*
- *Expectations and motivation*
- *Learning inside the classroom and out*
- *Classroom climate and management*

We trust teachers will use these themes, question sets, and exercises as they see fit. They can use the questions to spark discussion with their own students, or modify or replace our prompts to address the questions that most concern them. They can present our questions to students as a model, then seek from students their own alternative questions.

In the case of *Fires in the Bathroom*, we discussed some of the questions as a group; for others we had students write down individual responses. How many questions or exercises to attempt in any one session will depend on individual schedules and the pacing that best suits students' capabilities.

A final note: each of the sets below consists of several individual questions. For both writing and discussion sessions, we found that asking students the questions one at a time produced the best results; it allowed students to focus on the topic at hand without looking ahead to what came next.

Theme 1: Personal Connections to the Teacher

Students appreciate being asked what helps them feel respected and engaged in the classroom, and they can often give specific examples from their experience. To keep the discussion from turning too negative, follow up any complaint with the question, "What would have been a better way for the teacher to handle that situation?"

Question Sets

Describe the teacher you liked the best. Describe the teacher you learned the most from. Are they different? If so, why?

Do you need to like a teacher to be able to learn from a teacher? Does the teacher need to like the students? Can you tell if a teacher likes some students better than others?

Have you ever had a teacher who especially liked you better than other students? How could you tell and how did that make you feel? Have you ever had a teacher who especially didn't like you? How could you tell and how did that make you feel?

When a teacher is different from you or from most of the class in some way, what are the things he or she can do that can help make a connection anyway? What are the things that don't work?

Exercise: A Questionnaire for Teachers to Give Their Students

Student authors of *Fires in the Bathroom* compiled the questionnaire shown in Figure 7.1 as a way for teachers to get to know their students. They suggested teachers distribute it to their classes on the first day of school. It reflects the information that they wanted their teachers to know about them; different groups of students, of course, may have different ideas.

Exercise: Questions Students Would Like to Ask Their Teachers

Though adolescents often hide it, they are interested in their teachers' lives. The students who worked with us on *Fires in the Bathroom* listed the following questions as ones they'd like to ask their teachers. Teachers can either answer these questions for their students or use the list as a starting place to solicit questions their own students would want to ask them.

Figure 7.1   Sample Questionnaire of Student Information

Who Are You?
A Questionnaire for Students on the First Day of School
Note: I will not share your answers with anyone without your permission.

Basic information:

Name: _____   Name you like to be called: _____

Date of birth: _____   Place of birth: _____

Phone number: _____   E-mail address: _____

Parents' or guardians' names: _____

Any siblings? What ages? Do they live with you?_____

Others who live in your household: _____

What language do you speak at home? _____

Are you new to this school? Where were you before? _____

About your activities and interests:

What time do you usually get up in the morning? _____

When do you usually go to bed at night? _____

How do you get to school? _____ How long does it take? _____

What do you do after school? _____

_____

What are your other interests? _____

_____

What do you imagine yourself doing ten years from now? _____

_____

- Where did you go to college?
- Did you have other jobs before this one? What were they?
- Why did you become a teacher? Why this subject?
- Are you married? Do you have any kids?

Theme 2: Expectations and Motivation

These next questions ask students to think about their own learning—and as they do, to identify the conditions under which they either do well or lose heart. Not only does the discussion give the students practice in higher-order thinking, but their answers can help teachers enormously in shaping a more effective classroom practice.

Question Sets

How does a teacher give little signals that she expects you to try hard and do well? That he expects you *not* to try hard and do well? That she thinks you are smart or not? How might a teacher act in ways that make it safe to try hard and to do well? That make it unsafe?

In or out of school, have you ever felt that you were learning something and it was important to *you* to learn that, not just because you were supposed to? If so, what made those things so important? Have you ever had that feeling in a class? If so, describe that time.

Has your teacher ever asked you a question that really made you think about something in a new way? That made it clear that you weren't supposed to think?

In your life in and out of school, what pressures are on you to do well? What pressures you *not* to do well?

Was there ever a time in your life that you felt that you hated school? If so, why? Was there ever a time in your life that you felt that you loved school? If so, why?

Theme 3: Learning Inside the Classroom and Out

These questions aim to identify the situations in which students act most like confident and independent learners—whether they are learning on their own, from their peers, or from mentors in or out of school. Students' responses can help teachers design tasks that dovetail with students' own interests and expertise.

Question Sets

Have you ever been in a situation where you're learning from other students, not just from the teacher? If so, how did that happen? (Did the teacher's actions have anything to do with it?)

Teachers often are told not to do all the talking, but instead to set up situations in which students are more active—group work, hands-on activities, discussions or seminars, projects and presentations. What do you like about these strategies, and why? What do you dislike about them, and why? If they're not working, what could teachers do to make them work better?

Make a list of everything you know a lot about, whether you learned it in school or out of school. Next to each item, say who helped you learn that thing. Next to each thing on your list, make a check if one or more of your teachers knows about your expertise in that area.

Has there ever been a time (in or out of school) when you really wanted to write something? If so, explain. Have you ever wanted to make a piece of your writing the best it could possibly be? If so, explain why.

List all the situations in your life (in school or out) in which you read anything at all. Put a plus mark beside any of the items on your list that you enjoy. Put a minus mark beside any of the items on your list that you don't enjoy.

Exercise: A Student Questionnaire on Individual Learning Styles

Our student coauthors created the questionnaire shown in Figure 7.2 as an aid to help teachers understand their students' various learning styles. They suggested distributing it early in the school year or semester.

Theme 4: Classroom Climate and Management

Some of the following questions get at issues filled with tension and strong emotions on the part of both teachers and students. To keep the discussion from slipping into defensive responses or arguments, it can help to take turns speaking and listening, without interruption. Writing in journals afterward can also provide a way to reflect on what participants hear, with the benefit of time to think over new perspectives.

Question Sets

Describe a classroom in which you felt safe and comfortable speaking up or asking questions when you didn't understand something. What made it feel that way? When does it feel bad for a teacher to call on you in class? Why? How does it feel when a teacher singles you out for praise? For criticism? Why?

Sometimes teachers aren't experts in the material they're asked to teach you. Make a list of all the things teachers should do and shouldn't do when they're in that situation.

Teachers sometimes have trouble managing their classes. What kinds of trouble have you seen teachers run into? When you see them have trouble like that, can they ever recover from it? What does it feel like to be in a class when the teacher is having trouble?

How should the teacher act when students in a class act mean or cruel to each other? How should the teacher act when a student disrupts the class?

How does a teacher know when a kid has been disrespectful? What's the way the teacher could best deal with it? Describe an example of when you or another student has been disrespected by a teacher. Can a teacher fix a situation like that? If so, how?

Do you (or other students) test out a teacher? How? What's the worst thing a new teacher can do?

Figure 7.2   Sample Questionnaire on Individual Learning Styles

---

How Do You Learn?
A Questionnaire for Students

Do you like this subject? Why or why not? _____

What would you really like to learn about in this class? _____

_____

_____

How much homework do you expect? _____

_____

What's fair for me to expect from you? _____

_____

Describe the way you learn things best. _____

_____

_____

How do you feel about working in groups? _____

_____

Is there anything that could make this class especially hard for you? ____

_____

_____

Can you think of a way I could help you with this? _____

_____

Is there anything else about you that you would like me to know? _____

_____

_____

Exercise: Understanding Student Behavior

Fires in the Bathroom student authors explained that a teacher's display of fairness, trust, and respect has an important effect on students' classroom behavior. If a teacher knows and cares about the material and treats kids with respect and fairness, students say they generally will pay attention, do the work, and play by the rules. But if teachers signal unwillingness to keep up their part, kids will immediately act to right the balance, a struggle that many consider an "out-of-control classroom." Our student authors created and completed a table (see Table 7.1) as a way to help

Table 7.1 Sample Table: Disruptive Student Behaviors and Suggestions for Teachers

Understanding Student Behavior

When We Feel . . .	We Act Like This . . .	How a Teacher Could Change That Feeling
Bored	Inattentive, passing notes, playing cards, reading magazines, eating or drinking, talking to friends, giggling, pestering teacher with irrelevant questions	Use curriculum and activities that relate to our interests or call on our strengths
Physically restless		
Insecure about our status among peers		
Upset or worried about personal or family troubles		
Anxious about not being able to do the work		
Unseen and unheard, disrespected or disliked by the teacher		

teachers understand what lies behind certain types of disruptive student behaviors. Teachers can ask their students to fill in their own answers or add to Table 7.1.

Conclusion

We want to conclude by reiterating that teachers should use and modify the themes, question sets, and exercises included in this chapter as they see fit. By presenting our questions to students as a model and then seeking from students their own alternative questions we can begin the necessarily ongoing process of inviting students to help teachers make their classroom practices more effective.

Note

1. Originally published under the title "First Ask, Then Listen: How to Get Your Students to Help You Teach Them Better—A Teacher's Guide."

Part III

Listening in Action: Educators Learning from Students' Perspectives

In this section, I have gathered stories of how prospective and experienced teachers, school leaders, and teacher educators make learning from the student's perspective central to educational practice. Each of these chapters takes up from a slightly different angle the challenges and possibilities of putting into practice the principles identified in Part I and the strategies discussed in Part II.

Chapters 8 and 9 are written by teachers at the very beginning of their careers, one an undergraduate at Bryn Mawr College who completed an English major and her certification in English and one a graduate of Haverford College with some teaching experience who returned to complete his secondary certification through the Bryn Mawr/Haverford Education Program after teaching in China for two years. In Chapter 8, Darla Himeles narrates key moments in her early years as a student and tutor of other students during which she learned to listen to what students said and what they did not say. She discusses how developing the capacity for reflective practice deepened her ability to listen and to know what to listen for and how to change her practice in response. She then applies these early lessons to her work in education courses and preparation for student teaching, and she draws on the reflective papers she wrote during her student teaching to represent the thinking and work she did as an English teacher in a magnet school in an urban setting. This chapter offers to prospective teachers a rare glimpse into a student teacher's thought processes and into how her evolving commitments played out in her practices.

In Chapter 9, Brandon Clarke provides a before-and-after narrative pivoting on his realization that, while he thought he was listening to students, he really was not. Brandon learned through critical analysis and reflection and through a willingness to reexamine the assumptions he had made that he was not genuinely valuing or attending to students' perspectives or voices, even as he considered himself a student-centered teacher. He returns to moments of assumptions he made while participating in Teaching and Learning Together (see Chapter 13) and transcribing the tapes of the student discussions that constitute a critical component of that project. He also focuses on the revisions of those assumptions that were necessary to make him more of a genuine listening teacher. In the second part of his chapter, he discusses how he attempted to act on his realizations and revised commitments during his student teaching in an urban charter school.

Darla's and Brandon's stories illustrate that becoming a teacher who learns from the student perspective is a challenging and ongoing process. While they are at the beginning of that process, Chapter 10 is written by a teacher at the other end of her career: a newly retired teacher who completed thirty-four years of teaching in an urban school district. Caught off guard in that final year by being assigned a notoriously challenging senior English class at the highest ranked magnet school in Philadelphia, Marsha Rosenzweig Pincus uses the process of reflection on the way she structured that class to trace her evolution as a teacher committed to putting students at the center of their learning and her teaching. Impeded in her early years as a teacher by performance evaluations and her own lack of confidence, Marsha developed, with the support of several programs as well as her experience of becoming a mother, not only the conviction but also the capacity to learn from her students' perspectives and to shape her courses around their needs. Marsha's success within her classroom locally—along with the national recognition she has received—attests to her individual capacities but also to the power of learning from the student's perspective.

These narratives offer vivid illustrations of teachers working within their classrooms to listen to students. Chapters 11 and 12 offer glimpses into how several school leaders have created educational contexts that put students at the center not only of learning but also of conceptualizing and revising the daily and long-term workings of the school. Chapter 11 offers a principal's perspective: Peter Evans discusses how he developed a forum in his public high school in Vermont that created a space for student voices to be heard and included in decisionmaking processes at the school. He discusses the origin, the evolution, and the maintenance of his approach, weaving throughout his discussion the perspectives of students who have worked with him. Peter's description of the process and his analysis of the challenges and possibilities of creating such a space for students offer other school leaders useful guidelines and inspiration for creating similar forums.

In Chapter 12, Lois Easton and Daniel Condon describe how the Eagle Rock School in Colorado, an intentionally small, independent school for students who have dropped out of mainstream school settings, is built around student voice and prepares teachers through the Professional Development Center at Eagle Rock. Lois and Daniel present the premises and the features of Eagle Rock School, describe the professional development center and fellowship program, offer the lessons they have learned from students that shape the school, and share the perspectives of fellows who have visited the Professional Development Center at Eagle Rock and taken lessons learned back to their own school contexts. In these chapters, readers can find discussions of administrators' perspectives and examples of how listening to student voices and perspectives, as well as placing students squarely at the center of imagining and administering the school, can be implemented on a school-wide basis. In the students' words included in these chapters, we hear echoes of what the students from other school contexts had to say in Chapters 1 through 5—about relationships, positive learning environments, engagement, respect, and responsibility.

Moving from stories of classroom and school practices to stories of how teachers can be prepared to teach in ways that attend and respond to student perspectives, in Chapter 13, I discuss how I position secondary students as teacher educators in the semester prior to student teaching in the Curriculum and Pedagogy seminar I teach through the Bryn Mawr/ Haverford Education Program at Bryn Mawr and Haverford colleges in Pennsylvania. Through a four-part project within which high school students are positioned as teacher educators in direct dialogue with prospective teachers, I aim to foster the development of teachers committed to consulting students during their student teaching and beyond. In Chapter 14, Bernadette Youens discusses a program at the University of Nottingham in England in which secondary students serve as mentors during the teaching practicum of initial teacher preparation. She describes the genesis, structure, and challenges of this project, emphasizing the possibilities and drawbacks of positioning students as mentors.

These chapters are written by educators at the beginning, in the middle, and at the end of their careers, educators who work in urban and rural settings and with student populations ranked highest and those who were never expected to complete high school, and educators who work with prospective teachers in both the United States and England. They were written independently of one another and the authors did not read other sections of this sourcebook. The stories told here and the remarkable consistency of themes—such as relationships, respect, and responsibility— speak to the power of learning from the student's perspective and suggest that it can happen anywhere and with anyone if it is done carefully, deliberately, and reflectively.

8

Learning to Be Heard and Learning to Listen

A Preservice Teacher's Reflections on Consulting Students during Practice Teaching

Darla Himeles

Chapter Overview

Focus of this chapter: One preservice teacher's reflection on her journey from a student who wanted to be heard to a tutor and student teacher who attempted to listen to her students.

Discussed in this chapter:

- Context for this discussion
- Learning to be heard: The origins of my thinking about consulting students
- Learning to listen: Transitioning from student to private tutor
- Learning to listen better: Discovering reflective practice
- Focusing on learners
- Transitioning to teaching: Revising my writing, revising myself
- Incorporating students' perspectives in my classroom
- The risks we take in learning with and from students
- Learning from our narratives: Noting and reflecting on transitions

Context for This Discussion

In September 2006, four months after graduating and becoming certified to teach secondary English, I visited the Curriculum and Pedagogy seminar that Alison Cook-Sather teaches at Bryn Mawr College and that I had completed almost a year before, the final class that certification candidates in the Bryn Mawr/Haverford Education Program take before their student teaching semester. My purpose for visiting these students was to discuss with them how I came to reflect on and utilize student perspectives in my own student teaching, as well as how that practice has continued to inform my life and work since graduation. To give them an idea of where I was coming from, I felt like I needed to start at the beginning, *before* I was in their position. By showing them a fuller narrative of myself, I thought, I might encourage them as they proceeded to write about, plan for, and ultimately invite student input into their teaching.

The following is an expanded version of what I talked about with those students. When appropriate, I weave in excerpts written during my transitions from college student to student teacher to graduate. These excerpts sound the echoes and dissonances between myself in the midst of these transitions and myself a year removed. In learning to recognize and value our own growth and change, we better position ourselves to value others'—and particularly our students'—evolving perspectives and selves. I hope this narrative will be useful to other student teachers as they consider integrating their students' input into their teaching practices.

Learning to Be Heard: The Origins of My Thinking about Consulting Students

Like many students, I first became aware of the phenomenon of student voice when I was a young student myself, discovering the difference between those teachers who asked students what we wanted or thought and those who assumed they already knew. Most of my early education involved my participation in other people's stories: the narratives prescribed by textbooks, standards, and teachers. I valued these narratives and took my prescribed (mostly passive) role within them seriously, but I did not understand that my voice was necessary until I realized late in elementary school that submissive silence would result in a kind of academic suffocation. I came to believe that my ability to learn and a degree of my self-respect depended on my voice playing a part in the class, school, and world narratives that I was being asked to accept. Looking back, I think I was on the right track.

My shift from passive to more vocal student was initiated when I realized I was being left out of conversations about my future. In fourth grade, several peers were invited to take a GATE (gifted and talented education) test, and I was not. I spent the year feeling robbed and wondering why my performance or potential did not strike my teacher as "gifted" instead of just "good."

I saw each exam and project as an opportunity to show my teacher her mistake, but she was not aware that I was seeking her approval. The following year, as a fifth grader, I waited to see if my next teacher would recommend me for testing. Once again, I was overlooked. I nervously went to talk to her at lunch, asking her if I could have the chance to test into the program; I did not know whether I was gifted, but I thought I should have the chance to see. I was so nervous that I forget her end of the conversation now, but I remember my mother teaching me about analogies (which were a significant portion of the verbal test) and then my later taking and passing the exam. When I finally attended the GATE class and began my special "gifted" projects, I came to realize that the label was somewhat useless and unsatisfying (except for the few field trips and class exemptions it earned me), but I was proud to have spoken up and gained the opportunity to be there. To this day, however, I wish my teachers had made their selection process more transparent or democratic instead of issuing lists of special children without giving other interested students the chance to prove themselves.

Asking my teacher to listen to me when she had not sought my input was not easy or pleasant. She allowed student-initiated dialogue about student needs, but much more welcoming and, perhaps more rare, is the teacher who naturally checks in with her students during her planning and teaching. One such teacher taught tenth-grade English at my high school. When assigning a large project, she would pass out her guidelines with the due date left blank. For just a few minutes, she would ask our class when major exams and projects were happening in our other classes and she would write these dates on the board; she would then give us two options for due dates and we would vote. Though not a perfect system, this inclusion of our needs and preferences—and proof of her trust—made us feel respected. It demonstrated for us that for this teacher, our completing our work to the best of our ability was more important than to complete it in time for an arbitrary due date. I do not think it is a coincidence that many of my classmates viewed her as someone with whom they could talk about life, someone who cared.

As a student, learning to be heard can be difficult when teachers do not invite your input. Even as I have matured and become more thoughtful, I still usually only speak up to a teacher when my silence would allow serious misunderstanding. With a more mature sense of self has come a more mature understanding of power: if I question too much, I may lose favor and my grade in a class may suffer. This hesitation is something we, as former and current students, should remain sensitive to when we teach. We also should remember the impact of teachers who, even in small ways, include student perspectives and needs in their planning.

Learning to Listen: Transitioning from Student to Private Tutor

When I began tutoring privately after high school, I quickly realized that if I did not seek input and feedback from my students about their needs, preferences, and experiences, I risked being the kind of teacher I had resented as a student. One of my first students, a seventh-grade ESL (English as a second language) student named Kathy, taught me an important lesson about listening. After about six weeks of trying to help Kathy to build her vocabulary and fluency through reading a novel, I was frustrated with our seeming lack of progress. Although she was learning the new words I had listed for her, words taken from the novel we were reading, her comprehension of the story remained limited. After trying a few different methods, I was running out of ideas and decided to just ask what her independent reading process looked like. As it turned out, she was doing what she thought I wanted: she was quickly reading to find the vocabulary words I had listed and then using the sentences around the words to figure out the words' meanings. Once she said this out loud, we both realized that she was not actually reading the book; she was doing a variation of a word search. I almost asked Kathy, "How come you never told me this was what you have been doing?" I realized, however, that she never told me because I never had asked. Although I had been committed to helping and had spent a lot of time preparing assignments for her, I had been assessing our progress and making adjustments solely based on my own perspective. We decided together that she should just read for content without my lists, circling and defining new words as she encountered them. This new method proved the most successful, which is not surprising. I was much better equipped to help Kathy once I had consulted and worked with her to find a successful method.

The disconnect between my learning goals for Kathy and her interpretation of my expectations illustrates the importance of constructing learning together. Unfortunately, this kind of construction, or even consultation, does not naturally take place in most learning situations. Particularly where more traditional teaching models persist, students are often not accustomed to being asked questions about their needs, so they have to adjust to this new role. Because I had a genuine interest in my students' input, I learned to listen to what they could teach me about their learning and they learned to take the opportunity seriously.

Learning to Listen Better: Discovering Reflective Practice

At one point I worked for a small tutoring company that required tutors to submit biweekly reports about each student's progress. The more I tutored, the more my writing strayed from dry reporting and moved into goals, questions, challenges, and successes that the student and I were sharing. This note-taking process became a valuable part of my practice; I found that by recording and analyzing my work with students, I could be more effective. When I read through these notes before my sessions, I could see whether I was oversaturating or ineffectively challenging a particular student with a certain method, and I could enter our meeting reminded of where we had left off and of any academic or personal issues I wanted to check on. These notes, scribbled in my car after a meeting or at home over dinner, were informal, and they served what I felt was a strictly practical purpose. Working another job while also being a college student meant I could not hold this information in my head; I needed to record it or it would be lost. I would write details of what we had done together followed by ideas for a future session. This practice became indispensable once I began to invite my students' input because it forced me to integrate their ideas with my own. Listening to your students is important, but if you do not document and meaningfully process what they tell you in order to then respond to it, you risk rendering their words meaningless.

When I entered the Bryn Mawr/Haverford Education Program, I discovered that a more formal version of this kind of note taking—observations coupled with reflections that are analytical and catalytic—is essential to reflective practice, which, in turn, is essential to effective and responsive teaching. Meaningful reflection asks us to be open to revision, and revision is central to education if we believe that all actors in teaching and learning are "unfinished," as Freire asserts, continuously working and re-working their knowledge of their worlds and themselves.[1] Our reflective notes should encourage us to be teacher-researchers, wrestling with the hard questions about our classrooms; to be intentionally thoughtful about our students, our pedagogy, and our curriculum; and to habituate weaving the analytical and theoretical with the practical so that these remain integrated in our practice and we continue to learn and grow as teachers. My little notebooks were a starting place, but none of these above goals were explicitly clear to me until I transferred to Bryn Mawr and started taking classes in its education program.

For me, getting certified to teach through an education program that held me accountable to being reflective was important. Because reflective practice is foundational to the Bryn Mawr/Haverford Education Program, much of the writing we did in our Curriculum and Pedagogy class asked us to take stock of our learning narratives; our classroom experiences as observers and students; our various course readings and writings; our dialogues with peers, high school students, and teachers; and other influences on our teaching philosophies and plans. Our main repository for this writing was our final portfolio, a collection we drafted and revised throughout the fall semester. Our writing progressed through four categories—our own education and teacher preparation, focus on learners, focus on curriculum, and focus on pedagogy—that would form our portfolios' organizational structure. Our process, for which we had been prepared by previous education courses in the program, involved our creating an extensive series of artifact/reflective pairs, each of which consisted of an artifact (broadly construed to signify anything representable in two dimensions that was both significant to our learning and/or teaching and relevant to one of the four categories) and a single-page reflection that would respond directly to the artifact, explain the artifact's significance to us and to the educational issues with which it resonates, and explicitly state responsive plans for our student-teaching classroom. In an essay I wrote in my spring portfolio after completing student teaching, I reflected on the personal significance of my fall portfolio:

> Building and reading my portfolio was my most personal and successful source of encouragement for student teaching: when I needed the reminder, I could open it and revisit the reasons why I was teaching in the first place, what I thought really mattered in English education, and who I wanted to be as a professional. The portfolio was a final, required project for my class, but more than that, it was an enlightening and beautiful process of digging into myself and merging the academic with the experiential, the theoretical with the personal. It was my written transition from college academic life to student teaching.

This "digging into [one]self" is central to the reflective process that prepares us not only for a career of articulating our goals and struggles in teaching but also for hearing and processing our students' goals and struggles in learning. Using students' perspectives involves more than asking students what they think or what they experience; it involves hearing what they say and processing it deeply, digging into ourselves for meaningful ways to integrate students' voices in our practice.

When we no longer have the assignments of a college program to remind us to be critical and reflective, we need to have a practice in place to ensure that we remain so. Whether it means building a formal portfolio or simply journaling in a way that strives to push our thinking, learning, responding, and teaching further, we need to remember that without reflecting meaningfully on our practices and on our students we close off ourselves—and often our students—to genuine learning.

Focusing on Learners

The students I visited in the curriculum and pedagogy seminar were about to compose the "Focus on Learners" section of their portfolios when I came. I brought my portfolio and passed it around our small circle of desks as we talked. The students were interested in seeing the kinds of artifacts I had chosen as well as the specific issues I had focused on in my reflections. My artifacts came from a wide array of sources: a questionnaire from one of our course readings that asks students how they learn, a student quote from one of our course readings; a copy of a classroom activity in which we wrote responses (in silence) to printed-out quotes from our readings and also responded to each other on the printouts, an excerpt from a nonacademic piece of writing I had composed about racism's role in a particular student's self-perception, and transcripts of high school students' conversations during Teaching and Learning Together in which we and local high school students participated.[2]

Looking back at these artifacts, I am struck by the diverse resources I tapped to represent my thinking. In hindsight, I see assumptions undergirding my process that were not obvious to me at the time but that I now see are crucial to a democratic, learner-centered teaching philosophy.

First is the assumption that valuable knowledge and meaning-making come from more than academic theorists and their texts. My college preparation taught me to value those sources, but it also taught me to recognize the often equally valuable sources in classroom conversations, nonacademic writing, and classroom activities. Surely focusing on learners meaningfully means valuing their perspectives, and one cannot value a young person's perspective significantly if that perspective is assumed inferior to an adult expert's. Second is the assumption that I, a current student myself, had the authority to make claims about teaching. It was a given in our program that college students were expected to articulate their perspectives alongside the voices of theorists, teachers, and other students. Being prepared in a context that gave my student self authority made my transitions natural: both from authoritative student to authoritative teacher, and from being heard to wanting to listen.

On a literal level, my artifact/reflection pairs' content in my portfolio's "Focus on Learners" section was about listening to students and using their perspectives in my teaching, but what is most striking to me are the assumptions behind the portfolio assignment that support the kinds of listening—and speaking—necessary in a learner-centered classroom. Our portfolios, multilayered in their purpose and in their practice, were representative of the kinds of thinking and planning we generally did during our curriculum and pedagogy seminar. Our assignments and activities had an obvious content value—discussing a reading, articulating a hope or apprehension about teaching—but they also generally had a deeper teaching value, offering us pedagogical tools and demonstrating practices that would be valuable to us as teachers who sought to focus first on our students' needs. In other words, our assignments and activities were always explicitly about something important, but they were also implicitly demonstrating the kind of practice in action that we as future teachers were striving for.

For example, as I mentioned, one of my artifacts came from a silent discussion activity we did in class. We responded to half a dozen different quotes from various texts, one of which was a student's quote on teacher strictness from Wilson and Corbett's *Listening to Urban Kids: School Reform and the Teachers They Want*: "My teacher is strict. He always yelling at us and makes us do stuff we don't want to do. I prefer a teacher to be strict, but not like that. He is always yelling at people when they not even saying something."[3] My classmates, our teacher Alison Cook-Sather, and I responded to this quote and to each other silently, writing on the paper on which the quote was printed:

> Instead of yelling at students, I would try to organize the class with reinforcement methods that would structure the class without having to raise my voice at them.

> Students should be aware of the expectations the teacher has for them, and the expectations they have for themselves and their fellow classmates. . . . This enables the teacher to maintain order without resorting to yelling.

Yelling solves nothing. It only causes students to feel powerless and voiceless. As a result, they will tune out the teacher and not learn anything. Also, it makes them feel like they are at fault.

I reflected on this activity as an artifact in my portfolio:

> The handwritten comments surrounding the [student's] quote were written by my classmates and me as part of our class discussion. . . . What this created for us was a sense of multiple voices addressing each other, as if in conversation, about the same theme. There is the student's voice, of course, and then there are our voices, the voices of future teachers, relating how we would try not to be like this particular teacher.

This activity was literally about us wrestling with key concepts and questions raised in our readings; it was about us being students. I later realized that it also modeled a method of discussion that encourages thoughtful response and incorporates every student's voice *alongside the teacher's*; I had not considered at the time the significance of our instructor participating in this activity with us. Beneath its content, the activity was about creating spaces to dialogue as differently positioned learners; it was about teaching.

When I student-taught ninth graders *Romeo and Juliet* and twelfth graders *Mrs. Dalloway* at an urban public school, I used this silent discussion activity to discuss quotes and questions from the literature. In both classes, when I asked my students to share their experiences of the activity, students remarked that it was neat to hear from their quieter classmates. One of my students, Yvonne, said on her final course feedback form that the silent discussion was "my favorite learning technique," and another student wrote that "the silent discussions . . . [were] fun & interesting ways to learn *Romeo & Juliet*." Reflecting on the silent discussion activity now, I am struck by just how connected my work as a student was to my work as student teacher. The content focus of our curriculum and pedagogy activity (students' perspectives on school), the practice of the activity itself, and my portfolio reflection on it all ended up informing my student teaching in meaningful ways.

Transitioning to Teaching: Revising My Writing, Revising Myself

After talking with the Curriculum and Pedagogy students about the "Focus on Learners" section of my fall portfolio, I showed them the ways in which it informed my student teaching and the related but more practice-oriented spring portfolio. In the fall portfolio, our reflective writing was meant, in part, to inform our classroom teaching the following semester. When it came time to create our spring portfolios, we added the new artifacts that come with having lesson plans and the other artifacts of actual teaching. Many of us went through the illuminating process of revising our reflective writing from a focus on our hopes to a focus on our actual classroom practices.

Here is an example of how this worked. For one of my artifacts for my fall portfolio, I quoted a high school student, John, with whom I corresponded through Teaching and Learning Together: "I think it's important for a teacher to be understanding and understand the needs of students. And rather than mold the students to fit their teaching style, they should mold the way they teach to the needs of the students because what may work for some group of students may not work for another, or maybe even on a student basis." My reflection tied in some of our reading: "As the authors of *Consulting Pupils* put it, 'if we want to improve pupils' achievements and commitment then we may need to take our agenda for change, at least in part, from what they can tell us about teaching, learning and schooling.'"[4] After all, students are the ones being taught, so they are half the equation. But the main focus of my reflection was on how I could use John's words, along with what I had learned from readings and experiences, to make a better classroom: "My lesson plans, I hope, will act as a flexible framework in which I can adapt to the various learning styles of my students. Just because I am a successful learner when given certain kinds of instructions does not mean that my students will be as well, which is important to remember. I want a classroom in which each student is addressed meaningfully through my lessons, so that each student, if willing to learn, will have meaningful daily opportunities to do so."

When it came time between semesters to plan for my first days as a student teacher, I looked back at reflections like these for confirmation that I had specific goals for my classroom, but also with nervousness that I would not figure out who my students were quickly enough to give them the meaningful opportunities I sought for them. I wrote Alison Cook-Sather an e-mail to ask her advice, and she offered an idea for how to seek my students' input about their preferences and experiences at the very start of my time with them. Below is an excerpt of the lesson plan that her idea became, as documented in my portfolio:

(15–20 minutes) Since I'm going to be teaching this class for the next eleven weeks, I would like to take a little time to generate, as a class, some guidelines that we can use to ensure constructive learning for everyone.

I pass out one index card to each student. On it, students will write 2–3 qualities that make an English class inspiring, exciting, or successful in their minds; 2–3 qualities that make an English class problematic, hard, or unsuccessful in their minds; and 1–2 suggestions for class guidelines or rules that will help support what they want and avoid what they don't. We will discuss and then I will collect them.

Discussion: Students may add things to their cards if they are inspired by what a fellow student says. Discuss 5–10 minutes. I collect them. I will take them home and consider them, as well as my own responsibilities and goals, and bring in the product in a few days.

This lesson plan, inserted after John's quote about wanting teachers to pay attention to students' needs, rounded out this particular artifact for my spring portfolio. Now I did not just have a student's words about what he wanted, as I'd had in the fall, I had a lesson plan for other students that showed how I had tried to respond to this desire. The motivation behind this activity was clearly informed by the ideas and ideals I discussed in my fall portfolio, which is why that process was important for me. It helped me to focus from the beginning on how to seek and use input from my students. When I revised my fall reflection for my spring portfolio, I shifted my language from what I had hoped to what was, and from my vague idea of my future students to concrete reflections on who my students were. Here is the same excerpt I used in my fall example, revised for the spring:

> My lesson plans are a flexible framework in which I adapt to the various learning styles of my students. Tyrone has Asperger's and needs clear and direct instruction. Stephanie learns best by doing and is inattentive during most discussions. Loriel feels smothered if she cannot voice her opinions and thrives in discussion. Peter is more likely to share his opinions if he gets to share them with a peer first. I want a classroom in which each student is addressed meaningfully through my lessons, so that each student, if willing to learn, will have meaningful daily opportunities to do so. I refer back to their note cards often, and tune into their feedback every day.

When I look at this version beside the original, the parallels between revising my writing and revising myself are clear. In order to get from my classroom aspirations to a place in which I could reflect on how those aspirations had become action, I had to spend weeks watching and listening to my students, discussing them with other teachers and with their parents, asking them questions, trying things that sometimes were not successful, and revising my plans (and my assumptions) to find the balance of structure and freedom that would allow my students to be their most successful. By the end of my student teaching, I had not come close to mastering this, but I had come a long way from the hopeful reflections of my fall portfolio.

Incorporating Students' Perspectives in My Classroom

To gather and use students' input throughout our time together, I had to earn my students' trust by showing them that their input would be taken seriously in our class. I mention above that my weeks of student teaching began with a note card activity in which I asked students to write to me about their English class experiences and hopes. Here are some examples of the input students shared with me, in their own words:

Qualities that make an English class inspiring, exciting, or successful:

- You can use your imagination more and your own thoughts more.
- Open discussions and point of views on the books that we read.
- Having stand up activities.
- Deep discussions.
- Insightful discussion—no one is forced to talk, laid-back, debates.
- Group activities.
- Skits & Plays.
- Incorporating other things (e.g., art, music) into class activities.

Qualities that make an English class problematic, hard, or unsuccessful:

- Too much reading. Constant reading.
- Doing off topic work that don't help the subject.
- Not being able to speak your mind.
- Individual work through the entire book.
- Doing busy work in class.
- I can't formulate what I want to say right away so I end up being a jester.
- Group work—please just individual.
- Objective questions; pointless projects/activities.
- Bad undeveloped discussion.

Suggestions for class guidelines or rules:

- Not to give homework *every night.*
- Make it fun, modern—ways we can relate.
- No busy work.
- Not a lot of homework assignments, but each is detailed and important.
- No real rules because that ruins the laid back environment.
- Must be at least 1 class period devoted to discussion [per book].
- Ask students if the workload is too heavy.
- If there's too much work, mention something.
- Respect.

Looking at these comments now, I am struck by how instructive they are. These students used this opportunity to tell me that they take their learning seriously: they want to think, to discuss, to relate to what they study, and to use their creativity to interact with the content; they don't want their time wasted by excessive or unnecessary work, questions or projects that are limiting, or discussions that don't go anywhere. They want a relaxed and stimulating learning community in which they feel comfortable to "mention something" when their load is too heavy, but also in which the teacher "ask[s] the students if the workload is too heavy." In other words, they want to be respected and trusted, and they want to trust their teacher to create situations in which they will learn. These comments also reinforce that students have different opinions about activities (like group work). One student wanted me to know that he goofed off because he didn't feel he could come up with something meaningful to say fast enough in class. These students demonstrate that they took my invitation to share their ideas seriously; although I had not yet earned their trust, they were giving me a chance, probably because their regular teacher, my cooperating teacher, also consulted them in his planning and assessment process. Not all students give a new teacher this token of trust, but it can be earned by making space to listen to students from the start.

If I had proceeded to run the class without incorporating these students' ideas clearly into our class, I would have lost their trust as quickly as I had been offered it. Two days later, I passed out a guidelines sheet that incorporated their ideas, I passed out a chart that showed them how many students had made certain comments, and I held a brief discussion with the class about the decisions I had made in response to their input. A few students had requested eating privileges during class, but school rules forbade it; I had to turn down this request. Many students had requested that they never be given busy work. I discussed with them my intention to only give them assignments that were meaningful, and that I would explain the goals I had for the assignments given, make room for their feedback, and be flexible within reason.

By starting my time with these students by having this explicit dialogue, I demonstrated that their voices would be valued in our class. During our time together, my students continued to make suggestions or express hopes or frustrations to me that clearly effected changes in our classroom. In my final reflective paper for Curriculum and Pedagogy, I wrote about the effect one of my students, Lakeesha, had on our poetry unit:

> When [Lakeesha] later complained that the poetry I was teaching was dreadful because it wasn't about love, I brought in love poems the next day. Lakeesha thanked me, as did several of her friends; they realized that their opinions held weight, and that my plans would change if I felt they weren't learning as well as they could. The poems I had originally brought in were not "dreadful" to all of the students, but I realized that the appreciation I wanted all students to gain for poetry would only come if I were willing to bring in work that would speak to their various interests and passions; I was then more successful at pushing them beyond their preferences. Lakeesha's feedback, which she offered naturally during class because she trusted that I would not be offended, informed the rest of my poetry unit.

When filling out her final feedback form for our class at the end of my student teaching, Lakeesha wrote, "You used a lot of our suggestions. Most of your lessons were based on our learning styles . . . you respected my opinion of love poems and how they are ever so lovely." It was not hard to respond to Lakeesha's comment, and she appreciated that her input mattered in our class.

Disruptive students often are the ones least listened to, the ones most often told how to be and how not to be. I learned with one of my students,

Evan, that an effective "discipline" method is responsive dialogue, which I described in my final reflective paper:

> Evan is what most teachers would call "a pain." He loves to talk, and when he's not talking, he's humming, and when he's not humming, he's dancing in his seat, and when he's not dancing in his seat, he's gesturing across the room. He and I talked regularly about his behavior. At first, I tried just asking him to be respectful and to participate in class productively, but that would only go so far. At best, I'd have twenty minutes of uninterrupted class time before I'd begin to hear some R&B from the corner of the room, his sneakers squeaking on the floor in dance as he raised his eyebrows at the student next to him. It was exasperating. But I wanted to show Evan that he and his learning mattered to me. So, finally, I asked Evan why he found himself so easily distracted. More than anything else, he found it difficult to sit still and listen when he was thinking about a girl he liked and the music that reminded him of her. It was that simple! We talked about ways he could use that distraction productively within some of the creative work options I had offered students: he made a soundtrack for *Romeo and Juliet* that used love songs he could relate to personally while also relating them meaningfully to the text. He and some friends put together a "research rap" in which they combined interesting research they had found on Elizabethan England into a brief performance. He started to speak more (on topic) in class, relating himself to Romeo in interesting (and sometimes amusing) ways. Evan never stopped being a distraction, but he helped me help him to use his energy productively in the class.

In the end, Evan appreciated being taken seriously and not being yelled at, as he often had been. In his final feedback, he wrote: "I know I've been a hassle at times so thanks for putting up with me. You have a way with people & you can keep them disciplined without having to yell. . . . [The discussions] were fun & good and I really had a voice in them." By asking Evan how I could help him stay focused instead of by simply telling him what I needed him to do, I helped him to contribute to our learning community as a whole in valuable ways instead of shutting him down. I made room for his voice and showed him that his learning mattered to me.

The Risks We Take in
Learning with and from Students

On my final feedback form I asked students whether they felt their voices were valued in our class by their peers and by their teacher. Here are some of their comments, in their own words: "[You] always took into account the thoughts of everyone and the needs of the class and everyone's opinion was used and respected"; "I felt like I was heard by everybody"; "You actually listened and took our suggestions into consideration." Not all students were as celebratory of their experience in our class, however: "With the students, it was the same as always [and we didn't value each other's voices]"; "Being one of about 5 speakers in most class discussions, I doubt the class paid attention (their fault, not yours)"; "My only criticism is that you did not have complete control over the class. (Frankly, I don't blame you)." My students were kind to forgive me for flaws in the class dynamics, but I know better. I was successful with my students in a lot of ways, but I could not create a space free of disrespect, rowdiness, and misbehavior. I believed that if I valued my students' voices and perspectives, they would do the same for each other. This was often true, but not always. In trying to keep our class active and interesting, and in trying to encourage a sense of free speech and open discussion, I had to let go of total control in my class. At times, this was freeing and productive, but at other times (particularly Fridays and at the end of the day), it was not.

Reading my students' critical words, though they were gentle, is difficult. No matter how much we try not to, teachers inevitably will take criticism personally when they care deeply about creating a successful learning community. I reflected on this risk in my final reflective paper:

> Asking students for feedback on their learning experience is not easy because their learning experience is so influenced by your teaching. You risk, always, disapproval. You risk students telling you that the activity or text that you put your heart into was, for them, useless. You risk hearing that what you are trying to do is completely irrelevant to a given student. Since it is impossible to please everyone—especially when you have sixty or more students daily—these responses will come. Knowing that ahead of time might not make teachers immune to feeling hurt, but it should make them immune to feeling discouraged. We have to remember that in asking, we are trying to learn, and we learn nothing if students just tell us what we want to hear and keep their criticism to themselves.

I realize now that it is risky not only to ask for feedback but also to make space for student input. Once you ask students what they want, your risk of letting them down increases. Once you say that you will make a change in response to their input, you are responsible to be careful and consistent in keeping your word. Of course, the act of learning necessitates risk. To learn, we must admit that we want or need something we do not have— we must admit that we are indeed "unfinished." This admission may make us vulnerable, afraid, or courageous, but it is always necessary for growth. As teachers who hope to learn with and from our students, we must take the risks that come with wanting to learn.

Learning from Our Narratives: Noting and Reflecting on Transitions

Not only does learning necessitate risk, but it also necessitates transition— change—from one state to another. Looking back on the transitions between my stages of learning about student perspective, I am struck by the ways in which I have grown for, with, and in response to the teachers and the students in my life. Reflecting on these transitions through writing about them, as well as through meeting with the students enrolled in the Curriculum and Pedagogy seminar, has helped me continue to recognize the ways my different learning experiences inform one another. By noting the moments of transition between them with analytical and catalytic written reflection, I have been able to remain responsive to my own and my students' needs as learners and to continue to push toward growth in myself and others.

Current or soon-to-be student teachers might find a similar process valuable. Examine your own learning narrative, your own experiences with learning to be heard and learning to listen, and note your transitions as well as your ongoing questions. Push yourself to be critically reflective of your learning stories and to recognize the ongoing risks and changes inherent to learning with and from your students. Encourage your students to invite you into their own learning narratives; find out what excites and disturbs them about school, your subject, your class, and your assignments; and push yourself to respond to what they tell you. Care and show your students you care through respecting them as individuals with their own learning narratives. Build trust through including your students meaningfully in your planning, teaching, and assessing processes, reflecting with them and by yourself on your evolving classroom. Take the risks together; learn together; and never stop writing, revising, and rereading your own learning stories as a learner, as well as a teacher.

Notes

1. Freire, 1998.
2. Teaching and Learning Together paired each certification candidate enrolled in the class with a student who attended a local high school, with the high school student positioned as a teacher-educator. See Chapter 13 for a discussion of this project.
3. Wilson and Corbett, 2001, p. 77.
4. MacBeath, Demetriou, Rudduck, and Myers, 2003.

9

Rethinking Listening to Students

A Preservice Teacher's Revisions

Brandon Clarke

If I ever were to become a teacher I would try to talk to my students about how they want to learn, like what's the best way for them instead of me lecturing or me just doing group [work], but how they want to learn, because that's what I'm there for is to teach them, to benefit them.

—Rodney, high school student

Chapter Overview

Focus of this chapter: An early career teacher returns to the college from which he graduated to complete certification to teach at the secondary level. In the course of his preparation, he realizes that he was not listening, as he thought he had been, to students, and he works not only to listen but also to act on what he hears.

Discussed in this chapter:

- My perspective prior to student teaching
  - Variety
  - Relationships
  - My assumptions
  - Summary
- My perspective after student teaching
  - Variety
  - Relationships
  - My assumptions
- Conclusion

When a student is having difficulty in my class, it's easy to blame the student. It's easy to say that the student wasn't learning because he is lazy, unruly, or inattentive. What's far more difficult is for me to look at myself and see how I can change to better serve my students. While I might consider myself a progressive teacher who has the best interest of my students at heart, I have found that I have been guilty of failing to take the appropriate actions needed to help them. I have come to realize that I didn't act because I didn't know what to do, and the reason I didn't know what to do is that I hadn't genuinely listened to my students to find out what they needed.

In the penultimate course required for certification through the Bryn Mawr/Haverford Education Program, I, like most teachers, readily agreed that listening to students is an important thing to do. I even claimed that it's a practice that I already used in my lessons as a teacher of English in China. I might have called attention to the constant stream of questions I asked my students, such as "Do you understand?" "Why are you late?" and "Did you do your homework?" And I would have used students' responses to these questions as evidence that I was listening to them.

What I have learned is that there is an important difference between listening to students and genuinely listening to them. Listening is a simple act that involves simply hearing what is said, but to be genuinely listening I must be much more active and engaged. I must seek a student's honest response and be prepared to respond productively to a student's problems or concerns. "Do you understand?" should never be asked as a rhetorical question or in an offhanded way; it should be a genuine question that I am prepared to respond to by finding a way to help the student understand better. "Why are you late?" and "Did you do your homework?" should be asked in a nonjudgmental way. I should ask them because I care about the student, not as an act of discipline.

Students themselves state the importance of teachers genuinely listening to them. In the semester prior to my student teaching, I participated in a project called Teaching and Learning Together (TLT) based in my methods course (see Chapter 13) through which high school students shared their perspectives with those of us preparing to be teachers. The high school student participants wrote in their final reflections on the project not only about how nice it felt to be listened to and to feel that what they said might actually make a difference but also, as Andrew, one of the student participants, explained, "It has also made me more assertive, which has benefited me because it has caused one of my teachers to stop picking on me. The experience also made me more willing to express myself and now I will tell my teachers if I have a problem." Conversely, if students feel their voices are either ignored or carry no weight toward change, they will not make any effort to tell the teacher their concerns.[1] Not listening genuinely, I learned, is as bad as, if not worse than, not listening at all.

In the pages that follow I reflect on what I have learned by trying to genuinely listen to students, both at the end of the semester immediately prior to undertaking student teaching and subsequent to that experience. However, the most important lessons I gained from the project were not about the students or the school but about me. I began to recognize many of the flaws in my thinking about education and flaws in myself, a topic I will address in the section concerning my assumptions.

My Perspective Prior to Student Teaching

During the nine conversations the high school students who participated in TLT had as a group at their school and in their weekly writings (both of which those of us enrolled in the methods course had access to each week), the students thought deeply about numerous topics affecting them and their school. Their discussions on the importance of variety and reform in the classroom and the relationship between the teacher and the student struck me as particularly significant themes, and I will address each one separately. I will also discuss the way the discussions challenged my own assumptions about listening to students.

Variety

I don't like lectures very much, like in Latin class my teacher sits at the overhead and sits there and just like keeps talking over and over. I feel better when we're like moving around and interacting with each other and doing projects, and not just someone sitting there and me taking notes down. It makes me want to sleep; it's tiring. So I don't really like lectures like that. I like to interact.

—Rodney, Dialogue 7

I think also in my experience when a teacher has a routine that they do every day, it kind of made me dread the class because I knew what I was going in to every day and there was nothing new to look forward to; I knew exactly how the entire class was going to go.

—Rebecca, Dialogue 1

It shouldn't be too . . . carried away, like every day you have a new assignment, if you get too carried away the students get confused about what's going on in a class and they won't actually learn, but I think once in a while to have activities for various different topics that you're learning is always helpful and different kids have different learning styles.

—Maria, Dialogue 6

The teachers make the curriculum and the students have to follow it. And if the students were to approach the teacher and the teacher would want to accommodate the entire class . . . that teacher has to answer to someone else above him, they have a curriculum for the entire year that they're supposed to get through so if they cut the students some slack they're going to fall behind in their schedules and mess up the entire process.

—Jennifer, Dialogue 2

As an education minor at Haverford College, I always had a sense that there was a "right" and "wrong" way to do things in school. When I began studying for my education certification, I maintained this idea that to be a successful teacher I had to find the "right" method and then use it appropriately. Like a doctor performing an operation, I merely had to follow the appropriate steps to be successful. However, what I learned from the students who participated in TLT is that there is no single perfect pedagogical method. Any method, used too often, becomes dull. When I first listened to the TLT discussions, I found Rodney's description of his Latin class all too familiar. I was reminded of my chemistry classes in high school where I was forced to sit through hours of lecture and overhead projector slides. I had always imagined the tedium would apply only to the traditional lecture classes, and I imagined that all of my students would hold views similar to my own. I had forgotten the rich diversity of student perspectives that play such a central role in the classroom.[2]

The students in TLT pointed out my mistake and showed me that any style of class could become a bore if used too frequently. Prior to student teaching I had become quite enchanted with the use of group work and cooperative learning as a result of both my own experience using them to teach English abroad and what I read in the readings assigned in my Curriculum and Pedagogy course. However, I had not stopped to consider that by relying too much on such a method I might create the same dull atmosphere I was trying to avoid. In paying too much attention to the experts, I had forgotten to consider the students.[3] My students would not be put to sleep by lectures, but they might still, as Rebecca states, "dread the class" and secretly moan every time I assigned yet another group work assignment. They needed variety—a need confirmed by students in other contexts.[4]

What I had forgotten is that every student and every topic is different, and a teacher cannot expect one pedagogical method to work in all instances. The key to successful teaching is not, as I had thought, to find the universally "perfect method," but rather to find the best way to teach a given topic to a given student. To a student who enjoys interaction, like Rodney, a discussion or group work assignment might work well, but another student in TLT believed that some students really want to stay on topic and would prefer lectures to a teacher who doesn't directly tell the students what information is most important for them to know. A teacher should not dismiss all routine and "get too carried away"—as Maria points out above, a teacher who constantly changes all aspects of the class will simply confuse the students—but each lesson should not feel like a mere cookie-cutter reflection of all those taught previously.

Along with a variety of pedagogical techniques, it is also necessary that the teacher employ a variety of assessments. I was so repulsed by traditional methods, such as tests, and so attracted to the alternatives, such as projects and presentations, that I risked choosing a form of assessment or evaluation simply because it wasn't a test rather than because it was the best method. By listening to the students I was reminded that a teacher cannot adequately assess a student without employing a variety of methods. Just as there are some students who have difficulty taking tests, there will also always be some students who will excel at tests, but struggle to explain what they've learned in a presentation. I can't really say it much better than Rebecca:

> I think there can't always be a test every day, and having little projects shows how involved people are and if people are learning and paying attention, but solely that I think is a little unfair because there are kids who don't feel comfortable presenting in front of a classroom and they would much rather have a test where they can silently show the teacher everything that they've learned. So I think a little bit of both would be good. (Rebecca, Dialogue 9)

Of course to find out what pedagogical styles and which assessments will work for a student, I will need to be able to communicate effectively with the students. I need to break away from the belief that only the teacher knows what's best for the student. The best way is simply to ask, but that's far more complex than it might sound. A teacher needs to create an atmosphere of trust and respect in which the students feel safe honestly expressing themselves to the teacher.[5] It takes building a strong relationship between the teacher and the students.

Relationships

I feel the main points that I gave to the college students [who participated in TLT] are that, when you become a teacher, try and be as cool as you can with your students, don't be a hardcore teacher, and try to have a relationship with each one of them because that will help you out a lot. Students tend to feel more comfortable around you, and with you if you make a bond between you too.
—Rodney, Final Reflections

I think that your attitude and the relationship you have with the teacher and how much you're willing to put into the course [are really important]. If you really enjoy what you're doing, then how can you not do well? Because then you're going to do the work, you're going to study, you're going to understand it. I mean, if you have a patient teacher who is willing to explain it to you, then it's pretty simple to do well, maybe not in A, but in B–A range, I think, if you enjoy it.
—Jennifer, Dialogue 1

I think that the teacher is also a big part of the classroom environment. . . . I think there is a fine line between a teacher and a friend, but when a teacher makes it clear that they're available for extra help and that they're on your side, the entire environment of the classroom is always better. . . . They're still in control and they're still the adult teacher, but they want you to do the best job that you can and they want to help you.
—Rebecca, Dialogue 6

But sometimes we don't understand, sometimes it's really scary and, I don't know, it doesn't feel nice. . . . I'm not afraid, it's just how to approach it and respond to it.
—Maria, Dialogue 2

It's just that we are speaking and the teacher's just really nice . . . is niceness a part of pedagogy?

—Andrew, Dialogue 5

Without a doubt the single most prominent theme in every student's discussion was the importance of a strong relationship between the teacher and the student. When they reflected on their experience in TLT as a whole, the students all wrote that forming a good relationship was their main advice to college students preparing to be teachers. Each echoed Rodney's sentiment that a teacher needs to "try to be as cool as you can with your students."

As a new teacher, I worry I might become caught up in trying to spend most of my time preparing lesson plans and grading homework and forget that my first priorities are not the lesson plans, the grading, or the paperwork, but the students. What will ultimately make the biggest difference for them will be the time I spend helping them. As Rebecca stated above, my students will want to know that I'm available to give them the extra help they need and I'll have to be clear that I intend to be. I'll need to be a teacher who asks, "Do you understand? If not, how can I make you?"[6] Of course, it's one thing to say I'm available and quite another to actually accomplish this. For the moments that I am working with a student, I need to put aside all the other work I have and focus completely on her.

I have to make myself approachable. Students might have a desire to ask for help, but they might be apprehensive about actually approaching the teacher. As a teacher in China, I told students they could get help from me and I even set aside time to be available, but I forgot the crucial step that Maria describes above: I forgot that the initial effort a student makes to talk to a teacher about their concerns or ask for extra help can be incredibly intimidating. If I expect students to actually take me up on my offer to help them, then I need to create a comfortable atmosphere conducive to students being able to approach me. Even school dropouts, when asked what would have helped them stay in school, said among other things they wanted teachers who were "easy to talk to . . . [would] actually sit down with me and help me with my work . . . talk to you politely when you are not in lessons . . . someone you can turn to when you're struggling with your work,"[7] and their feeling that there was a lack of such approachable teachers was a factor leading them to leave school. I'll need to do better in creating an environment where students feel comfortable seeking help.

Creating that comfortable atmosphere must be a central goal as I plan out how I want to present myself to the students. Throughout the dialogues, Andrew describes how much he likes positive teachers, teachers who are "just really nice." He struggles to explain exactly what this actually looks like, but with the help of his classmates he describes some distinguishing characteristics that I can use to guide my actions in the future. As a teacher, I'll need to recognize each of my students is an individual and treat them as such. I'll need to give encouragement and work patiently when giving help. I'll need to pay attention to every student, not just the ones who are doing the best in the class, and recognize when they are struggling or even just having an off day. Perhaps most importantly, I must not reject any student or let any student maintain the perception that he or she has been rejected. Andrew described a math teacher who sought participation, but then dismissed Andrew's own attempt to participate. Andrew was hurt because he did not understand the teacher's reasoning. I'll need to be clear to my students when I take actions the students might dislike and ensure none of them feels rejected.

Rebecca's comment above provides one other important reminder: trying to be a caring teacher is not the same as trying to be a friend. The teacher must maintain the line between the student and the teacher and continue to act as a responsible adult. It is a very difficult balancing act to be perceived as a teacher who genuinely cares for my students and can make a bond with them, but who is also strong enough to remain a role model. Instead of trying to be liked, I need to focus on being respected.[8]

My Assumptions

Every now and then the students say something I find thought provoking, but in general the students' backgrounds are so similar to my own that I find them simply repeating things I've already noticed.

—Brandon, e-mail to Alison Cook-Sather

Terms that evoke roles . . . have preconceived limits or parameters that are assumed and often unquestioned; set meanings become inscribed in fixed terms. Thus roles have a way of shifting parts one can play to permanent states. Translation is a way out of this fixedness.

—Cook-Sather, 2007a, p. 840

Perhaps the greatest lesson I learned from engaging in TLT was that I had to learn to swallow my pride and realize that I too was guilty of many of the flaws that I saw in other teachers. As soon as I began listening to the high school students' voices in the first dialogue, I made assumptions about them and judged them. I egotistically assumed that I knew who these students were based on the very little information I could glean about them from their conversations. This was especially true for Andrew; as soon as Andrew introduced himself by mentioning video games and the film club as his interests, I assumed he was a kind of social outcast. In all his subsequent statements I always interpreted what he said in terms of the role I had created for him. The same was true of Rodney; as soon as I heard him speak I assumed he was black, though I had never seen a picture of him. I also assumed he was from a less affluent family than that of the other students. I created roles for all five students as soon as I heard them and while I was mildly aware of what I was doing, I didn't acknowledge that having done so was coloring my view of what they said. Ironically, I labeled my students' responses as naïve or as being limited by their position in the school when in fact, as Alison Cook-Sather describes, by assigning words to define the students I had limited *my* ability to listen to and understand them. I believed that only I, with my superior knowledge of school workings, could see the bigger picture.

I believed the school the students in TLT attended was a high school similar to the one I had attended with students similar to those who had been my classmates, despite having never actually set foot in the school. The community is somewhat similar to my own, so I assumed the school must be as well. When the students discussed the relationship between their school and the town's other high school, I framed their conversation in terms of my own experience with the two schools in my own town. I assumed I knew the whole situation even better than the students, and I judged Rodney as being ignorant of the unequal divide between the two schools because he was against integrating the curriculum of the two schools. In reality, I have no idea if such a divide even exists. I had co-opted the students' voices and made them what I assumed them to be.[9]

I didn't realize what I was doing until I put my judgments into words. After the eighth dialogue I wrote an e-mail to Alison discussing my frustrations with the whole project. In the course of it I suggested that the students' backgrounds were so similar to my own that I could learn nothing new from them. Almost as soon as I sent it, I was shocked at what I had just written. I had always imagined the assumption that "secretly, adults generally believe that they know best" was limited to the old traditional teachers who dismissed reform efforts. I was surprised to realize that Cushman was describing me.[10]

Much of the literature on good teaching states that teachers must be learners, and I thought this concerned primarily maintaining knowledge about a teacher's content area and the latest pedagogical approaches. I learned from this project that these are just small parts of what it means for a teacher to be a learner. Kathleen Cushman recognized that good teaching also "requires humility to admit one's own mistakes and to keep trying. It requires empathy, to hear and feel what someone else is experiencing."[11] Making assumptions and judgments about students is unavoidable, but what a good teacher must do is recognize when he is doing this and not let these assumptions get in the way of actively listening to the students. Teachers need to admit that they don't know everything about their students, that every student is an individual, not a "role," and that as such there is always some new viewpoint that can be heard if the teacher actively listens. Even if I know a student's background, it is impossible for me to truly understand his or her experience.[12] I will never really know about Rodney unless I listen to him.

Summary

What I realize now is that the categories above into which I divided my analysis are far more connected than I had initially envisioned. There is really only one category: caring and what it really means to be a caring teacher.[13] As a caring teacher I must care for all students equally, see them as individuals, and understand the necessity of diversifying my lessons to respond to their varying needs. Caring is not about making friendships with the students; it's about showing I value them, pushing all of them to be better, and giving them the individual support they need to reach those higher standards. As a caring teacher I work to make students feel valued and respected. Their classes become environments where students feel like partners in their own education, not silent patients being worked upon by the better knowing and unquestionable doctor. Additionally, as a caring teacher I question myself. I follow the same criteria I lay out for my students and seek out my own assumptions and question them. I must never believe that I "know" my students, no matter how many similar students I've taught or how many books I've read. The great power of reflection is not that it lets me see how something else has changed or how I changed in the past, but that it changes me in the process.

My Perspective after Student Teaching

As I entered the classroom to complete my student teaching, I tried to do more than just hear my students speak. I tried to actively listen and pay attention to what it was they were actually saying. As I struggled to put the ideals I had developed during the TLT project into actual practice, I met with both success and frustration. I've learned that patience and perseverance are among the most important characteristics needed to genuinely listen to students. The only way a teacher truly fails to listen is when he or she stops trying. In the following pages I discuss the ways that I attempted to act on what I had learned about genuinely listening to students. I revisit the issues of variety, relationships, and my assumptions from above; discuss how I tried to manifest those ideas in the classroom; and reflect on the insights I gained from my efforts.

Variety

In the first dialogue of the TLT project, Rebecca explained how she often would "dread the class because I knew what I was going in to every day and there was nothing new to look forward to." It is difficult to generate any interest or enthusiasm among the students if they enter the room wishing they were somewhere else, so among my top priorities as I planned my curriculum was to avoid too much repetition of a single pedagogical or assessment approach. Additionally, I hoped that with a variety of lesson styles I would appeal to my students' different styles of learning and that I would "provide each student with every possible chance to succeed."[14]

I embraced a wide range of methods throughout my student teaching. During the second month I began a new unit with my seventh grade students on traditional African cultures. I began with a mapping activity, first with students working in pairs to identify and draw key geographic features of Africa and later with the entire class working together to assemble a giant map of Africa's resources on the floor of the classroom, an activity that involved the students actually walking around the map and manipulating the various "resource cards." The students then individually researched the geography of a single African country, the first part of a unit-long project. The following day, the students walked around the classroom on a "museum tour" in which they looked at an ensemble of traditional African art objects, reflected on each one, and then later learned about the real use of one to share with the rest of the class. We continued our exploration of African culture on the third day of the unit in a more auditory manner; I told traditional stories from different regions of Africa and the students listened, reflected on what they could learn about the lives of the people who created the stories, and then we discussed their reflections together. Finally, on the fourth day the students went online to the Museum of African History at the Smithsonian, found art objects from the country they had chosen to research, and individually researched their country's culture.

As I generally assessed students with large-scale projects rather than exams, I was concerned that my students would worry about their grades being adversely affected by changes in the form of assessment. However, I found that interest and engagement generally seemed to trump grades. The students' engagement with the content of the lessons was clear. I saw all three of Schlecty's three characteristics that show students are engaged: "(1) they are attracted to their work, (2) they persist in their work despite challenges and obstacles, and (3) they take visible delight in accomplishing their work."[15] The students became increasingly curious to learn about Africa's culture, and many were eager to have a chance to explore it on their own in the individual research component. Even if a student had difficulty grasping the material during one activity, the fact that the content of each activity overlapped, but was presented in a different manner, meant students with different learning styles had the chance to catch up. One thing I observed that I had not initially expected was that by employing so much variety I gave students a chance to surprise me. A student who had been struggling with the material the day before sometimes seemed to find a different lesson particularly appealing and would suddenly become the star of the class.

One of the problems with striving to employ variety is that there are such limitless options. Sometimes students get so carried away in the newness of the activity that they don't really notice what was supposed to be learned. I soon discovered that it is important to have the students engage in reflection on the activity: "It is only in the critical contemplation of experience that one can really make sense of it—a meaningful connection between what was lived and what was learned."[16] Additionally, it can be very difficult to decide how to teach a particular lesson, and I frequently felt that my creativity was at risk of burning out. To guide my choices I asked myself, "If I were a student, what would interest *me*? What would make *me* engaged?" However, it was not really the best question I could have been asking because what might help me learn is not necessarily the best thing for many of my students. I need to ask, "What interests *my students*? What would keep *them* engaged?" Furthermore, this shouldn't be a mental exercise for myself; I need to go out and actually ask my students. As I student-taught, I paid attention to students' comments on my lessons, such as "That was really fun today!" or "This is stupid," and I tried to use those comments to guide my future lesson plans, but I never made a concentrated effort to get more details from my students until the last day of the semester. By engaging in an earlier dialogue with my students about what they felt they learned the most from, I hope that in the future I can focus my choice of pedagogy and topics to better serve my students.

Relationships

Rodney advised aspiring teachers to "try and be as cool as you can with your students. . . . Try to have a relationship with each one of them because that will help you out a lot." What strikes me now about that passage is that Rodney believes that both the student and the teacher will benefit from this bond. As I forged relationships with my students during my student teaching, I found that not only did the students show greater engagement with the class and a greater willingness to look to me for guidance, but also I had an easier time controlling the class, meeting students' unique needs, and quite simply, I enjoyed myself more. Relationships are what make teaching more than just a job.

I strove to make myself as approachable as possible. I smiled and appeared eager to help. I responded to or acknowledged students' requests for help as quickly as I could. I also tried to maintain "withitness"[17] in the classroom and notice when a student was frustrated or confused. When a student began to get unruly, I tried to view it not as a discipline problem, but as a sign that the student was struggling with the material or with staying attentive, and I addressed such students by asking, "Do you need help?" rather than just "Be quiet!" I let students know I was available during lunch if they needed extra help. I tried to "encourage them to feel that they belong" in my class and to feel that they had important knowledge that I wanted to hear them share.[18] While I tried to make it clear that I was not looking to be "friends" with the students, I also allowed myself to be humanized. The more I felt comfortable sharing about my own experiences, the more my students seemed willing to do the same. At times I was surprised that a small action, sometimes something as simple as a joke and a smile in the hallway, could pay off remarkably in student performance in the class.

As I worked to build constructive relationships with my students, I found myself confronted with several difficulties. I sometimes took advantage of students with whom I felt I had a strong relationship by counting on their continued support while increasingly demanding them to help their classmates or take on greater responsibilities. Meanwhile, I spent large amounts of class time dealing with a few disruptive students and possibly neglecting others who were quiet or never asked questions.

I was too passive in my efforts to help, often assuming that if I made myself as approachable as possible, then students would let me know if they had a problem. I need to be more proactive in helping students who may seem to be working, but who would benefit from increased assistance. During one project in which students were doing research and writing on their own, one student was working hard every day and seemed to be getting a lot done, so I assumed she wasn't having any problems. When I finally went by to check on her, I found that she had been copying word for word from a website that only marginally related to the assigned topic and that she didn't really understand the assignment. All her work was useless. Had I been more proactive I could have avoided having her waste so much time.

I also sometimes felt I left myself vulnerable. Some students responded to my offers to provide extra help outside of class by simply never doing the work during class time. At other times my efforts to get a disruptive student to focus on his or her work merely came across to the other students as me being too lenient with a troublemaker. I expected my students to honestly express themselves and share their experiences with the class so I felt I had to do the same, but it was sometimes hard to do. At one point a student took advantage of my hesitation and embarrassment in answering a personal question and what had perhaps been a passing question became a massive issue that occupied some of the students for weeks. If I'm going to build relationships in which I expect genuine responses from the students about their experiences and needs, then I'm going to have to be willing to give them the same in order to avoid confusion, mistrust, or ridicule.

My Assumptions

I acknowledge that "the great power of reflection is not that it lets me see how something else has changed or how I changed in the past, but that it changes me in the process." It was only after my student teaching that I began to understand the importance of that continual change in my teaching practice. The largest impediment to my goal of genuinely listening to my students continues to be my own ego. I have great difficulty in stopping myself from believing that I know best because only I, the teacher, can see the "bigger picture" of the students' educational needs. When I had a problem, I would analyze my teaching practice, but in general I believed that the answer would be found in my own reflection or in the advice of more experienced teachers, not in engaging in discussion with the students about what I could do to better serve them.

One of the challenges of listening to students is that much of the communication is unspoken. A student who wants to be treated differently may never say it, but if given the opportunity, he or she may embrace a change. A student may never get that opportunity if I allow my ego to get in the way and constantly assume that I know what's best for each student.

Guided by my ego, I might do many of the things that the students in TLT recommend, but in doing them for the wrong reason I would get inferior results. If I am guided by my ego I would embrace variety because it's what *I* enjoy, and I appeal to multiple intelligences because that's the way *I* learn best. Guided by my ego, I would strive to build relationships with my students because I want to be treated with the respect I believe I deserve as the teacher, and I would be rewarded with the students' goodwill for my extra efforts in creative lesson planning and maintaining a positive attitude. And guided by my ego I would make choices about what is best for my students based on my own assumptions of their abilities.

Conversely, as a caring teacher I might do all of the same things as when guided by my ego, but my reasoning would be completely different and the ultimate results would be far superior. In every instance I make choices guided by what is best for my students and I use the students' own voices, not my assumptions, to guide me in determining what is best. Guided by my ego I will rarely be surprised by my students because I never give them a chance to surprise me. As a caring, listening teacher I will provide those chances and will have to continually reevaluate my own teaching and embrace fresh ideas as my students surprise and impress me with their knowledge and abilities.

Conclusion

The moment I stop being surprised by my students is the moment that I have to admit that I have completely failed them. It means that I have limited them to only who I assume them to be and have ceased to give them any opportunity to be who they might want to become. It's the reason why I need to keep experimenting with different pedagogical methods that appeal to different learning styles, even if no one objects to the old methods. It's the reason why I need to always recognize that I'll never really know my students and I must continually reevaluate our relationship and continually work *with* the students to meet their needs and not simply impose on them what I assume is best. "To learn is to be in motion. And because learning is ongoing, there is a perpetual need to reinterpret students' experiences of that learning."[19] If I can succeed in putting my students first, proactively listening to them, and working with them, rather than egotistically assuming I already know them, passively waiting for them to speak to me, and forcing them to accept my "teacher knows best" decisions, then I will never fail to be surprised by my students' capabilities and insights.

Notes

1. Rudduck, 2007, p. 595.
2. Oakes and Lipton, 2007.
3. SooHoo quoted in MacBeath, Demetriou, Rudduck, and Myers, 2003, p. 2.
4. Corbett and Wilson, 2007.
5. MacBeath, Demetriou, Rudduck, and Myers, 2003, p. 8.

6. Cushman, 2003, p. 91.
7. Smyth, 2007, p. 645.
8. Cushman, 2003, p. 19.
9. Thiessen, 2007, p. 480.
10. Cushman, 2003, p. 188.
11. Cushman, 2003, p. 184.
12. Rudduck, 2007, pp. 593–594.
13. Noddings, 1997, p. 471.
14. Orlich, 2001, p. 380.
15. Schlecty, 1994, quoted in Strong et al., 2001, p. 85.
16. Cook-Sather, 2006, p. 24.
17. Kounin quoted in Lipton and Oakes, 2007, p. 262.
18. MacBeath, Demetriou, Rudduck, and Myers, 2003, p. 2.
19. Cook-Sather, 2007a, p. 856.

10

Beyond "Wiggle Room"

Creating Spaces for Authentic Learning in a Twelfth-Grade English Class

Marsha Rosenzweig Pincus

Chapter Overview

Focus of this chapter: A case study of a challenging senior English class built around student interest and perspectives as an occasion for an urban teacher to reflect on her thirty-four-year career.

Discussed in this chapter:

- Prologue: The last act
- Inquiry across the lifespan: "I used to be an English teacher"
- Creating "wiggle room"—designing the course
- Sample of student choice in text selection
- Moving beyond "wiggle room": The intellectual autobiography
- A fitting final: Student-generated exam questions
- Conclusion: Student voice and teacher integrity

I would like to see a curriculum that is not so structured and restricting, with some wiggle room. I'd like to have a variation of different teaching methods and materials: a class that isn't so predictable. I'd like to read books that make sense and have actual meanings. I'd also like to do different types of writing instead of just essays.

—Brent

It is possible that my previous English classes restricted me from my constitutional pursuit of happiness and that my subconscious saw this as a violation of my inalienable rights. As you have not prohibited enjoyment in the class, I think you've already made English matter more than it has in the past.

—Tiffany

145

The class would be more interesting to the students if we really had a say in the class. For example, most English teachers will force students to analyze every minor detail in a book because they feel that there are so many metaphors, symbols, and motifs behind the text. However, when this happens, students leave simply knowing those metaphors and motifs without really understanding the deeper concepts in the text. Thus, if we could really share our opinions on different books that we read in class without being confined to finding the symbols, the class would be much more meaningful.

—Shanita

Prologue: The Last Act

As the summer of 2007 was winding down, I was preparing myself for what was to be my thirty-fourth and final year of teaching in the School District of Philadelphia and my tenth year at J. R. Masterman Laboratory and Demonstration School. I was all set to teach the same courses I had been teaching for the past five years—two sections of an Honors English 3 class with an emphasis on American literature and two sections of a popular senior elective entitled "Drama and Inquiry." I was looking forward to a pleasant but uneventful school year to cap off an interesting and rewarding career when I was shaken from my complacency during the last week of August by an e-mail from my principal. In addition to my other courses, I was told, I would be teaching a section of English 4. This was not good news.

Masterman, a magnet high school for academically talented and mentally gifted students from every neighborhood in Philadelphia, is considered one of the most successful high schools in the country. By most accounts it is a desirable place to teach. That is, of course, unless you teach seniors, who are notoriously difficult to engage. Under huge amounts of pressure and understandably worried about their finances and their futures, they spend the first half of the year preoccupied with the college application process. During the second half of the year, once their midyear reports have been sent to the colleges and their acceptances start to come in, they turn their eyes toward prom and graduation.

As a successful and experienced teacher, it is hard for me to admit that I was cowed by this assignment. The last time I had taught the class was in 1998, my first year at Masterman, and I remember what a struggle it had been. Nearly half of the students in the twelfth grade took Advanced Placement (AP) English. That meant that the students in the "regular" English 4 class didn't have either the scores or the inclination to take AP English. It was either a subject they disliked or one in which they weren't particularly skilled—or both. In addition, it is a gateway class—required by the state for high school graduation—making the stakes high for the students, who in turn put pressure on the teachers to make the class relatively easy to pass. Knowing all of this, I spent the days prior to the opening of school obsessively writing and rewriting the syllabus and the nights having the kind of teaching dreams I hadn't had in years.

The comments by Brent, Tiffany, and Shanita above represent a sampling of student responses to the syllabus for the English 4 class that I taught at Masterman High School in 2007–2008. Why I was so terrified of this class and what I learned in my attempt to create a meaningful and engaging course for these students in my final year of teaching is the subject of this chapter.

Inquiry across the Lifespan: "I Used to Be an English Teacher"

I used to be an English teacher. I taught vocabulary on Monday, grammar on Tuesday, literature on Wednesday and Thursday, and composition on Friday. I taught well-planned lessons with behavioral objectives and specific learning outcomes. My students completed worksheets selecting proper tenses and placing commas in appropriate places. After reading a story, poem, or novel, they would answer my meticulously developed literal, interpretive, and evaluative questions. And my principal saw my work and said that it was good.

—from my teaching journal, 1988

When I was a beginning teacher, this traditional conception of the teaching of English was the only one available to me. It was how I had been taught in middle and high school, and it was how I was taught to teach in college. Every now and again, I would deviate from this schedule, prompted by boredom and a desire to try something new. In my first year of teaching, 1974, I invested ten dollars and bought a class set of S. E. Hinton's brand new novel *The Outsiders* for twenty-five cents apiece. Together, my eighth graders and I read this book, rewriting chapters from different characters' points of view, converting parts of the novel into a stage play, drawing portraits of Ponyboy and his brothers, and writing personal narratives about family, friendship, and violence. One day during this unit, my principal came to my door, announcing that he was here for my formal observation. He looked around the room and he saw thirty-five adolescents sitting in groups, some of them on the floor. Some were acting out their original scripts. Others were creating a giant collage. All were talking. All were engaged. My principal paused, and I watched him look disapprovingly around the room as he peered down at his clipboard one last time before saying with disdain, "I'll come back when you're teaching."

The following day, fourth period, he did indeed return, and I dutifully taught a lesson about parts of speech, complete with examples on the board, followed by a question-and-answer session with a skill sheet for reinforcement. My thirty-five rambunctious adolescents sat quietly in rows and politely completed the lesson. My principal sat in the back row taking notes and checking items off on the checklist and with a few minutes left in the period handed me a copy of his evaluation with my high scores.

For many years, I was troubled by that incident. While I didn't abandon the kinds of activities that we did in response to *The Outsiders*, I did them less frequently and with more trepidation, despite the fact that I *knew* through my observations of my students' written and oral responses that this kind of teaching was more engaging and effective. Additionally, *I* felt more engaged and alive when I was teaching in this manner, eager to see and hear the multiple ways in which my students were making sense of the novel, relating it to their own lives and raising questions about gangs and loyalty, violence and social class. Their responses sparked in me a genuine interest, and as I learned more about them and how they saw themselves and the world, I was better able to understand what they needed from me individually and collectively as their teacher.

Unfortunately, during this period of my life and career, I lacked the confidence to value my own knowledge. I was grateful for my superior rating, and it never occurred to me to ask for an appointment to speak with my principal to discuss the evaluation, let alone to explain and defend what I was doing in my class the day he'd announced that I wasn't "teaching." And it certainly didn't occur to me to examine the items on the evaluation checklist to critique the conception of teaching embedded within. I lacked the experience and sophistication to understand that the evaluation tool was constructed by those in power and it perpetuated a particular teacher-centered, authoritative, skills-based approach to teaching.

Before a teacher can engage her students to live life consciously, she must find the courage to question and live consciously herself—face her own fears, analyze and understand her own desires, and see herself as a living human being capable of doing meaningful work in the world. A teacher who has not been awakened to her own possibilities for growth cannot inspire such growth in her students.

—from my teaching journal, 2002

Interestingly, it was my time away from teaching that sparked my transformation. When my children were born, I took a two-year maternity leave. During those years, I would spend my days with my infant and toddler, watching them closely and figuring out how they were making sense of the world. I can still remember the satisfaction and pride I felt as a mother when I finally understood that the sounds of "*bruh bruh bruh bruh*" that my nine-month-old daughter was making as she toddled after her brother were not random. They represented her first word—"brother." When I took my two-year-old son to the zoo, I listened as he pointed to every animal, excitedly calling each one a "dog!" When we got to the elephant, he shouted, "Dog! Dog!" Another time, he pointed to the moon and uttered with surprise and wonder, "Egg in the sky!" This little two-year-old was using language to make connections based on size, shape, and space and as his mother and teacher, it was my job to lead him gently to new words for concepts he already understood. Before I could engage my children in naming the world, I first needed to understand the ways in which they were doing it and see the patterns and logic of their systems.

Becoming a mother gave me the confidence in myself that I lacked as a teacher. I came to value my abilities to interpret my children's needs and questions and respond to them in ways that would enable my children to grow. When I returned to the classroom in 1985 after my maternity leave, I was not the same young woman who had left two and a half years earlier.

Unfortunately, I encountered the same expectations for "good" teaching that I had left behind. Only this time, I was becoming increasingly uncomfortable with my role as the purveyor of the standardized curriculum and the literary canon. Upon returning to teaching, I was transferred to Simon Gratz High School, a large comprehensive neighborhood high school in the heart of the African American community. All of my students were African American and I, a young Jewish woman, often found myself questioning why I was surrounding the classroom with pictures of "great" American authors like Melville, Poe, and Emerson and teaching books by Twain, Hawthorne, and Fitzgerald.

During this period in my career, I experienced a great deal of dissonance between what I was doing in the classroom and what I *wanted* to do. I was still standing in front of the class lecturing about books I had assigned from the book list, writing study guides with comprehension questions, and developing tests asking the students to identify literary devices. Yet, I was also listening to my students, asking them to speak and write about their lives and their dreams, trying to understand who they were and who they were hoping to become, much in the same manner in which I had learned to engage with my children. This gap between who my students and I were as human beings and what I was teaching them continued to widen in the months following my return and made me feel increasingly uneasy in my role.

I honestly don't know how long I would have remained a teacher if I had not become a participant in the inaugural summer institute of the Philadelphia Writing Project (PhilWP) in 1986. A site of the National Writing Project (NWP), a professional development network dedicated to the teaching of writing, PhilWP was founded by Susan Lytle, a literacy professor at the University of Pennsylvania, and several teachers in the School District of Philadelphia. The NWP was founded on the belief that teachers are the best teachers of other teachers and that the teaching of writing was a complex process involving issues of language, power, culture, and identity. It was during the summer institute that I read the work of Paulo Freire for the first time and learned of his approach to literacy teaching and learning in Brazil. In the very first reading assigned during the summer institute, his autobiographical essay, "The Importance of the Act of Reading," I encountered for the first time the idea that language and reality were dynamically interconnected.[1] One sentence in particular caught my attention and caused me to question my fundamental beliefs about teaching English: "In a way we can say . . . reading the word is not merely preceded by reading the world but by a certain form of writing it or *rewriting* it, that is transforming it by means of conscious practical work."[2] I began to see that I needed to provide my students more such opportunities to read, write, and rewrite the world and the word.

Maxine Greene writes that a teacher willing to undertake inquiry into her practice is "no longer content to be a mere cipher, a functionary, a clerk."[3] In the summer institute, I learned about teacher research for the very first time and how it was possible for teachers through "systematic and intentional"[4] inquiry into our own practice to "reclaim . . . the classroom"[5] from bureaucrats and policymakers, thereby generating a body of knowledge that would enable us to learn from each other, improve our teaching, reform our schools, and ultimately transform the lives of our students. This vision of an empowered teacher, intellectually engaged in the world, learning with and from her colleagues and her students to effect positive change, energized me and made me particularly excited about returning to my classroom in the fall.

At first I struggled. While PhilWP had given me the vision and the theoretical underpinnings, I still lacked the classroom practices to engage my students in meaningful ways that would honor what they brought to the classroom. Once again, I was incredibly fortunate. In 1987, I became a participant in the very first year of the Philadelphia Young Playwrights Festival (PYPF), a nonprofit, arts-in-education organization whose mission is to "tap the potential of youth through playwriting."[6] The program pairs professional theater artists with classroom teachers in a yearlong partnership designed to teach students to write, revise, and stage their own original plays. From the moment J. Rufus Caleb, an award-winning playwright and Philadelphia Community College professor, entered my classroom and introduced my high school students to playwriting, I knew that something special was happening.

In the playwriting workshops, students were able to tell stories that were important to them. They were able to create worlds and people those worlds with characters and give those characters dialogue to speak made up of the words and sounds and rhythms of their lives. I was struck by the way this enlivened students who had been previously unengaged—those students who sat quietly in the back of the room, doing just enough school work to earn a D. These students had been awakened by the playwriting process and through my observations of and conversations with them, I was able to have access for the very first time to their thinking about themselves as writers and the ways in which they could use literacy to impact their lives and the lives of those around them.

Terrance Jenkins, one of my Simon Gratz students in the early years of the playwriting program and winner of the National Young Playwrights competition in 1992 for his play *Taking Control,* initially wrote the first draft of his play because it was an assignment and he wanted to earn a good grade. As he continued to write and revise his play about a teenaged girl from a shattered family trying to "take control" of the situation when her younger sister becomes pregnant, he shared emerging drafts with different audiences. From that experience, he developed a sense of himself as a writer and saw the possibilities for using writing as a way to bring about positive change. In an interview for a documentary about the playwriting program, he said, "I had a message to get across, I had a story to tell. I wanted people to see this [play] and I wanted them to make a change."[7] It was through this playwriting program that I learned the powerful impact that adults could have on young people simply by listening to their stories, voices, issues, concerns, and questions and responding to them in thoughtful and respectful ways.

In the years that followed, I learned how to adapt the lessons I had learned about student choice, voice, and agency in the playwriting program to other aspects of the English curriculum. I became more adept at designing projects that engaged students in the process of inquiry, structuring their interaction with texts and each other in ways that honored their perspectives and questions.

This kind of teaching contributed to substantive reform in some Philadelphia high schools in the 1990s. At Simon Gratz, I cofounded a school-within-a-school called Crossroads, which joined 300 students—ninth graders to seniors—with sixteen teachers from all of the major disciplines into an academic community who stayed together for all four years of high school. Our program was interdisciplinary, writing-intensive, and inquiry-based. Each year, our curriculum was centered on an "essential question," a curricular organizer we adapted from the Coalition of Essential Schools, a network of schools whose goal is to create and sustain personalized, equitable, and intellectually challenging schools. Teachers worked together to make sure that our individual curricula addressed that question in ways that would allow the students to make connections across disciplines.

The first year of Crossroads, we, the teachers, decided on the essential question, "How does learning connect to your world?" This question worked in two very important ways: (1) it pushed the students to see how what they were learning could have an impact on their lives, and (2) it forced the teachers to think hard about the sense our students would be making of the material we were presenting to them. After the first year of the program, students and teachers gathered together in June to evaluate the effectiveness of that year's essential question and to engage in a collaborative process to select the question for the following year. Some of the questions we explored in the eight years I was part of Crossroads included:

- How do people, events, and conditions influence change?
- What are the roads to the future?
- What is the relationship between power and inquiry?

Each question presented its own unique challenges; however, discussing and addressing those challenges throughout the year became part of the inquiry process for teachers and students alike.

Students maintained portfolios of their papers and projects and were taught how to engage in self-reflective processes, evaluating their strengths, weaknesses, and progress as writers and learners. As seniors, they presented samples from these portfolios to a panel of teachers, parents, community members, and juniors as part of their senior exit project, which also included the writing of a substantive research paper relating to an aspect of the year's essential question.

This reform effort has been documented in many places, most notably Michelle Fine's 1994 book, *Chartering Urban School Reform: Reflections on Public High Schools in the Midst of Change.* The essays in the book illustrate the inextricable relationships between and among school reform, teacher inquiry, and student agency. In order for meaningful, positive change to occur, teachers have to be willing to engage their students in a dialogue about issues that impact teaching and learning. At Simon Gratz, I learned how to interact with my high school students in the same ways I had interacted with my small children while on maternity leave. I learned to put their questions, concerns, and desires at the center of their learning, accessing their prior knowledge, then creating learning experiences in which they could pursue those questions in meaningful ways.

I transferred to Masterman in 1998, just as the new structures implemented by the reform movement of the 1990s were being slowly dismantled by a new local administration and a shifting national trend toward reliance on high-stakes testing as the primary measure of a school's progress.

While the students at Masterman scored well on these tests (after all, high scores were required in fifth and sixth grade for admission and again in ninth grade for readmission to the smaller and more select high school), I immediately sensed an undercurrent of dissatisfaction among the students. I soon learned that Masterman students would often begrudgingly comply with teachers' assignments; they would less frequently actually engage.

My first year at Masterman, I tried to include the playwriting program in my English classes. I soon discovered that it was not a good fit; the academic requirements and the pressure for students to perform well on standardized tests did not allow for this kind of curricular "deviation." I became dismayed by the implications of this kind of content-centered, grade-oriented, competitive approach to teaching. My new students often told me that it wouldn't take long for me to be "Mastermanized" and succumb to the pressures of delivering a traditional curriculum with a teacher-centered pedagogy.

With the support of the Carnegie Academy for the Scholarship of Teaching and Learning (CASTL) I began to explore alternative approaches to what I was doing in my classes at Masterman. Using the terms "main stage" and "second stage" as they are referred to in the theater as a metaphor for school reform, I developed a theory of "second stage reform" that I thought might be possible at a school like Masterman. Many theaters have two performance areas: a main stage upon which works are performed with a wide audience appeal and a second stage, sometimes called a black box, where new plays and experimental works can be developed. The second stage often serves as an incubator for main stage productions. In rethinking my approach to my teaching at Masterman, I developed an elective class called "Drama and Inquiry" that grew out of my decade-long association with Philadelphia Young Playwrights and was consistent with my critical pedagogy approach to teaching and learning. While my English classes remained "main stage" productions, my elective became the alternative, experimental space: my "second stage" on which I could enact a different kind of pedagogy that might eventually have an impact on the pedagogy of the main stage. Table 10.1 illustrates the differences between the main stage practices I saw occurring in the major subject classes and the second stage practices I tried to enact in my Drama and Inquiry elective.

For three years of their high school experience, Masterman students follow a very rigid, prescribed academic program with little choice in their course selection. In their senior year, they are able to select from among a small number of electives that take the place of some of the more selective AP courses. The purpose of the Drama and Inquiry course, as I stated to the students in the syllabus, was to use drama to "explore questions about multiple perspectives, shifting identities and our coexistence in a diverse, complex and ever-changing world." It was my hope that we could "become a true intellectual community filled with members who raise heartfelt and complex questions and explore answers together in an engaged ethical dialogue."

In this course, we read plays by contemporary American playwrights that dealt with issues of race, class, gender, ethnicity, and identity. Students wrote their own monologues and dialogues and eventually wrote and acted in their own one-act plays. They participated in alternative types of classroom discourse, including Socratic Seminars, collaborative inquiry, reflective conversations, and journal groups. In the early years of teaching the course, I was still required to create written midterm and final exams, to be given by proctors during times designated by the administration. In more recent years, I was able to get permission for alternative assessments that were more compatible with the nature of the class. I was able to count the text of their original plays as a final exam and institute a series of in-class performances instead of written midterms. At the end of each year, we produced a Drama Showcase, which consisted of original scenes

Table 10.1   Differences in Practices

Main Stage	Second Stage
Emphasis on answers	Emphasis on questions
Individual achievement	Group accomplishments
Lecture and debate	Dialogue
Argumentative	Reflective
Competitive	Collaborative
Knowledge transmission	Knowledge construction
Certainty	Uncertainty
Test-driven	Process-driven
Anesthetic	Aesthetic
Preserves tradition	Transforms tradition

written, acted, and directed by the students, performed for a small audience in an intimate space we created in our basement classroom or on the stage of a local theater.

In "Learning from Laramie: 'Urban High School Students Read, Respond, and Reenact *The Laramie Project*,'"[8] I document one class's involvement with the course and discuss what happened when we read, researched, and performed *The Laramie Project* by Moises Kaufman and the Tectonic Theater Company. After seeing the work performed in my classroom, the director of the high school play decided to do *The Laramie Project* as the high school play onstage in the main auditorium. The performances were followed up with peer educators leading workshops about homosexuality and homophobia. The play had literally made the journey from second to main stage.

I would spend the rest of my teaching career at Masterman trying to infuse second stage practices into my main stage English classrooms.

Creating "Wiggle Room"—Designing the Course

In designing my English 4 course, I had a little more leeway than I had in developing my English 3 courses because twelfth grade is not a "tested" grade for either the state of Pennsylvania or the school district. And while I did have to adhere to English Department guidelines that had been approved by the district (we all agreed, for example, that every student would write a literary research paper in twelfth grade), choose texts of literary merit from world literature, and assign a range of writing, I was relatively free to design the course and select texts that I thought would interest and engage my students.

All of the students had read Orwell's *1984* over the summer, so I selected novels, films, plays, and nonfiction that I thought would enable us to continue to explore issues about language, power, identity, and storytelling that *1984* was sure to evoke. I named the class "21st-Century English Studies: Literature, Language and Lives in the Age of Globalization" and wrote the syllabus in the form of a letter to the students explaining my goals and rationale and soliciting their feedback. I included these questions as my guiding principles:

- How can we co-construct an English 4 class in an academic high school that engages the students in meaningful ways? How can we make English matter?
- What are the ways in which we can co-construct the curriculum of this course so it can better reflect the realities of human interaction in a global environment?

For their first homework assignment, I asked the students to respond to the syllabus, to tell me what they thought, raise questions, share suggestions, and recount their past experiences in English classes. The three responses that open this chapter are representative of the ones I received from all thirty-two of the students. Like Brent, Tiffany, and Shanita, many expressed their disdain for the restrictiveness and predictability of some of their former English classes.

Amit, echoing the desire for relevance and variety, explained, "I am really looking for a class that avoids the basic pitfalls of most English classes: tedium and boredom. A lot of English classes just have you read a story then write an essay on it. The simple response to this is to create a large array of techniques to tackle an objective. It can be research papers, skits, discussions, or whatever the students can think of. . . . If the class reflects our wishes, we'll be more willing to interact and get involved."

Sayeed suggested a way to make the literature more meaningful to the students: "My final suggestion is to sometimes move the 'lens.' When reading books, we don't always have to focus on the book with blinders on. We can talk about what's going on in the world and in our lives."

Amit added, "Even if you think that there are certain ideas the students must have about a book, you have to be willing to accept the view of those students who don't see things your way or the way of the scholars. If you don't accept those with opposing views, all respect will be lost and you'll be forced to grade papers that just say what you said to your students. Never suggest that a student try and change his/her views, though it is acceptable to ask them to take a different viewpoint for a moment. It's one thing to look through someone else's eyes. It's another to have your eyes replaced."

Using metaphors of sight, Amit and Sayeed offered powerful critiques of main stage teaching practices and echoed Greene's warning about teachers becoming functionaries and clerks in a bureaucratic system.

In going forward from here, there were three things that I did in response to the students' letters:

- Organized the material into loosely structured inquiries into dystopias, language, and storytelling;
- Varied the types of texts and writing assignments that I assigned to the whole class;
- Offered several opportunities for the students to select their own texts and/or the ways they responded to those texts.

In addition, I began our reading and discussion of every text by assigning a personal response. This way I was able to have access to and understand the sense the students were making of each text while they were reading (see Table 10.2).

Sample of Student Choice in Text Selection

Several times throughout the year, students were able to follow their own interests and select texts within the context of the organized inquiry units. Table 10.3 shows the range and variety of texts read or viewed by several students. During these times, students often shared books or movies with

Table 10.2   Some Common English 4 Requirements

Major Texts: Read or Viewed by All
Orwell, George, *1984* PBS Video, *American Tongues* Sophocles, *Antigone* Fugard, Athol, *The Island* Wiesel, Eli, *Night* Erdrich, Louise, *Love Medicine* Cruz, Nilo, *Anna in the Tropics* Eggers, Dave, and Valentino Deng, *What Is the What?* Satrapi, Marjane, *Persepolis*
Papers and Projects: Completed by All
Film scenario and screenplay: Modernization of *Antigone* Missing scene from a play: In response to *Anna in the Tropics* Literary research paper: Formal research paper, student-selected text Collaborative response and research journals: *Love Medicine* Intellectual autobiography: Long, complex personal narrative project Final exam: In-class essay with student-generated personalized questions

Table 10.3   Student Choices

	Jeff	Andy	Katrina	Aaron
Dystopia Inquiry	*Republic of Plato*	*A Clockwork Orange*	*Wicked*	*Escape from LA*
Native American Storytelling Inquiry	*Bury my Heart at Wounded Knee*	*Yellow Raft in Blue Water*	*Doe Boy*	*Genocide of the Mind*
Literary Research Project	*On the Road*	*Maus I*	*The Secret Life of Bees*	*Like Water for Chocolate*

each other and engaged in informal conversations about what they were discovering.

Moving beyond "Wiggle Room": The Intellectual Autobiography

Midway through the course, I sensed a trend toward disengagement among many of the students. The spaces I had opened in the syllabus for student choice of texts and student voice in response to those texts were losing their novelty and many students seemed to be going through the motions, not much differently from the way they would have even if the curriculum and assignments had been more traditional. I was very anxious to reengage them to create assignments that would be personally meaningful to all. I thought back to my own educational experiences and recalled an assignment I was given in graduate school that really made a significant difference in my life: an intellectual autobiography in which we expressed our current philosophy of education, tracing our intellectual journeys and laying out the roadmaps for our future research and studies. This assignment prompted me to think long and hard about how my life experiences influenced my choices and how they connected to the books I had read and the questions I had explored in my academic work. I remembered how I had been galvanized the first time I read Paulo Freire, and how I found deeper meaning and purpose in my teaching life after reading Maxine Greene. More importantly, this assignment allowed me to discern the themes and patterns in my life thus far and gave me a sense of agency and purpose for my future, a way of integrating who I am with the kind of work I wanted to do in the world.

I began to modify this assignment for high school seniors. The students would each write a proposal for an intellectual autobiography of their lives so far, including a title, book abstract, annotated table of contents in which they describe the contents of at least six chapters, one sample chapter, and a book cover. Later, at the students' request, I added an artistic component; these included paintings, poetry books, CDs with representative songs, photography, or websites.

The project was introduced slowly and was worked on over a period of three months. The first phase of the project was personal reflective writing in response to prompts I would give the class. The students would write their responses in their notebooks and would only share with others if they elected to do so. The prompts related to their literacy and educational histories. They wrote about learning how to read and write, their favorite childhood books, teachers who had made a difference in their lives, powerful learning experiences in and out of school, and images they had of themselves as students.

Because the students had been together since fifth grade, they had shared memories of books and teachers. The conversations in class on the days we would work on these prompts were lively and engaging. Many of these reflections and discussions became personal as students talked about the impact on their lives of losing family members or surviving serious illness. It is important to note that this assignment in which the students were writing about their own lives was done within the context of a yearlong inquiry into language and storytelling through the literature we were reading. While I deliberately did not make this connection explicit, many of the students began to comment on how their own writing was similar to or different from Eggers's or Wiesel's or Erdrich's. Still others addressed issues of language, culture, power, and identity in their own reflections.

The final in-class activity we did before the students were assigned to write the autobiography at home was to look at a portfolio of their writing since eighth grade. Each year, their English teachers would have them select two of their best pieces of writing and write about how they had grown as writers that year. By twelfth grade, they had ten pieces of writing in their portfolios. Examining their writing portfolios in the context of the intellectual autobiography gave more meaning and purpose to what could have been a perfunctory activity.

For the first and only time during the school year, every single student handed in his or her intellectual autobiography on the day it was due. Sayeed, who entitled his book *Rounded*, wrote about his experiences living in two very different contexts—a rural university town and a large urban city. He explored issues of language, race, and identity in his own life. After the project, Sayeed wrote, "It was as though you let us go with all of the knowledge you taught us all year. The project basically wrote itself as we knew nothing else but to make the inevitable connections."

In her chapter, Jasmine described surviving cancer as a child and how that experience inspired her to become a nurse. In an e-mail to me after the school year had ended, Jasmine wrote, "I started forgetting about you as the grader and I started to really focus on me and my accomplishments, my hard times, the lesson I learned and the person I still wanted to improve on. . . . After completing this project, I felt a bit changed, relieved. Writing it was healthy for me."

Another student, Kathleen, was inspired to write the entire book. Each chapter told of a significant event in her development. But what was remarkable about this work is that each chapter was told in a different way; Kathleen had experimented with her writing. She emulated the different storytelling techniques used by the authors we had been studying, writing one chapter as a play, another as a story within a story, another as a graphic novel, still another as a poem. Upon completion of the project, Kathleen wrote, "The intellectual autobiography . . . helped me create a place for myself in the world, or rather, helped me see the place I've simply been overlooking."

As for Brent, the student who had asked for "wiggle room," he too wrote a compelling narrative about his early years in school. In his chapter, he described an elementary school teacher who rewarded his students with money for answering questions correctly. Young Brent was very good at that game and continued to "play the game" right through middle school, where he won academic awards at eighth-grade graduation. By high school, he had decided to opt out, no longer motivated by extrinsic rewards. I am somewhat sad to say that I was not successful in motivating Brent to make his learning in my class more intrinsic; for most of the texts we read and essays we wrote, he continued to "wiggle" his way through them, relying on Sparknotes, in-class discussions, his native intelligence, and excellent writing skills to fake his way through essays and other writing assignments. However, he did engage in the process of writing his intellectual autobiography, and by reading it, I was able to come to a better understanding of who he was and what he needed (or didn't need) from my class.

A Fitting Final: Student-Generated Exam Questions

This past year, you gave us options and different strategies to go about looking for the "right" answers to questions . . . and there was no one answer, it was whatever we thought the answer was, so long as we backed it up. Also, the fact that we could create our own essay topics that were used on tests and such kind of blew me out of the water. The fact that you had faith that we were smart enough to think of intelligent, well-rounded, involved questions really made me think I wasn't as low on the "Masterman Scale" as I thought.

—Barbara

At Masterman, all teachers are required to create final exams that are given to seniors during the first or second week of May. After having taught the class in a way that solicited their input into the texts and interpretations of those texts, it seemed inconsistent for me to create a "one-size-fits-all" final exam. Instead, I proposed that each student create his or her own essay exam question. The only criteria for the questions were that they had to relate to one of the issues we had explored in class during that year and that they had to include content from at least four texts (whole class or self-selected) in their response. For those students who chose not to write their own question, I created three questions from which they could choose. Twenty of the thirty-two students chose to write their own questions.[9]

Barbara's comments address the way in which just being asked to create her own exam question changed her image of herself as a learner. No longer was she "low on the 'Masterman Scale,'" one that ranks students by their grades and test scores; she was "smart" and "intelligent" and capable of completing this complex task. Because I, the teacher, had faith in her and classmates, they could reconstruct their images of themselves as valued learners, echoing Greene when she wrote, "The teacher who believes in stimulating and developing potential will be challenging—at least implicitly—the inhumanity of credentialing systems which sort and rank people according to market demand."[10]

And in a fitting outcome for me, the teacher, I was spared the fate that Amit warned me about in the beginning of the year. The essays I read and responded to for their final exam were varied, interesting, and enlightening, reflecting and refracting the course I had designed for them through their diverse lenses and perspectives.

Conclusion: Student Voice and Teacher Integrity

Alison Cook-Sather has written that when students have the opportunity to develop a metacognitive awareness of their learning both in order to engage and as a result of engaging in serious dialogue with adults, they not only construct their understanding of subject matter content, but they also construct themselves anew.[11] This reconstruction of self is evident in my students' responses shared above. But what is the impact on the adult who so engages with her students? Greene finds the seeds of the answer in Martin Buber: "In learning from time to time what *this* human being needs and does not need at the moment, the educator is led to an ever deeper recognition of what all human beings need in order to grow."[12] Including herself. A teacher who seeks this kind of dialogic relationship with her students will not need to move out of the classroom to grow professionally and personally. She will be able to find the work meaningful and challenging over the course of a lifespan.

Back in 1973, Greene railed against the bureaucracy that was paralyzing schools and forcing teachers into the role of bureaucratic functionaries. Thirty-five years later—in the wake of required tests implemented in response to the No Child Left Behind Act of 2001, her words echo with pointed urgency as teachers once again are called upon to abandon their own goals, desires, beliefs, and expertise; ignore their own knowledge about their students and what they need to learn; and implement restrictive and often meaningless curricula designed solely to raise scores on standardized tests.

In a talk in 2008, Lee Shulman, then-president of the Carnegie Foundation, discussed integrity in teaching.[13] Teachers, he says, need to align their knowledge, purpose, design, and action. I believe that it is impossible for a teacher to separate her true self, her values, her beliefs, her background, her experiences, and her questions from her work as a teacher and remain in the classroom for any length of time. There have been times in my past when I have been forced to "teach against myself"—that is, to present to young people ideas, texts, and positions that I did not believe in. I've been forced to present material to them in ways that I know neither connected to nor engaged them. I have been forced to give them assessments that measured skills that are neither relevant nor necessary for real learning. When I have done these things, my actions have not been aligned with my beliefs.

I have struggled over the years to bring my actions and beliefs in line. Of course, there has been no easy resolution—only the tension that comes from trying to reconcile disparate ideas, perspectives, and approaches. I have tried to listen to my students and respond to their questions and needs in meaningful ways. The constant investigation into my own teaching and a serious attempt to listen and respond to my students' voices, questions, and desires are the threads that have held me together and allowed me to teach with integrity.

Notes

1. Freire, 1987, p. 29.
2. Ibid., p. 35.
3. Greene, 1973, p. 7.
4. Cochran-Smith and Lytle, 1993, p. 23.
5. Goswami and Stillman, 1987, p. iii.

6. Information is available at www.phillyyoungplaywrights.org.

7. Strosser and Patterson, 1993.

8. Pincus, 2005.

9. The student-generated exam questions and other materials related to this chapter are available at www.marshapincus.com/beyondwiggleroom.

10. Greene, 1973, p. 92.

11. Cook-Sather, 2006.

12. Martin Buber quoted in Greene, 1973, p. 94.

13. Shulman, 2008.

11

Student Voice on a High School Decisionmaking Team

A Principal's Model of Listening to Students

Peter M. Evans

Chapter Overview

Focus of this chapter: A principal's story of working to develop a mechanism for ensuring that student voice and participation are central to decisionmaking processes at his high school

Discussed in this chapter:

- Aspects of our program
- Implementation of Solon Circle
- Experiences
- In their own words: The voices of students participating in Solon Circle

The vision that the stakeholders of our school community have for our students is that their experiences in high school will prepare them to take their first steps after high school on to postsecondary studies or work but also equip them with the skills necessary for life after college as they assume roles as active and engaged members of the democratic society. My work as a principal has allowed me to witness the achievement of these goals, not by a singular focus on raising the test scores of students, but rather by allowing students to follow their natural desire and need to find their voices through activities that are meaningful and engaging.

In many ways, trying to decide the first steps to take in making substantive changes in the way we engage students in high school can be the most difficult. With the complexities of meeting the requirements of No Child Left Behind, state mandates, and initiatives and policies created by local school boards, at times it seems there is little opportunity for autonomy. Despite that, our high school's stakeholders determined that students' perspective and voices were of critical importance. Therefore, we, the adults, had to begin by accepting students' perspectives and then provide students with opportunities to practice their new skills.

Aspects of Our Program

The cornerstone of democracy is an open and transparent process of making decisions, and, in my opinion, that method provides the strongest indicator of a school's willingness to honor student voice. Our school was willing, but only after coming to the realization that decisionmaking is a source of tremendous power and control in a high school where tradition is closely guarded by faculty, staff, administration, community members, and even students.

When I became principal in 2003, I was certain that the process of making decisions was going to be the cornerstone of a foundation that subsequent changes would be built on. This became very clear to me after meeting with teachers, parents, and students during the summer prior to the start of my first school year. What I heard described was student apathy, teacher frustration, and parent concerns about a wide range of issues, from out-of-control students to lack of consistent expectations from the teaching staff. I believed much of the concern was rooted in the fact that none of the stakeholders clearly understood how decisions were being made. This resulted in each of the constituent groups forming strong opinions about various aspects of school, but did little to reveal a process for making decisions. In fact, the teachers—by default and as a result of their numbers, their control over curriculum, and their close interaction with students during the course of the year—held and controlled the greatest amount of power in the school. Creating a new process for decisionmaking, one that included students, would likely reduce teachers' amount of power and as a result would likely be met with opposition. Rather than create a new process, I looked to an existing model that could be redesigned to allow for more voices in decisionmaking.

I had the good fortune to inherit a management team structure put in place by my predecessor as a way to receive guidance from key school staff. The team was made up of department heads, two faculty at-large members, the discipline coordinator, and me. In addition, two students had been invited to attend meetings in order to offer the "student perspective." After the first few meetings, it was clear that the model, although effective when it was created five years earlier, was no longer viewed or perceived by stakeholders as a functioning structure. In fact, many of the staff and students stopped attending because they were uncertain of its purpose, value, and ability to inform decisionmaking. It had evolved into discussion time with no clear beginning, end, or outcome. I quickly saw the potential for the management team to be the vehicle for decisionmaking, but only if it could be transformed into a decisionmaking body that provided equal voice for all stakeholders.

Late in the spring of my first year, I offered to organize and fund a retreat during the summer with the goal of reestablishing the design and purpose of the management team so it functioned as a decisionmaking body for the school. I sent out an open invitation to all students and staff to take part in the retreat. Students were hesitant because they couldn't imagine the work leading to anything much different than what already existed. Some staff members questioned what the process might lead to and went so far as to suggest that if they refused to take part, changes could not be made without them. The status quo was far better for some than a model of decisionmaking that could lead to a change in their role and a flattening out of the power they held.

I was pleased that twelve offered to participate. Nine of the twelve were teachers and staff from various academic disciplines as well as a guidance counselor, the school's discipline coordinator, a special educator, and one support staff member. It was a diverse group and represented a variety of disciplines as well as those in favor and opposed to changes in the management team. The balance of the group was students—a future valedictorian, a student who had experienced considerable challenges in her young life including learning disabilities, and a talented visual arts student. It was as much diversity as our school provides.

I was able to use some professional development money to pay for the two-day retreat and an excellent facilitator with a passion for and knowledge of student voice. The retreat was located about six miles off a main road with the last mile being a grassy, wooded path that our vehicles barely squeezed through. The location was ideal as we were forced to focus on the work at hand rather than the many distractions that would have come our way had we been at school. It also afforded us a neutral setting where students and staff came together to meet as equals and colleagues working toward a common goal.

Our facilitator led us through a process that allowed us to look at our high school through the widest of lenses and gradually transitioned to a close-up look at the issues surrounding decisionmaking. During the process, we agreed on a statement of mission and purpose for the team. We agreed that our management team was going to be "vested with the responsibility of continually assessing our school's capacity to meet its stated mission," which includes three goals: (1) students learn at the highest levels; (2) teachers excel; and (3) the community and schools collaborate to support learning for everyone. We also agreed that the purposes of the team would be to:

- Assess the school climate of the high school and recommend action as needed.

- Serve in an advisory capacity to the principal regarding issues requiring input from multiple perspectives.
- Ensure that curriculum, assessment, school climate, and the supporting protocols and systems are consistent with the mission and initiate action to alter or modify the protocols as needed.
- Provide a vehicle to ensure that all students, staff, faculty, and parents have a forum to be heard.
- Monitor and continually improve communication systems.

In order to further articulate the methods by which we were going to work together to make decisions, we agreed that:

- We will accomplish this in a variety of ways, including action research, open communication, reflection, discussion, and a decisionmaking process that ensures that all members of the school community (students, parents, community, and those employed by the school) are heard.
- In the event of noted inconsistencies between the mission and practice, the team will ensure the implementation of an action plan to effect the desired change by working collaboratively with the existing decisionmaking bodies in the school.
- The team will also serve in an advisory capacity to the principal regarding any issue that warrants broader input.

As we moved from a broad to more narrow perspective, we found ourselves engaged in discussion and dialogue that were increasingly difficult. Ideas did not come as easily, and some of the twelve participants appeared apprehensive about the direction the discussion was moving. From the document that was written after the retreat and mailed to all of the school's stakeholders, it is clear that the issue of student involvement was a key issue and one area that was discussed more fully than any other issue. The document described what we could find agreement on:

> We recognized the importance of students serving as members of the management team. While this will seem uncomfortable to some, we understand that it will take time and commitment on the part of all of the school community members in order to have each engaged in a meaningful and genuine way. Our goal is to move from a place where any member is viewed as an object to a place where all are seen as equals in opportunity. We believe this is essential if we are to become fully engaged in the learning process. This is supported by William Lofquist's theory that describes four stages in the process of moving toward greater involvement.[1] His continuum of involvement defines the role that each member of the school community can assume in each of the four stages when we are seen as:
>
> - Objects: exercise arbitrary and near total control over others.
> - Recipients: determine needs, prescribe remedies, implement solutions, and evaluate outcomes with little input from others, but in their best interest.
> - Resources: accept help from others in the planning, implementing, and evaluating work.
> - Equals in opportunity: members of the group have opportunities to share decisionmaking equally.

The level of concern about the role that students would play on the team became even more apparent when our facilitator introduced the Lakota Sioux concept of the Circle of Courage—to reclaim is to recognize the worth of youth who have been devalued, to cultivate courage in environments of belongings, mastery, independence, and generosity.[2] Of the four qualities, belonging was the most difficult concept for the participants to consider and the one that moved us closer to arriving at a solution.

The students shared their belief that they did not feel they belonged at the school other than to soak up the information, knowledge, and content that teachers were there to pour into them. They also said that they could remember few times when anyone asked for their perspective on a school issue, and yet they all indicated that they had definite opinions. That realization led us to talk about what we might do to help all students feel that they belonged. We agreed on a full value statement as the basic principle of our school and the new management team. The full value statement consisted of a list of the qualities that all members of the school's management team agreed were essential if the team was to be successful. The qualities are:

- Open, honest, and respectful communication
- Genuine listening
- Active research
- Confidence
- Equal voice
- Productivity, determination, and timeliness
- Fun and humor
- Creative process
- Integrity
- Clear path for task completion
- Open-mindedness
- Confidentiality
- Focus/refocus
- Emerging shared vision
- Diverse membership
- Accountability through documentation and communication
- Trust

An issue that acted as the turning point in our discussion was the idea of equal voice. I am not sure, looking back, why I should not have anticipated this from the beginning. This is when teachers realized that decisionmaking would be shared equally with students, but in order to accomplish that, they would have to share their power with students. During this part of the discussion, I decided to tape the dialogue we were having because I knew that we were at the point in our work that was the most critical. We were finally looking at the issue upon which everything else seemed to hinge—student voice. Thinking back to this discussion, I recall feeling that this one issue had the potential to make the work we accomplished at the retreat a tremendous success or a huge failure. As I played this part of the tape back after the retreat, I realized it would be hard to forget the conversation between one of the students, Kristen, and one of the teachers, Betty. It went like this:

KRISTEN: So, this means that students will have as much say about the decisions that are made as the teachers on the management team.

BETTY: Well, I don't think that's what we really are saying . . . is it?

KRISTEN: I think that is what we're saying; votes are equal, regardless of whether you're a student or a teacher.

BETTY: I don't think so. What if students vote against the teachers? . . . How's that going to be seen by teachers . . . by parents . . . by the community?

KRISTEN: If we work together to make decisions by looking carefully at what our school is all about, I don't think that will happen.

BETTY: Maybe not if you're on the management team, but what about students who don't have the best intentions and what do students know about what's right for them? Aren't we opening up a huge Pandora's Box with this? How can I go back to school and tell the teachers who aren't here that I agreed to give students a voice in running the school? I'm not ready to face them.

KRISTEN: I think you've got to give students a chance, especially if you are serious about getting students more involved in the school. I don't think bad things will happen. In fact, I really believe this will work. If this doesn't happen, if students don't have an equal voice on the team . . . well, nothing has really changed for you or us.

We were in a big circle as this discussion unfolded. I think we all knew that it was the most critical part of the retreat, and our silence after Kristen finished talking served as evidence of just how important this discussion was. We sat there in the circle, not a word spoken for what seemed like a long time but really was about a minute, before our facilitator interrupted the silence to ask whether we were in agreement with students having an equal voice in the decisionmaking process. We went around the circle one by one; everybody nodded in agreement.

The last piece of work was to name our new management team. We drew heavily on the work we had done in learning about the Circle of Courage and liked the image that the circle created. The circle is about equality: no one person can dominate in a circle, and staff and students would be able to see each other throughout a meeting. It was suggested that we use the wise lawmaker Solon as part of the name, since that was what we saw our duty to be. It also was an easy decision because our school mascot is the Solon. After a few more minutes of discussion, we settled on Solon Circle as our new name.

We left the retreat feeling that we had accomplished something really great. There was hope, anticipation, and optimism mixed with concern and a bit of anxiety. The latter was a result of realizing we had to return to school and explain to the rest of the school community what we were about to embark on.

Implementation of Solon Circle

Since its advent in 2003, Solon Circle has continued to grow, change, and evolve. Membership in Solon Circle is open to all students and staff. We decided that instead of electing or assigning members to serve, membership should be open to all. Any member of the school community has the right to take a seat in the circle. The meeting takes place each week in the middle of the day and falls during one of the lunch periods, so lunch is typically munched on throughout the meeting. While having the meeting during the day means some are not available to attend, it does ensure that all participants are able to make this an integral part of their day rather than have to add it on at the end. Having the meetings during the day also sends a message that the work of making decisions is important. Two participants share the responsibility of capturing the conversation that takes place during the meeting, and as soon as the meeting is over, the document is sent via e-mail to all staff and students. This provides quick and accurate feedback to all members of the school community and ensures a more transparent process. Decisions are not made behind closed doors with a few people invited to participate. The feedback that is received from the previous week becomes the first item of the agenda for the next meeting. After feedback, agenda items are suggested by participants and can range from issues involving school climate to policy issues to facility concerns. Students and staff may request time to share a concern they have, or other times they just come to the meeting to add to the dialogue. There are times when a decision is reached right away and other times when it is not possible to reach a decision.

When a recommendation is made by Solon Circle, it typically comes before the student body and the faculty for additional discussion by all. A few stories might provide a clearer picture of how Solon Circle works as a way to give students and staff a voice in decisionmaking.

Arriving at the solutions shown in Box 11.1 and others would not have been possible without a forum like Solon Circle that provides open and honest discussion of schoolwide issues and concerns. Including the ideas and voices of all stakeholders provides a solution that is embraced by all because of the level of trust that participants have in each other. Early on we decided that "Solon Circle will strive to make decisions using a process to achieve consensus. Consensus is achieved after a thorough discussion of an issue takes place and the group finds a solution that everyone can agree on. While the benefits of this process are that everyone is given an opportunity to express their opinions and feel valued, the challenges are that this process is time consuming and requires good facilitation." As Figure 11.1 indicates, decisions are made only after an issue has been thoroughly discussed and consensus is reached.

Box 11.1   Solon Circle Decisionmaking Flow

Each year, as students return to school, there is renewed interest on the part of students to create a student center run by and for students. The purpose of the center is to provide students a place of their own in the school where they can go during free periods. When a few students came to one of our Solon Circle meetings after school started, they clearly were intent on making the center happen. One of the group's leaders was Elvira, whom I interviewed after a final decision was made about the students' request for a lounge.

> School is interesting and fun, but definitely there's room for improvement. It's fun to be in a school that's not perfect and so I like being able to work on being better. This first quarter was great because of the work I did on the student lounge. I really loved working on that and working to make the school better. . . . I really got into that on my own time. . . . I noticed something lacking in the school and I realized we could do something about it. We could change this hellhole into a great place. It would be a place where students could spend their free periods and have a place to go. I really got into it because it was respected by teachers and you, and I felt that I was part of the community and had power. I was doing something very productive and in a worldly way . . . real ideas that I was thinking about and making happen.

If there's irony in the comments that Elvira made to me about how she felt working to make a change at the school by creating a student center, it is that the student center did not become a reality. It did not happen because, in the end, we all—students and staff—agreed that we did not have a space in the school for the center that was adequate and that could be taken away from other uses. Toward the end of my interview with Elvira about the experiences she had while working with other students and staff to plan the student center, I asked her, if she had to do it all over again, would she work as hard as she did knowing that it might not happen? She hesitated for just a few seconds and then she told me she would do it all over again. She repeated the statement about feeling like she was a real part of the school for the first time, and how powerful it was to feel that.

*   *   *

One of the topics brought up by students attending Solon Circle on a regular basis is our school's requirement that all students take a minimum of one and a half years of physical education. While there have been a lot of complaints, and some adjustments made to the way the school awards physical education credit, one student, Tom, decided to come to Solon Circle with an alternative that he felt would better meet his needs. Prior to coming to the meeting, Tom wrote me a letter. In his letter he explained some of the reasons why he needed an alternative to the current requirement. He wrote:

> I have come to realize the merit of dance class for what it really is . . . a forum for exercise without competition or monopoly that relaxes the body and rests the mind. The class connects two inseparable human desires: music and movement while remaining physically challenging and developing. The current system of awarding credit is flawed because it assumes that taking a physical education class is the only way for students to learn about keeping their bodies in good physical shape.

continues

Box 11.1   Continued

Tom came to the Solon Circle meeting the following week and shared with participants that he had learned the power of dance in his life and wanted to use the dance class as a way to meet his physical education requirement. He presented his reasons calmly and honestly. We had a lively discussion about the pros and cons of allowing Tom to do this and also whether it was setting a precedent that would allow other students to follow. Some staff also shared their concern that this could lead to all students wanting to create their own curriculum and how could we manage that as a school? In the end, it was the power of Tom's passion around dance and his argument for wanting to satisfy his physical education requirement through dance that persuaded us. Tom shared with Solon Circle, "I am not saying that no one benefits from gym class, but for me it's drudgery. The dance class has enriched my days and given me a chance to perform, which I love to do. Please let me and other students—if they want to—meet their PE requirement how they choose." The week after Tom made his request to the Solon Circle, we invited the physical education teachers to the meeting in order to expand the discussion to include them. Tom restated his request to use the dance class as a way to satisfy his physical education requirement. There were questions back and forth, a few heads nodding, and by the end of the meeting we had reached consensus that Tom's request made sense. We also agreed that if this worked for other students, we should open up the opportunity to them as well.

* * *

Some of the issues discussed in Solon Circle are more difficult to reach consensus on and therefore appear on our agenda for a few weeks or in some cases, the whole school year, before they are resolved. A case in point is the policy we've had concerning students coming to school late. Our rules call for students to serve a detention after school in the event they are tardy three or more times. My observation was that despite having this rule, there were no changes in the number of incidents; in fact, we started to note an increase in incidents as well as the length of the tardiness. I shared the data we had been collecting that clearly showed the increase in incidents and length, but staff members attending Solon Circle were convinced that detention still served a purpose and should not be eliminated. During one meeting, one of the students commented that part of the problem with the policy was that it was not really a deterrent to students because it did not matter if you were two seconds late to class or thirty minutes late; the amount of detention was the same. She suggested that we consider a different approach that really took into account the actual incident. That idea shifted our thinking to ways to create consequences that were more consistent with the incident. We finally came to consensus on a policy that eliminated detentions and instead put the onus on students to demonstrate, through their actions, what their level of commitment was to attending class. In essence it spells out that students are expected to attend all of their classes and be on time. In the event that students have a continuing problem with attending class on time, a meeting will be called that will include the student, teacher, parent, and guidance counselor to find ways to remedy the tardiness. However, it took two years of discussions about this issue before we were able to reach consensus.

continues

Box 11.1   Continued

*   *   *

Some decisions can be reached during a meeting while others require more intense scrutiny of our school's culture. A case when the decision came easily was when Lindsay came to Solon Circle. She was very upset about not being able to eat her lunch in the school's lobby. We had a long-standing rule that the only place students were permitted to eat was in the cafeteria. Lindsay expressed frustration at not being trusted to eat outside of the cafeteria in a more relaxed and quieter environment. She argued that students were responsible and were willing to pick up after themselves. We agreed to modify the rules during a pilot period. After two years we decided that the change had little negative impact, but rather a very positive impact on the school climate during the lunch periods.

*   *   *

When Marcie and Lishia came into the room where Solon Circle meets and seated themselves at the circle of desks, it was clear they were agitated. We started with agenda topics for the meeting, and they immediately asked why the school was not doing anything to celebrate Black History Week at school. Being two of a very small number of students of color, they said that they represented the other students of color in the school. It was disturbing to them that the school had not done anything or said anything about Black History Week. They wanted to know why. I shared with them the fact that the faculty had talked about it and decided that learning and celebrating black history should be an integral part of every day rather than just one week out of the year. One of the teachers asked what they felt should be done to celebrate during the week and whether they might be interested in organizing something for next year. The tone quickly shifted from blaming to thinking about solutions for the future. One of the other students present, not a student of color, offered to help out with the planning. Another said that he could work with them to get other students involved. The two students promised to work on the plan and left thanking everybody in the room for their help and support.

Experiences

Solon Circle has become the cornerstone of a foundation we're building that will allow all members of our school community, and especially students, to feel confident that their perspectives, hopes, and dreams for high school are valid. I watch as students speak up at a Solon Circle meeting and can see them learning the skills of dialogue, debate, and patience as they try on the democratic process. Occasionally, no students are present at our meetings, and I am struck by how unproductive the meetings are without their voices. We have come to expect them at our meetings, to ask questions, offer opinions, and share concerns. We have learned that adding their voices to the decisionmaking process is essential.

Figure 11.1 Decisionmaking at Montpelier High School

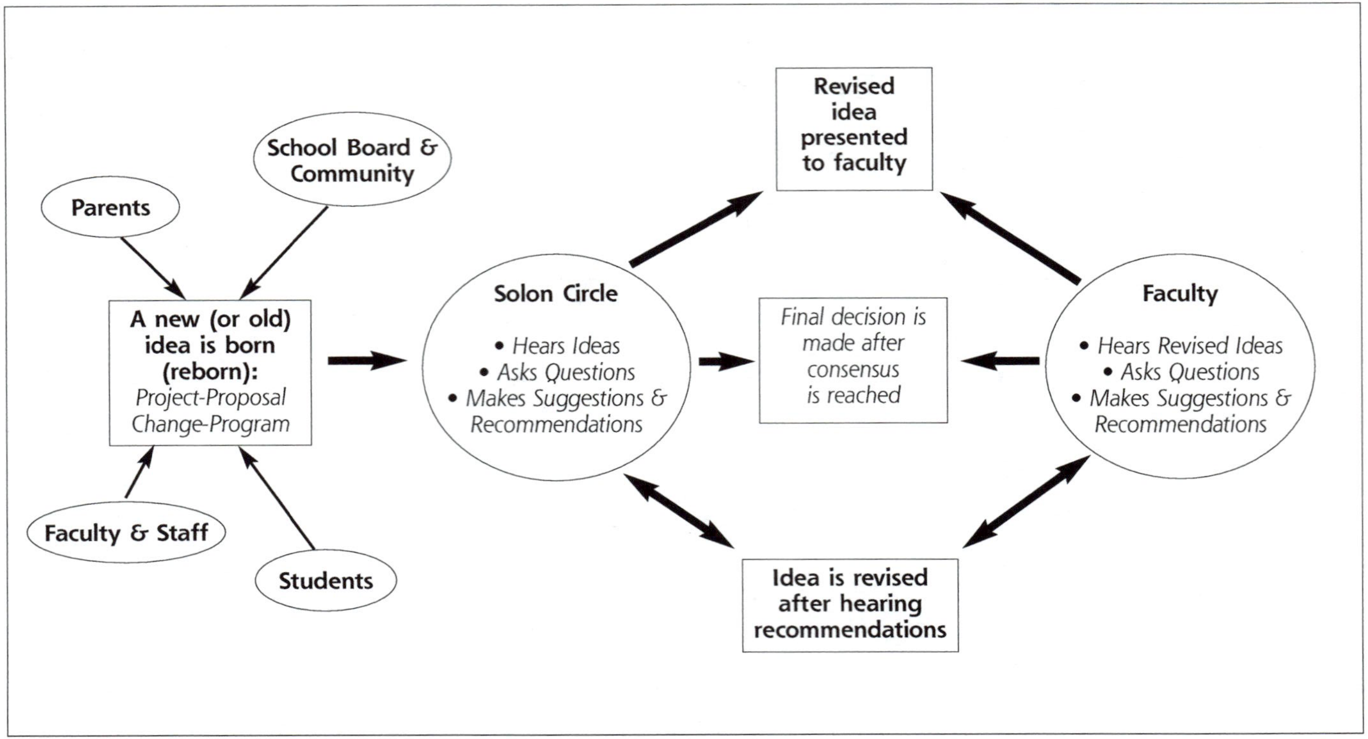

There are times when I am amazed at how far we have gone down the pathway of considering students' perspectives, and then there are times when I wonder if we have moved at all. The latter was true when I read the final edition of our student newspaper that came out just a few days before the last day of school one year. In that edition was an editorial written by one of the students about the many changes that had been made at school during that school year. Among the changes that were highlighted, the student writer mentioned how physical education credit is earned, study areas in the school being closed temporarily due to a lack of care by the students, and the midterm and final exam schedule being changed. In the middle of the editorial, in a box, was the question "Where is the student's voice?" All three topics had been discussed at Solon Circle, during two of the first three years of its existence.

As I read the editorial, I reflected on the way decisions are made at our school with Solon Circle at the center of the process. I specifically reflected on the way the decision to change the method of administering midterm and final exams was made. Of the three changes that the student editor highlighted that lacked student voice, this one was probably the most significant. I made changes to the method of administering final exams to students with little input or feedback from any of the stakeholders, including teachers. The reason for making the changes and the dilemma I faced in making them will shed light on the paradoxical situation I faced as a principal and the challenges that Solon Circle have presented to me.

Without going into great detail about the change, I can say that the way our school administered exams was taken out of a page of the handbook on running a high school circa 1939. All of the exams for a given subject area were administered at the same time throughout the school. This made it impossible for a teacher to be with his or her five classes for more than a few minutes to answer questions and then rush off to check on other classes. Proctors, who were not teachers of the subject being tested, were assigned to the classroom and instructed to do the best they could answering questions and beckoning the teacher of record to the room as needed. The model prohibited teachers from using methods of assessment other than paper and pencil tests to assess student learning. As a result, assessment targets other than those that could be described as knowledge, such as dispositions, skills, reasoning, and products, were not assessed. This dramatically impacted assessment practices, but more critically impacted instructional practices. Most importantly, the old system did not provide a way for students to be a part of or lend their voices to their own assessment.[3] I was determined to design a new model that provided teachers and students with a means of assessment that was more accurate, appropriate, genuine, and allowed for more student voice.

I spent a few years discussing the schedule with teachers, students, and parents, and despite what I thought were sound educational arguments for a new model, I was met with opposition. There were many reasons for the opposition. The teachers were opposed to anything other than the model in place because it meant giving exams throughout the week as opposed to during one block of time. The old system, they argued, gave them more time to correct exams and even provided each teacher with a day off when he or she could stay home from school. They were also hesitant—and in some cases unwilling—to commit to trying new ways to assess student learning. The students preferred the old system because it allowed them to do group studying for each subject and provided them with more time off during the exam days. In the end I realized the best decision educationally was to do away with the old model and design a new one. I came to the realization that this decision was not one that stakeholders would make on their own. I reflected on Fullan's assertion that changes at the high school level and the challenges of changing culture could only be achieved by making substantive structural changes.[4]

When I made the final decisions, I shared these same thoughts and conclusions with students and staff. It was the first time I had, without reaching consensus with stakeholders, made a decision without the involvement and voices of others. I wondered, could I ask students to offer their perspective on issues and then make a decision without consulting with them? In the end, I decided the impact of not changing the way we assess student learning was more critical than working longer to arrive at consensus. I also realized that I was using this more autocratic method of decisionmaking at the risk of discouraging future student involvement in the process. The writer of the editorial said it better than I could have:

> In any environment everyone should have a voice—in our country the government has guaranteed that no one group gets too much power with the checks and balances system. While of course there are differences between our school and the national government, the relationship between adults and students should not give the administration the authority to lay out mandates for change without student input. Equality will require change in both sides—stronger students, and a more representative administration. School is a place to learn both educational and social skills. It is the perfect environment for students to discover and express our voices and realize we can instigate change. Next year let's hope that the students speak up and the administration listens to them.

The editorial writer put the responsibility of listening to all voices on the shoulders of the administration, but she also concluded that students should use their voices and participate in the process. The editorial reminded me that just because we have established this mechanism, Solon Circle, it does not mean that we are done with trying to find ways for students to find their voices and offer their perspectives. I have a ways to go before I learn the challenges of including students' perspectives in the decisionmaking at our school. It is complex, fragile, and not often easy to understand. It is democracy at the most grassroots level, and my work has provided evidence that just because we live in what many refer to as the greatest democracy in the world, it does not mean we are born with the skills required to be active and engaged participants. When students' perspectives are considered, the first step in providing students the skills to achieve that goal has been realized. And while it is challenging, the end results can be powerful. The most important thing to remember is that once students' perspectives are considered, students expect that consideration to continue and increase, and they begin to expect that their life will be better for it. They might even gain enough confidence to write an editorial reminding the principal that if he is going to ask for students' opinions, he had better be listening. At the same time, if the principal is asking for students' perspectives, they had better be offering those or they should not complain about the consequences. Could there be a more important lesson in learning what lies at the heart of the democratic process?

In Their Own Words: The Voices of Students Participating in Solon Circle

In closing this chapter, I am reminded of the power of the voices of students. Through dialogue, listening, and sharing, so much can be learned that informs, strengthens, and enriches the experiences students have during their four years of high school. What follows are some of the words of students taken from Solon Circle meeting notes during the past three years:

> Most of my school years, up to high school, I had been made to feel inadequate in my learning as if something was wrong with me. I was taken out of many classes and put in a separate class with other students who were ADHD or had learning disabilities. It wasn't until a high school special educator told me that she would work with me by helping me find my voice in order to advocate for myself instead of trying to "fix" me. (Colleen)

> One of my teachers realized that I was a bright young student who learned in a way that was unique. Through my conversations and discussions with the teacher, I worked to design assignments that gave me a better chance at demonstrating my learning. (Amy)

> Everybody tells me that in order to get into the best college, I need to have a good transcript. . . . I hate it, but I buy into it. I think about the things that I do in school that I feel very positive about. It's when I've spent time in a class, learning about something that I'm curious about, and then I leave school and realize what I just learned is connected to other things I know about. That's what helps me make sense of stuff that I hadn't been able to make sense of before. That's when I realize how important school really is. The conflict for me is that being able to make those connections doesn't have anything to do with what my transcript looks like. (Elisa)

Notes

1. Lofquist, 1996.
2. Brendtro, Brokenleg, and Van Bockern, 1990.
3. Stiggins, 2001.
4. Fullan, 2002.

12

A Schoolwide Model for Student Voice in Curriculum Development and Teacher Preparation

Lois Easton and Daniel Condon

An Eagle Rock student will have the desire and be prepared to make a difference in the world.

—Mission of the Eagle Rock School

Chapter Overview

Focus of this chapter: A discussion of how Eagle Rock School (ERS) and Professional Development Center has put listening to students at the center of its work with students who have dropped out of traditional school settings and faculty who participate in professional development programs[1]

Discussed in this chapter:

- Eagle Rock School
  - The bare facts
  - The students
- The Professional Development Center (PDC) at Eagle Rock
- A principle-based school and professional development center
- The school's program
  - Culture
  - Structure
  - Curriculum, instruction, and assessment
- Teaching fellowships at Eagle Rock
- Licensure program
- What students teach

- How students affect professional learning
- Conclusion

"When I went to school myself, the staff didn't trust student voices. In fact, we were never asked our opinions on much of anything, except perhaps where the prom should be held."[2] Stephen Richards was a teaching fellow and alternative licensure candidate at Eagle Rock for a year. "What a loss!" he said. "Now that I'm at Eagle Rock, preparing to be a teacher, I cannot imagine *not* engaging students in discussions about what affects their lives profoundly—their own education. And, I cannot imagine learning about education in any better way. They are my best teachers."

Having voice affects not only teacher candidates and fellows, like Stephen. It affects teaching staff, who depend on students to help them help students learn. It also affects visitors to the school's professional development center. They dare to ask questions they think they cannot ask students in their own schools—and are surprised that students are so smart and knowledgeable about learning. Students, themselves, learn from having voice. They learn from each other, and they understand themselves better when they are given voice. "My school affects me by allowing me to hear my voice," said Leslie, a student. How beguiling to think that hearing their own voices, perhaps for the first time in their educational histories, helps students gain self-knowledge.

Eagle Rock staff are certain that Eagle Rock thrives because the school depends upon student voices to embrace the myriad challenges of education, especially the education of adolescents who have not succeeded in school. Eagle Rock is an intentionally small, independent school in Estes Park, Colorado; it welcomes visitors to its professional development center; and it hosts fellows and licensure candidates who are part of Eagle Rock's community for an entire year. Eagle Rock School and Professional Development Center was developed as a philanthropic project to serve two purposes:

1. Graduate young people who have the desire and are prepared to make a difference in the world.
2. Have a positive effect on education, primarily in the United States.

These seem like simple enough goals, until you realize that Eagle Rock intentionally enrolls students who many people think are the hardest to educate in U.S. schools—those who have dropped out and, perhaps, made decisions that jeopardized their lives (and the lives of others). The second purpose of Eagle Rock to some extent explains the first goal. Besides wanting to do something to help students who have been lost to the education system, the founders of Eagle Rock wanted to have an effect on education, especially in the United States. By selecting hard-to-educate young people—rather than those who are successful in school no matter what the conditions are—Eagle Rock gains credibility. The strategies that work at Eagle

Rock have validity because they work for those for whom success in traditional schools has been elusive.

The school would probably not exist were it not for the second purpose, improving education, not just in the United States but worldwide. The professional development center would probably not work were it not for the school, which is a living laboratory for educators.

Although Eagle Rock is an independent school because its founders wanted to free it from policies and regulations that might hamper its staff in finding the best ways to educate young people, Eagle Rock attends to most state policies, including the Colorado State Model Content Standards.

Eagle Rock School

In this section, we present the bare facts about Eagle Rock School and its students.

Bare Facts

Eagle Rock

- Is an initiative of the American Honda Education Corporation, a nonprofit subsidiary, a 501(c)3, of the American Honda Motor Company. Both the school and the Professional Development Center are fully funded by Honda.
- Is a full-scholarship high school for students and a low-cost professional development center for adults.
- Is located in the mountain resort community of Estes Park, Colorado, gateway to Rocky Mountain National Park.
- Opened in the fall of 1993.
- Admits and graduates students three times a year.
- Is year-round (three trimesters) and residential.
- Is purposefully small, with a capacity of 96 students.
- Is fully accredited by the North Central Association Commission on Accreditation and School Improvement, the Association of Colorado Independent Schools, and the Association of Experiential Education.
- Includes a professional development center for the continuing education of practicing educators and the preservice education of teachers-to-be.

The Students

Eagle Rock's students are between the ages of fifteen and twenty-one and have one thing in common: they did not expect to graduate from high school. They sat in the back of classroom after classroom, disengaged or belligerent. Many dropped out or were expelled, sometimes from several schools or several times, before coming to Eagle Rock. The school strives to maintain an even balance of males and females, and of Colorado and out-of-state students. Typically, about one-third of the students are Caucasian, about one-third are African American, and about one-third are Hispanic, with a small number of Asian and Native American students. Apart from that, Eagle Rock students share the diversity found in any U.S. high school.

Some students come from fully functional and caring families; others were abused, neglected, or abandoned or the products of messy divorces. Some turned to drugs or alcohol; others did not. Some ran away or joined gangs; some engaged in petty crime. Students themselves must commit to Eagle Rock; no matter how committed their families are, students are not admitted unless they choose to enroll.

Many Eagle Rock students were labeled in their previous schools: ADD, ADHD, special education, LD, gifted and talented, dyslexic. Some were not. Some had low skills in reading, writing, or mathematics before coming to Eagle Rock. Others were adept students, earning high grades but not sure they were learning anything. Nevertheless, Eagle Rock is a high school, not a therapy or rehabilitation center; students admitted to Eagle Rock must have dealt with their addictions and addressed emotional and psychological issues before enrolling. Once admitted, however, students receive support as they continue to stay sober or work through issues.

Head of school Robert Burkhardt describes Eagle Rock students this way: "Imagine a continuum. At one end are the students guaranteed from birth a spot at Harvard and probably editorship of the *Law Review*. At the other end are students guaranteed a bunk at Folsom Prison. If Harvard is 0 and Folsom 100, our students are between 60 and 80." In part, this profile stems from the needs of the Eagle Rock Professional Development Center—educators need to see whether strategies work with the most difficult-to-reach students.

The demographics of ERS graduates are as follows: 58 percent women, 42 percent men; 56 percent Caucasian, 44 percent students of color (47 percent African American, 37 percent Hispanic or Latino, 13 percent Asian, Native Hawaiian or Other Pacific Islander, 3 percent American Indian or Alaska Native). They have come from twenty-six states.

The Professional Development Center (PDC) at Eagle Rock

The Professional Development Center welcomes educators thirty weeks each year for professional learning. Individuals and groups of up to twenty-four people come for a half day to two weeks to become immersed in the school, learning both cognitively and emotionally what it feels like to be a student at Eagle Rock. They take their learning with them, reforming specific elements of their own environments and restructuring their educational programs. Although not designed to be replicated, Eagle Rock has influenced the design of numerous alternative high schools, high school alternative programs, charter schools, and public schools within a school.

As a mentor school for the Small Schools Project of the Coalition of Essential Schools (CES) and an Affiliate Center of CES, Eagle Rock has worked closely to help schools reopen as small schools and other schools start up as small schools. As a founding member of the League of Democratic Schools, Eagle Rock has worked similarly with other schools from around the country.

In addition to hosting visitors and various outreach activities (such as taking students to present at national conferences and consult with schools and districts), the PDC focuses on the education of young people who are considering teaching or working with youth as a career. The Eagle Rock Public Allies Teaching Fellowship Program and the alternative licensure program, discussed below, help to prepare young people for work in education or youth-serving organizations.

What is most remarkable about the Professional Development Center is how its activities serve Eagle Rock as a mirror, providing continuous feedback, leading to constant self-evaluation. Through their comments and questions, visitors keep the school involved in the continual development process found in thriving organizations of any kind.

A Principle-Based School and Professional Development Center

A set of principles serves as Eagle Rock's lodestar. Some of these were drafted as Eagle Rock was being created; others emerged as students addressed questions such as, "What does it take to have a safe community?" or "What is worth knowing?" The principles consist of eight themes, five expectations, and ten commitments, which all students sign when they enroll (see Table 12.1). Thus $8 + 5 = 10$. The mathematics begs correction, but the meaning is quite clear to students and staff alike: living these 23 principles yields a powerful learning community for everyone.

One important aspect of these principles is that they are "lived"; new students are acculturated to them—by both the faculty and veteran students—during their first three weeks at Eagle Rock. For example, the first class new students take is ERS (for Eagle Rock School) 101 so that they can get to know what ERS is all about and how to "live" Eagle Rock. The principles are maintained through a variety of academic and nonacademic rituals. For example, students reflect on $8 + 5 = 10$ in their Presentations of Learning (exhibitions, which are described below, that they give to outside audiences three times a year) and every Tuesday morning Gathering features a veteran student and a new student who explicate one of the principles for the other students, often through a skit or story.

The School's Program

The program at Eagle Rock can be understood in terms of culture; structure; and curriculum, instruction, and assessment. Many categories overlap, of

Table 12.1 Principles of Eagle Rock School

Eight Themes	Five Expectations	Ten Commitments
Individual integrity 1. Intellectual discipline 2. Physical fitness 3. Spiritual development 4. Aesthetic expression *Citizenship* 5. Service to others 6. Cross-cultural understanding 7. Democratic governance 8. Environmental stewardship	1. Expanding knowledge base 2. Effective communication 3. Creating and making healthy life choices 4. Engaging as a global citizen 5. Practicing leadership for justice	1. Live in respectful harmony with others 2. Develop mind, body, and spirit 3. Learn to communicate 4. Serve the community 5. Become a steward of the planet 6. Make healthy personal choices 7. Find and develop the artist within 8. Increase leadership 9. Practice citizenship 10. Devise a moral and ethical code

course, so that something that affects culture may be structural, and something that is related to curriculum may be related to a structural element.

Culture

Culture is affected by having adult involvement in intramurals (rather than interscholastic sports), band, orchestra, plays, and musicals. Adults and students alike attend the frequent all-community meetings and morning gatherings. Students have important roles in governance, admissions, and hiring.

Culture is also affected by the intentional diversity of its student body and staff as well as how new students are helped to enter the community. They are mentored as prospective students and throughout their first year. New students learn the culture during prospective student visits as well as before, during, and after a three-week wilderness trip. During the three-week wilderness trip, students spend the first week working hard physically, emotionally, and socially. They are challenged by the desert or mountains and long hours carrying a fifty-pound pack. They are challenged by their fears of being in a wilderness, and they are challenged to trust others. In the second week, they continue to work on personal and social growth, meeting in "strong circles" to address group problems, for example. In the third week, they capstone their experience by working together on a service project in the wilderness, help each other make it out of the wilderness (closely watched by staff, who can intervene in the case of trouble), and run back to the Eagle Rock campus triumphantly, often having surprised themselves, and ready to embrace the academic challenges of Eagle Rock.

Eagle Rock is both "home" and "school" to its students and staff. It's not just school culture that students and staff care about; it's their home culture as well. The presence of the Professional Development Center also affects the culture—the school functions as a lab school for the learning of adults and students alike.

Structure

Structure affects culture in two ways: time and space. In terms of time, Eagle Rock follows a block schedule, which allows students an extended period of time to learn and makes it possible for teachers to teach to a variety of styles and intelligences. Being year-round and 24/7 allows Eagle Rock to extend learning beyond its typical boundaries. Learning is divided into three trimesters, of two blocks each, separated by an Explore Week and followed by a week of Exhibitions of Learning—a schedule that, after much experimentation, seems to work for students. Students do not graduate according to instructional hours received (seat time) but according to their mastery of graduation requirements.

In terms of space, students live in small dormitories, which are called houses and function as much like a home as possible. Finally, several spaces on campus can be used by groups, large and small, and the whole community can gather together in one large area.

Curriculum, Instruction, and Assessment

Curriculum, instruction, and assessment at Eagle Rock are characterized by active and interactive learning, a social constructivist philosophy, and an effort to make learning self-directed.

Specifically, students document learning in order to gain credit; they do not get credit for seat time and adequate grades. In fact, students do not receive letter grades (A–F), nor are they separated into grade levels (9–12). They work on graduation requirements (related to the Colorado State Model Content Standards) until they demonstrate mastery according to rubrics, beginning on their first day at Eagle Rock. Classes are naturally integrated and interdisciplinary, with service learning forming the basis of many. In addition to documenting learning for credit, students make Presentations of Learning three times a year to a panel of people from outside Eagle Rock.

Although Eagle Rock does not participate in the state's testing system, it does test students when they arrive and when they depart to determine growth according to an outside measurement; scores soar upon graduation. Students also take the SAT and the ACT exams and match the national averages on these exams.

The curriculum is explored through a variety of structures. Classes can be all trimester or half a trimester. They can be all day or only one or two periods of three in a block schedule. Explore Week, between the two blocks of the trimester, allows students to take weeklong high-interest classes.

Teaching Fellowships at Eagle Rock

Fellowships are an important component of the Professional Development Center's activities. Fellowships are cosponsored with Public Allies, Inc., headquartered in Milwaukee, Wisconsin, with local sites in fifteen communities around the country. Public Allies identifies talented young adults from diverse backgrounds to become "allies" and prepares them for careers working for community and social change. Allies serve in ten-month paid apprenticeships at local nonprofits and participate in a rigorous and rewarding leadership development program with a diverse group of peers.

Eagle Rock's teaching fellowships have two perspectives: local and global. Locally, fellows contribute skills, energy, and knowledge to the Eagle Rock School community. As residents, they are involved in student activities and campus life as well as classroom teaching and administration. Like everyone else at Eagle Rock, they serve as role models, take on leadership roles, and live the values expressed through Eagle Rock's commitments. The global perspective relates to Eagle Rock School and Professional Development Center's mission of engaging educators in forging renewal and reform initiatives in schools across the country.

Fellows are expected to use what they learn at Eagle Rock in their next work environment and serve as emissaries for the kind of education Eagle Rock promotes. No matter what they do or where they go (but most especially if they enter public education) fellowship alumni act as ambassadors for the values that Eagle Rock honors.

Molding tomorrow's educational leaders begins with core training during which fellows are oriented to the school and begin the community-building process. Throughout the year, fellows gather as a cohort once a week for learning seminars facilitated by skilled professionals in the field; often these weekly fellow learning seminars explore the theory and practice of education. Fellows participate as a group in midyear and year-end retreats, and they join regular critical reflection sessions during which they connect their service to larger social and public issues. In addition, they fully participate in professional learning experiences with the rest of the faculty.

The fellows are coached by the local site director of the Public Allies Teaching Fellowship Program in coordination with each fellow's cooperating mentor teacher using a continuous learning process, which includes setting personal and professional goals, creating plans to achieve those goals, and giving and receiving feedback from peers, supervisors, and students while documenting progress toward specific service and learning outcomes. The program concludes each August with Presentations of

Learning, when fellows demonstrate their mastery to the entire Eagle Rock community, showing they have met their teaching goals and learning outcomes throughout the year.

Licensure Program

Some fellows become candidates for licensure (based on their meeting requirements set forth by the Colorado Department of Education, which certifies Eagle Rock's alternative licensure program). Licensure candidates teach approximately twenty hours per week under the guidance of a certified mentor teacher. This regular teaching experience is the bedrock for all of their learning. Two books about Eagle Rock anchor the licensure curriculum: *The Other Side of Curriculum: Lessons from Learners* and *Engaging the Disengaged: How Schools Can Help Struggling Students Succeed*, both written by Eagle Rock's first director of professional development, Lois Brown Easton.

The licensure program is divided into three phases. In the first phase, licensure candidates look at research-based best practices in instruction. Literacy strategies, the workshop model, gradual release of responsibility, and formative assessment are just a few of the many instructional moves the licensure candidates learn and practice. In addition to their own work on the practice, candidates engage in an assignment that involves analyzing the mentor teacher's moves and reflecting on their own decisionmaking. The focus is on action before theory because the candidates need immediate support and confidence.

The second phase of the program is based on adaptation of the Japanese lesson study model. Japanese lesson study is different from its U.S. cousin in a couple of ways. First, Japanese teachers take on both an academic and a personal/social growth challenge for the year; thus they may study mathematics and sharing with others. They make lesson study the centerpiece of their professional learning and engage in it at least weekly for an entire year. Their daily schedule includes professional learning time for lesson study. At Eagle Rock, candidates collaborate with others to design lessons that meet clearly articulated learning targets. Their mentors observe and videotape the classes and use protocols to reflect on how well the lesson went and what might improve the work. Throughout this phase, the candidates address advanced pedagogical theory. They look at what understanding really means and what is meant by "learning."

The final phase focuses on the use of critical friends group protocols to provide a sustainable method for the candidates to continue their own job-embedded professional development. Many of the protocols they use today were developed by the National School Reform Faculty, a part of the Coalition of Essential Schools, which also developed the concept of critical friends groups—groups of teachers who support each other for professional learning. Student work becomes the center of all discussions and protocols, and the candidates continue to relate greater theoretical background to their practice.

Michael Soguero, current director of professional development at Eagle Rock School, explains, "I think that job-embedded professional development with follow-up is much more effective than traditional models of professional development where teachers go off to a workshop and there's some hope they will transfer their learning back to their site. Our teacher preparation program uses the context of the current teaching experience as the source of the assignments candidates must complete to earn their teacher license. We do lesson study using real lessons delivered at Eagle Rock and use many critical friends group protocols to examine student work."

What Students Teach

Students literally teach at Eagle Rock, either in conjunction with adults or interns or by themselves, under the supervision of an adult staff member. Their teaching is the finest sort of learning for them—and for their peers who witness a student who has content and pedagogical responsibilities. More importantly, students teach staff, visitors, fellows, and licensure candidates what they need in order to learn. They teach when they go to conferences or visit other schools. Their teaching is informal, as when an adult "hangs out" with them at mealtimes and encourages them to talk about learning. Their teaching is more formal when the adults directly ask students what they need to learn, as they often do. It is even more direct when they talk with adult visitors during a shadowing experience. They may serve on panels or symposia for visitors or at other schools. Students are expected to make clear to adults (as well as to themselves) what they need to learn.

Below is a list of some lessons Eagle Rock staff, visitors, fellows, licensure candidates, and educators from other schools have learned from Eagle Rock students. Below the list, each point is expanded upon.

- The importance of culture
- Learning for learning also helps with testing
- Building relationships is more important to learning than content
- Intentional learning communities foster learning
- Principles govern a school better than rules
- A democratic community helps students learn
- Holding students to standards
- Innovative instructional strategies help students learn
- Learning from assessing learning
- The importance of looking at the student as a whole person

The Importance of Culture

Culture is too important to be left to chance. Culture needs to be intentional rather than assumptive. Culture is manifested through structure, governance, curriculum, instruction, assessment, and other aspects of school. It appears as beliefs, metaphors, artifacts, and practice. Eagle

Rock students regularly examine their beliefs and, in a part of the packets for their Presentations of Learning, present their Moral and Ethical Codes. Here is a segment from the code of a student, Lina: "In everything we do, we must make a choice. Preferably a choice based on one's beliefs, beliefs that are themselves based on a consciousness of choice and developed from honest contemplation. This is my preference, at least, and at most it could go much further. It, like the most appreciated things in life, could become an art, a creativeness and an intelligence of soul open to constant development. I'm working on it."

Learning for Learning Also Helps with Testing

It may seem obvious that learning improves test scores, but not learning in the "test preparation sense." The curriculum at Eagle Rock is unrelated—except accidentally—to the tested curriculum. The methods of instruction in no way match the testing formats (recall, choice among options). Yet, struggling students do amazingly well on these tests. They see the point of learning for learning but not for taking tests.

Students are clear about why they do not do well on tests: lack of confidence, lack of interest, revenge on a system they think is unfair and biased, fear and low self-esteem, group identification, differences in how they learn and how tests test, and doubt about the relevance or purpose of the tests. For example, Fahad said, "I just don't think that way. I think all the answers are right in some way." Jason added, "The hurry-up part of tests makes me nervous. I like to think about things."

They are also clear about why they do well on tests (and their reasons have nothing to do with test preparation): self-confidence as a learner, seeing testing as part—albeit a small part—of learning, seeing testing as "no big deal," wanting to perform well on tests, seeing the challenge in a test, knowing that tests are neither true indicators nor the only indicators of their worth, the school's lack of emphasis on testing, and the school's focus on learning. Michelle, a student, stated, "I know I'm good at some things now. I didn't need a test to tell me that."

Building Relationships Is More Important to Learning Than Content

Students repeatedly declare that what helps them learn—more than anything else, individually or in combination!—is the relationships they have with their instructors. According to Jonah, a student, "The critical thing is making it possible for students to trust staff and realize that staff can understand where they are coming from. A mutual trust and understanding is necessary for students and staff to reach a level that . . . benefits in improved performance in the academic setting (for staff as well as for students)." Relationships also soften the issues of status and hierarchy, power and authority, which often get in the way of student learning. Finally, students learn about good relationships by being in them. They feel accountable to those with whom they have built a relationship.

Intentional Learning Communities Foster Learning

Anthony, former gang member, Eagle Rock graduate, college graduate, and parent, recalled the importance of community to his learning. "The benefits of the whole school learning community are intentionality (one of my favorite words) and consistency. When all actions of community are in tandem, then goals are achieved easier and with greater success."

Students as well as staff benefit from an organization that considers itself a community of learners. The recent movement toward building professional learning communities (PLCs) does not go quite far enough. The entire community—students as well as all staff—should be a school learning community (SLC). Having a professional development center helps students and staff—as well as visiting educators—value learning. Seeing adults learning—and, sometimes, struggling with that learning—helps struggling students feel like part of a learning system, rather than an outcast.

Principles Govern a School Better Than Rules

Principles—not rules—result in a culture that is meaningful and important to struggling students, a culture they will defend! For one thing, rules bring out the worst in people, according to a graduate, Khadija: Rules "get us to 'buy in' to a concept through fear, reward, or punishment." Lana, soon to be a graduate, commented, "A bunch of rules which we might or might not be inclined to care about aren't sufficient to govern a structured community." Principles need to be built and reinforced through a "system of use."

A Democratic Community Helps Students Learn

Students study democratic values from kindergarten on, but in most schools, they do not live them. Struggling students understand the value and responsibility of power and authority. Anthony, a graduate, realized the importance of a democratic society: "Democracy is more than a vote. Democracy is inclusion in and responsibility for the everyday activities of a community. From the mundane to the enthralling, all persons who are affected by a decision must have some say in that decision."

He added, "What happens to the least powerful at Eagle Rock happens to the most powerful at Eagle Rock because we are all one. We all chose to participate and make efforts for the well-being of the community. Isn't that what democracy is, the people coming together to find solutions to common problems and then acting on those behaviors?"

Holding Students to Standards

Students want to be held to high standards; in fact, it is an affront to them to consider lowering standards for them. But they want support. They want flexibility. Students at Eagle Rock are scornful of the conventional way of giving credit to students (seat time and grades). They like knowing what they need to do; they like being given flexibility in terms of how they do what they need to do. They like being responsible for documenting their learning with a truly standards-based approach. Struggling students become engaged in their own learning when they are in charge of their own learning.

Crystal, a student, interpreted the notion of "seat time" in a concrete way: "Well, first of all," she said, "there is absolutely no seat time [at Eagle Rock]. Most of the time you are out and about doing things or having a really juicy discussion in class and it takes up all the class time."

Innovative Instructional Strategies Help Students Learn

Several instructional strategies help students engage in learning. Some are subtle and embedded in all lessons: power, voice, choice, accountability, transparency of the curriculum. "Teenagers want to be independent," student Erin said, "and choices help students gain a sense of independence." Erica, another student, said, "The more I am in control of my own choices, the further I am willing to take my own learning. I'm willing to push further and learn more."

Others are intentional: adhering to a constructivist theory with appropriate strategies; engaging students experientially; letting students teach; promoting self-directed learning, project-based learning, and problem-solving; and engaging in service. About service, Ernest, a student, said, "The hands-on relationship between you and the project at hand is what I liked." Aziza, another student, commented, "It's more hands-on and engaging. Also it's different from classes and interesting. It keeps me from being bored. I used to become disengaged and get bored. When I do service projects, I give learning a chance."

Learning from Assessing Learning

Learning happens for students and staff when assessment is assessment for learning.[3] Eagle Rock's documentations of learning (for credit) and Presentations of Learning (POLs)—thrice-yearly public exhibitions of learning and the packets that students prepare for the panel members who will witness them—are examples of educative assessment. Students appreciate the authenticity of documenting and presenting themselves as learners—they cannot "fake it." They feel honored by the responsibility of accountability.

The Importance of Looking at the Student as a Whole Person

Students do not like to be parsed into their academic selves and everything else about them. They live their lives as whole persons, and they appreciate educators who see them as whole people. Their personal and social growth is as important as academic growth. Everything about a school helps students understand whether a school's focus is on the whole student—beliefs, culture, structures, programs, curriculum, instruction, and assessment.

How Students Affect Professional Learning

Each year, when the dozen teaching fellows arrive for their yearlong term of service, they are told that their most powerful teachers will be the Eagle Rock School students with whom they will spend many of their waking hours. Below is a list of themes that emerge across participants' comments.

- Creating community within the classroom
- Allowing teachers to be students
- Recognizing the assets of students
- Relationship building and trust
- Allowing students to hold staff accountable
- The power of students as teachers
- Learning for understanding, not sitting for seat time
- Walk a mile in their shoes

Former fellows, some of whom became licensed teachers through Eagle Rock's alternative licensure program, explain these themes.

Creating Community within the Classroom

Mary Waters, former language arts and literature teaching fellow at Eagle Rock, explained:

> Eagle Rock helped me understand the importance of building a safe learning community, which allows students to take risks and grow. One method I applied at a Denver public school was the incorporation of rituals in the classroom. Each week we set aside time to publicly, yet anonymously, acknowledge each other. Students and participants counted on this time, and it was powerful to see how much it contributed to a trusting learning community.

Allowing Teachers to Be Students

Bruce Jeffries, former language arts and literature teaching fellow at Eagle Rock, reflected:

> Being a Fellow at Eagle Rock allowed me to be both teacher and student at the same time, as is the case in life. Instead of separating academics from practice, it gave me a chance to live both, to study myself as I interacted with others, and to look at myself through the lens of myself. Most importantly, it prepared me to live education by teaching me that the core of any meaningful experience is in the relationships.

Recognizing the Assets of Students

Irene McNichols, former visual arts fellow and licensure candidate, said:

Eagle Rock students taught me that I can set high expectations for my students and that not only will they rise to the challenge, they will exceed whatever I thought they were capable of. This is the case both in the material they are learning and also in how the class is run. At Eagle Rock, the students have a voice in nearly everything and they always surprise me with the maturity of their decisions. Because of this I make an effort in my own classroom and school to let the students have a say in most of what we do and in how things are run. As I continue to grow and learn as a teacher I try to keep giving the students more and more opportunities to make their voices heard in order to help them practice making better decisions in the school and in their lives.

Louisa Dorin, former fellow in the Learning Resource Center, added:

I learned explicitly that the knowledge "students" bring to the classroom is just, if not more, important than the knowledge I as the "teacher" bring. When the banking model of education is abandoned and everyone is encouraged to authentically and equally contribute, progressive and meaningful education can take place. This concept was easy to adopt at Eagle Rock specifically because I was working with a population who, more often than not, refused to adopt the typical structures of a conventional classroom environment (perhaps because they felt undervalued).

One example of this practice was when I was coteaching a gender studies class. My colleague and I designed a working syllabus before the class began, simply to provide conversational structure. Once the students were in the class, we decided, as a collective of learners, to brainstorm topics and compose the class around discussions of personal experience. Our flexibility in the role of "instructors" coupled with the "students'" desire to interact with the curriculum endowed each of us our own stake in the success of the class as an authentic model of collaborative education.

Relationship-Building and Trust

Irene McNichols, former visual arts fellow, stated:

Spending a year with Eagle Rock students has profoundly changed my approach not only to teaching but also in how I interact with my students. I had been working in youth development and education for several years before Eagle Rock but it was my time there that taught me how to really build relationships with students like I had never had before. I always felt that it was not possible to interact with students on such a personal level without compromising my authority.

Eagle Rock students taught me that not only is it possible but having strong relationships with my students does wonders for classroom management. It's much more effective to have a talk with a student about how their behavior is affecting the class and me rather than give them a detention. I now make an effort to spend time with my students, especially the ones who are really struggling, outside of school and the classroom. This has helped me to hold the students accountable for their behavior and grades in a more personal and effective way, much like the way it is done at Eagle Rock.

Allowing Students to Hold Staff Accountable

Nancy Westin, former world languages fellow, said:

> Eagle Rock students forced me to be real. The first year of teaching is generally "sold" as a terrifying one, and while I had heard these rumors before stepping into the classroom at Eagle Rock, I had never really felt it. I soon came to understand that I could not "hide" anything from my students at Eagle Rock. The realness of *their* lives, *their* struggles, and *their* joys were such a part of the community that it would have been almost disrespectful for me to walk around a classroom trying to hide anything.
>
> And so in a matter of months I saw my confidence and ability to portray myself improve tenfold. I taught with more vigor, more passion, and more confidence than I knew I had. And the more honest I was about everything, from not knowing the answer to a question to calling them out on disrespect, the better teacher I became. Since working at Eagle Rock, I've traveled and taught around the world and come to understand that teaching is more than a spitting out of knowledge; it is an honest conversation about learning. Eagle Rock students could see dishonesty and were not afraid to call me out on it, and now I see why the first year of teaching can be so terrifying. I've never felt so exposed. Now I can teach like I've always wanted to and without fear, because Eagle Rock students taught me what it was like to feel safe while teaching.

The Power of Students as Teachers

Jim Stone, former math fellow, said:

> I believe Eagle Rock students have made me a more compassionate teacher than I may have been otherwise. I came to ERS already holding the belief that mathematics instruction should focus on conceptual understanding, critical thinking (problem-solving, reasoning), and communication. Teaching such a diverse group of students has shown me many tangible reasons *why* this is so important and has continued to push my thinking about how to most effectively put those skills at the center of my classrooms. Two reasons are that it allows me to present material in an accessible way to a range of students and it also allows them to incorporate their diverse interests/experiences/ideas into the work we do.

Learning for Understanding, Not Sitting for Seat Time

Mary Golden, former human performance center (physical education) fellow, said:

> Honestly, before I set foot at Eagle Rock School, my only experience in education was my own learning. I rarely learned for the sake of learning, but in order to get a good grade, pass a class, etc. Outside of school was where a lot of my own learning occurred.
>
> Eagle Rock radically rocked my foundation of education. As a fellow and first year teacher, my eyes were opened to a new view of education, one in which the student learns in order to be a more aware citizen, a better global steward, or even to satisfy the thirst for knowledge. I learned that making the real life connection

in the classroom is necessary for both the student and for the facilitator. It was amazing to see so many young people wanting to learn and striving to take back their education.

Walk a Mile in Their Shoes

Charles Anton, former math fellow, said:

> I remember how the stress and anxiety would start to wear on some students at Eagle Rock as vacations approached. I used to think that the stress was from Presentations of Learning or portfolios or an otherwise school-related trauma. After a few advisees began to open up, I saw that the stress was from the reality of having to go "home" . . . and many didn't want to . . . partly because Eagle Rock was safe and comforting, partly because home life was awful, partly because they were concerned about old roles from their old ways catching up on them. While we tried to teach our students to live one life, the reality was that some of them had to focus on surviving, rather than living one life.
>
> I think often of those lessons now because I need to keep reminding myself . . . that I have no idea what my students face when they get home. I'm starting to learn more as I enter into my second year at [an] environmental charter high school in Los Angeles and kids are beginning to trust me more and open up. We started up an extensive after-school program this year, and many students stay simply because they don't want to go home. For them, 3:30 every day is what some Eagle Rockers felt three times a year: "How do I reconcile two different worlds, with two different sets of rules, conditions, modes of survival, into one meaningful life?"
>
> I need to remind myself that . . . to help [my students] face [the] challenges [they experience], I need to be deeply patient, teach from a place of love, and listen to what my students are saying and how they are saying it. Asking for help is not easy for many students. They don't know how to do it. And . . . while we teach them, we need to hear their asking in between the words and emotions they use. After all, when they're adults, I'd rather have them remember me for those kinds of lessons instead of the notes on page 576 in the text.

What makes the fellowship and alternative licensing program at Eagle Rock distinct from most other new teacher training programs is clarified by Tommy Johnson, a former math teaching fellow, who went on to be an Eagle Rock teacher, and is now a candidate in a traditional teacher education program. He explained:

> As a current student in a traditional teaching program, a main difference I notice between my experiences at Eagle Rock and in school placements is Eagle Rock's commitment to principles and practices is significantly greater than anywhere else I have seen in public education. Traditional education programs provide classes that teach about the values of inclusion, but mainstream practice in public education still mostly ignores these principles and attempts to create homogeneous learning environments by separating "those" students for a variety of reasons. Eagle Rock's commitment to inclusive learning environments provided me practical experience teaching in such settings, while my traditional teacher preparation program has provided me mostly with theoretical discussions about inclusive learning environments.

Conclusion

With few exceptions, such as those highlighted in this sourcebook, teacher candidate interactions with students prior to teaching usually consist of scheduled classroom visits during the semester preceding student teaching and a semester of student teaching. Sometimes, but infrequently, these experiences include dialogue with students outside of classes to discover them as learners. If they happen, these experiences are typically informal, occurring when the teacher candidates are able to "hang out" with students. Once graduated and working as teachers, adults rarely have time with students in order just to listen to their perceptions of school, teaching, and learning. In-service days and other forms of professional development seldom or never include out-of-class discussions with students about themselves as learners. Right there, within reach, accessible, and eager to share their experiences, are students. They have lots to say. As Nancy and Ted Sizer maintain in *The Students Are Watching*,[4] they have been watching us, and their ideas about teaching and learning have been honed over many years of sitting in desks in rows. We should listen.

Notes

1. Parts of this chapter have appeared in previous publications: Easton, L. B. (2008). *Engaging the Disengaged: How Schools Can Help Struggling Students Succeed*. Thousand Oaks, CA: Corwin Press. Also Condon, D. (2008). "From the Inside Out: Eagle Rock School Producing a New Generation of CES Teachers," in *Horace* 24 (Spring): 1. *Horace* is the journal of the Coalition of Essential Schools.

2. All quotations in this chapter come from ongoing research by the authors.

3. Grant Wiggins and Jay McTighe, 2005; also Rick Stiggins, 2001.

4. Sizer and Sizer, 1999.

13

Students E-Mailing Prospective Teachers

Listening before Student Teaching

Chapter Overview

Focus of this chapter: Teaching and Learning Together (TLT), a program that positions high school students as teacher educators.[1] The program is based in a teaching methods course offered through an undergraduate certification program in a liberal arts college in the United States.

Discussed in this chapter:

- The goals of TLT
- The components of TLT
  - How the four components of TLT unfold during the semester
- Essential features of TLT
- Challenges and rewards of facilitating TLT
- Critical lessons preservice teachers learn
- Students' experiences of participating in TLT
- Teachers' experiences of participating in TLT

Much of preservice teacher education at the undergraduate level is based on indirect links between those preparing to teach and those who spend their days in schools. Typically, during the first two years of their preparation, preservice teachers study educational theory with their peers at the college and spend an hour or so per week observing in practicing teachers' classrooms. Then, during student teaching, generally in the last semester of their undergraduate years, preservice teachers take responsibility for teaching several classes at a middle or high school. Neither during the more distanced preparatory period nor during the intensive student teaching semester do the traditional structures and forums of undergraduate teacher preparation afford preservice teachers the opportunity to engage in ongoing, thoughtful dialogue with school-based teachers and students.[2]

Teaching and Learning Together (TLT), the project I have facilitated since 1995 in Curriculum and Pedagogy Seminar, the secondary methods course I offer through the Bryn Mawr/Haverford Education Program,[3] forges a direct link between preservice teachers pursuing state certification to teach at the secondary level and high school students in area schools. TLT was born of conversations I had with a high school teacher friend and colleague during my first year as director of the education program. As I mentioned in the Introduction, when we discussed my friend's high school students' needs and interests and my preservice teachers' preparation to teach, we realized that prospective teachers were learning to teach without much direct interaction with high school students and, specifically, no interaction through which the high school students could inform the preservice teachers about their experiences and needs as learners. In response to this concern, we designed TLT as an integral component of the penultimate course required for certification to teach at the secondary level and offered in the semester prior to practice teaching. In 1995 we secured grant support from the Ford Foundation; we won three more years of funding from the Arthur Vining Davis Foundations; and once the project was established, Bryn Mawr and Haverford colleges continued to support it as an integral part of the education program.[4]

Goals of Teaching and Learning Together

When we originally designed TLT, we had two basic structural goals:[5]

1. To bring into direct dialogue those preparing to teach with a diverse group of students who are taught in U.S. schools and
2. To bring into conversation high school students separated by grade levels and by the tracking systems, both acknowledged and implicit.

Within these structural goals, we had larger political and pedagogical goals. These were:

1. To complicate the traditional model according to which educational theorists and researchers generate pedagogical knowledge and pass it down to teachers, who in turn are pressured to implement reforms based on that new knowledge, with students positioned as passive recipients of this transfer;
2. To alter the power dynamics that usually inform that teacher/student relationship, with the teacher conceptualized as the sole

authority and the student conceptualized as a blank slate or passive recipient of the teacher's knowledge;

3. To prepare teachers who are committed to eliciting and acting upon students' perspectives not only during their preparation but also over the course of their careers; and

4. To foster in high school students a critical awareness of their educational experiences and opportunities and the confidence and vocabulary to assert what they need and want as learners and to provide support and mentoring in wrestling with this responsibility.[6]

Concerned by the exclusion of student voices from conversations about learning, teaching, and schooling, we developed a commitment to taking seriously what students say about their experiences of being learners in school.

Components of Teaching and Learning Together

Through its four-part design, TLT uses various forums for interaction to expand the contexts through which preservice teachers learn about good teaching and the sources they consider authoritative.[7] Table 13.1 lists and briefly describes the four components.

How Teaching and Learning Together Unfolds

Each summer, when I know how many students will be enrolled in my secondary methods course in the fall (usually between five and fifteen), I contact my school-based collaborators and begin to discuss selecting high school students to participate in TLT. As soon as the high school opens in the fall, my school-based collaborators invite students from different grade levels, academic tracks, racial and cultural identities, and genders to participate. Each of these students is paired with a preservice teacher enrolled in my course (each preservice teacher corresponds with two high school students from different schools). We make some effort to create pairs that are likely to be productive, since we have only fourteen weeks to make the project work.

Once we have paired preservice teachers and high school students, we schedule an initial meeting of all participants at the high schools. During these first meetings, the pairs meet face-to-face, get to know one another a bit, and exchange e-mail addresses. Then, we complete the sentence, "A good teacher . . ." First the pairs complete the sentence and talk about their responses, and then as a whole group we map the responses on the blackboard so that both preservice teachers and high school students can see the range of hopes and expectations they have for teachers. Once we have mapped this range, we generate some initial thoughts about how teachers can meet the diverse needs of students.

Table 13.1 Components of Teaching and Learning Together

Component 1: Weekly e-mail exchange between preservice teachers and high school students	Each preservice teacher enrolled in my secondary methods course is paired with a student who attends a local or city high school. The weekly e-mail exchange these pairs maintain is based loosely on topics explored in weekly seminars at the college (i.e., what makes a good teacher, lesson plans, testing) but also includes topics the pairs feel are relevant to teaching and learning.
Component 2: Weekly conversations among high school students	These weekly conversations among all the high school student participants are convened by a school-based educator and held at the students' school. The discussions last for approximately thirty minutes and are held after school or at lunch. Like the e-mail exchange, they are based on the topics explored in the college seminar (see this chapter's Appendix), and the discussions are audiotaped, transcribed, and assigned as required reading to the preservice teachers.
Component 3: Weekly discussions in the college course	As part of the weekly meetings of the college-based methods seminar in which all preservice teachers are enrolled, we discuss how the e-mail exchange is going and what preservice teachers are struggling with, learning, and integrating into their plans for practice.
Component 4: End-of-semester analysis paper	Each preservice teacher selects a focus of the exchange with her high school student partner for a final analysis of what she learned. This analysis must draw on and quote excerpts from the e-mail exchange, transcripts of discussions among the high school students, and college-based class discussions.

Component 1: Weekly e-mail exchange between preservice teachers and high school students. Over the next several weeks and throughout the semester, the pairs follow up within their e-mail exchange on this opening discussion as well as address the topics we explore in the college-based class. To avoid logistical complexities and miscommunication, we generally designate a particular day on which the high school students send their e-mail messages (i.e., by Friday each week) and a day on which the preservice teachers send theirs. Issues explored in the e-mail exchanges or in the college-based class include how to learn to access, listen to, and respond to learners' perspectives on their needs; define and develop engaging curriculum; address state standards; create a classroom environment conducive to learning; handle classroom management problems; plan engaging lessons and differentiate instruction; and design effective approaches to assessment and evaluation. Pairs also explore other issues they feel are relevant to teaching and learning: relationships with teachers, dynamics among

peers, home responsibilities. Their e-mail exchanges are private: I neither see nor read any of the e-mails. The reason I structure the project in this way is that I believe it is important for the preservice teachers to have the opportunity to develop a relationship with a student on their own, within guidelines that I provide and with support from me and other preservice teachers when they need it, but primarily independently—without my management or surveillance. This opportunity prepares them for the responsibilities they will have as teachers, and it also gives all participants involved—preservice teachers and high school students alike—a chance to communicate more openly and frankly, knowing that their words are not being monitored by a college- or school-based authority figure. The guidelines I provide for the e-mail exchanges are simply these: that the preservice teachers need to inform me immediately (and the high school students need to inform my school-based collaborators) if (1) they are not maintaining a weekly exchange for some logistical reason (i.e., problems accessing the Internet, e-mails bouncing back); (2) if their partners reveal something in the letters that is of concern (i.e., a health, psychological, or safety issue); or (3) they feel unable to compose a response or want to check that their response is appropriate before sending it.

Component 2: Weekly conversations among high school students. The private, one-on-one exchanges described above are complemented throughout the semester by the weekly meetings of the high school students at their school. These discussions also address the issues that are listed above (learners' needs, classroom environment and management, lesson planning, and so on), but in this case the dialogue is not between a single preservice teacher and a single high school student but rather among students (see this chapter's Appendix for a list of guiding questions we use). Because of the diversity of the participating students, these conversations provide the preservice teachers a diversity of perspectives and, as important, afford the high school students an unusual opportunity to talk with one another across tracks and grade levels about issues they are rarely if ever asked to address. In addition, because these conversations are audiotaped and transcribed every week, the preservice teachers have the opportunity to hear voices other than those of their respective dialogue partners, and they get to hear their dialogue partners as they participate in the group discussions (often in similar but also often in different ways than they participate in the e-mail exchange).

Component 3: Weekly discussions in the college course. To process what unfolds within the e-mail exchanges and in the school-based conversations, each week in the college-based methods course, the preservice teachers raise questions and issues that they experience in the e-mail exchange and that are prompted by reading the transcripts. These discussions not only give preservice teachers a chance to share their excitement and frustrations, they also give preservice teachers the opportunity to ask for and offer advice to other members of the class. Each year, the kinds of questions that arise include how to pose questions that elicit student responses without being too prescriptive or overwhelming (too narrow or too broad); how to develop a reciprocal dialogue—one in which both parties ask and answer questions, not just a more traditional teacher-to-student question-and-answer exchange; how to respond to sensitive information about students or others that students reveal; and how to apply to practice the advice offered by students, particularly when it is contradictory (either to educational theory or to what others students advocate).

Component 4: End-of-semester analysis paper. Finally, at the end of the semester, we have another face-to-face meeting in which the pairs debrief the experience of the project, and we talk as a group about what went well and what they would like to see structured differently. After this final meeting and as the culminating assignment for this project, each preservice teacher selects a focus for an analysis paper. Drawing on and quoting the e-mail exchanges, transcripts of discussions among the high school students, and college-based class discussions, each preservice teacher reflects back over the entire semester's various exchanges and focuses on particularly important discoveries for him or her. The purpose of this assignment is to prompt the preservice teachers to reflect on how the exchange unfolded over the course of the semester, to realize what large and small lessons they learned, and to reinforce the importance of attending to students as sources of educational knowledge. It is often not until this point of reflection that preservice teachers realize how much they learned—from students, about themselves, about teaching and learning.[8]

Essential Features of Teaching and Learning Together

There are two essential features of TLT that facilitate my reaching the goals I have for the project.[9] The structure and participants in the project challenge traditional power inequities in teacher preparation and change the ways that student learning might be supported. The ways TLT (1) involves members of school communities in teacher education and (2) develops mutually respectful relationships between teachers-to-be and students echo key features student participants in TLT have reiterated as important to them: active participation and meaningful relationships.

Involving Members of School Communities in Teacher Education

Although the project is a central component of the college course, many of its key participants are based at the high school. The student participants are invited to interact with college students and a college-based teacher educator—opportunities they would generally not have—and they are invited as well to analyze critically their experiences in school and offer advice directly to those planning to teach. These invitations not only help the students gain new perspectives on what is important in learning to teach, they change their perspectives on their own education.[10] On another level, these invitations change the very structures within and assumptions according to which prospective teachers learn how to teach. TLT rejects the traditional conceptualization of students as empty vessels waiting to be filled and asserts instead that not only do students have unique and essential perspectives on classroom life, learning, teaching, and how to improve all three, they must also be invested with power and authority to share those perspectives.

In addition to the students, the school-based educators with whom I collaborate on the project play a crucial role. Teachers at the high schools of the student participants select the student participants, serve as conveners of their meetings, and facilitate the school-based discussions. They thus play a critical role in preparing, supporting, and guiding students through this new responsibility they assume for teacher preparation. Because students are invited through this project to think about and express their views, and because they likely have little experience with such invitations, part of the challenge facing the school-based educators is to help students learn the vocabulary educators use to talk about teaching and learning as well as how to gain critical distance on, analyze, and describe their own experiences and needs in that language. My school-based collaborators choose student participants who they know will participate constructively—a choice I could not make as the college-based facilitator. They frame questions for the students in a language the students can understand and prompt them to elaborate on their responses in ways that build on their strengths. This is an essential role, also not one a university-based educator could play, since students need to learn a new language and gain confidence in expressing themselves in order to constructively participate in these conversations—processes that require the ongoing presence of a known and trusted adult.

Developing Mutually Respectful Relationships between Teachers and Students

Through their participation in TLT, the preservice teachers and students develop relationships based on mutual respect within which knowledge about teaching and learning is co-constructed and that affect their conceptions of teaching, learning, and one another. As one preservice teacher explained: "[My high school partner] and I built our knowledge [together], rather than giving it to one another, and neither one of us was ever only a teacher or student in the traditional sense." And commenting on how the e-mail exchange with his preservice teacher partner shifted his sense of teachers, a student stated: "It made me respect teachers more. I never really thought that they wondered about some of the things that [my preservice teacher partner] asked me. And just to think that they actually wondered about that or cared about that made me respect them a little more."

Challenges and Rewards of Facilitating
Teaching and Learning Together

Because this project attempts to alter established educational structures and power dynamics, it raises a variety of issues, which are both challenges and opportunities. The following are the various challenges I have faced and how I have tried to turn them into opportunities.

Logistical Challenges

There are the logistical challenges of collaborating across educational contexts (high school and college) and the demanding schedules and numerous commitments that school-based educators and high school students have. The school-based educators with whom I collaborate try to select a diverse group of high school students who are also willing and able to commit to and follow through on regular e-mail correspondence and attendance at weekly meetings, and they must find a meeting time that fits into students' already scheduled responsibilities (we never take students out of class to participate in the weekly discussions). In addition, we try to find times for the high school students and the preservice teachers to meet—at least once at the beginning of the semester and once at the end— but since the college class meets in the evenings and preservice teachers have other courses scheduled, and since it is both a legal and a logistical challenge to take students away from school, I usually arrange for the preservice teachers to meet with the students in a half-hour slot after school at a time that works for everyone's schedule (this can be tough and isn't always possible). The lesson here is how busy everyone is, particularly students, which is important for prospective teachers to keep in mind as they prepare to make demands on students in their classes.

Psychological Challenges

There are the psychological challenges of convincing young adults on the brink of their first careers that they have something to learn from the people they are planning to teach. This challenge springs from the fact that authority has always been assumed to belong to educational researchers and theorists, not students. It is therefore difficult—even for preservice teachers within a project that frames high school students as authorities—to accept those students as authorities. As one preservice teacher put it, "Being in the [college] environment for four years, I just did not think that I could learn anything from [my high school partner]. . . . At the beginning I came in to [Teaching and Learning Together] with the idea that she could probably learn something from me."[11] This challenge presents me with the opportunity to strike a balance between insisting that the students have important perspectives to share (which I demonstrate by structuring the project in the first place and by making attention to students' perspectives so integral to preparation to teach) and letting preservice teachers develop their own awareness and commitments to consulting students and attending to students' perspectives and needs based on the experience they have through the project.

Intellectual Challenges

There is also the intellectual challenge of fostering communication between groups of students who speak different languages and move in different educational cultures. One preservice teacher stated: "When first talking with Kurt, I realized that the language with which I approach issues related to schooling (most likely resulting from three years of study in the discipline) is not a language that we share. Issues which I had pondered for extended periods of time may have been altogether new to him." This challenge gives me the opportunity to support preservice teachers as they learn new languages, ways of interacting, and ways of thinking—processes that transform their sense of communication, students, and themselves.[12]

Preparedness Challenges

In addition to these three challenges, there is the challenge presented by the fact that students do not always have helpful things to say. As I have written elsewhere, "Sometimes they have nothing to say, sometimes they say things they have not thought through, and they always speak from complex positions"[13] because their identities and experiences are multifaceted. The opportunity here is to help preservice teachers figure out how to elicit from students what both groups need to hear—what and how students need to learn, when, and why.

Despite and sometimes because of these challenges, facilitating TLT is always a learning as well as a teaching experience for me. So many issues of power, identity, role, relationship, and responsibility are at play that my primary focus becomes trying to keep possibilities open rather than letting old assumptions and fears close them down. When I am able to do that, participants in the project learn a range of critical lessons.

Critical Lessons Preservice Teachers Learn

One of the critical lessons that preservice teachers learn through participating in TLT is the importance and efficacy of listening to students.[14] This is, of course, the premise of the project, and some preservice teachers recognize and embrace it right away. For instance, one preservice teacher explained:

> What's so special about the project is that we are focusing on their voices, 'cause otherwise we could just learn all the theory, learn all this and never apply it, and never communicate to young people. And I think what was important, where I saw my role, was as a listener. I was going to listen to them. And as a teacher, that's what I want to do for my students. I'm going to listen to them because they are extremely articulate, extremely intelligent, they know what's wrong with school, they know what's missing, and they're constantly asking for it.

For other preservice teachers, however, it takes a while—sometimes a whole semester—before the premise becomes an embraced reality. Many preservice teachers assume that they will be the ones doing the teaching. But as one preservice teacher realized, upon reflection: "I was so wrong. I learned *so much* from her. . . . I put three main issues [in my final analysis paper] that I learned that struck me as, 'I'm not listening. I'm not listening. I'm just saying things to her, and not listening.' . . . She was listening to me and I was not listening to her. You need to hear the student's voice, because that's the reason for teaching."

Learning to listen to students has immediate and practical consequences for preservice teachers in their preparation for practice. It helps them remember what students experience in school. As one preservice teacher explained: "I can look back and into the mind of a high schooler. Even though that was only a few years ago, being in an environment like [Bryn Mawr and Haverford colleges], I have become so accustomed to the lifestyle here and have forgotten what it used to be like. Having this pathway to experience what it was like helps me to understand what I can do in my classroom to teach as best as I can."

Attending to students and letting the students' words reflect back to the preservice teachers what they intend—or do not intend—to enact in their practice gives the preservice teachers an unusual opportunity to critically reflect on their commitments and approaches before assuming formal teaching responsibilities. In some cases, it throws into relief discrepancies between espoused theory and enacted practice. As one preservice teacher explained:

> [There] was a really big turning point . . . where I realized that I was dominating discussion [in the exchange of e-mails] and that's not what I believed. . . . I know on paper I can say, "Oh, I really want student voice to be a dominant part of my classroom." But, when it really comes down to it, can I somehow foster an environment where that's true? And it's a real student that is depending on you and a real situation that is depending upon your decision or the decision of the two people involved. And it's a real negotiation, and it's real interaction, and although we're not teachers yet, we're in the mindset of prospective teacher, if not teacher already, mindset, and this is definitely a student. . . . So I wrote [in my final analysis paper] about, "How do I support my theory with my actions in this real experience?" Because it was very real.

When preservice teachers have the opportunity to engage in this kind of learning, they embark on their teaching practice with greater confidence and with greater skill.

Students' Experiences of Participating in Teaching and Learning Together

Students' comments on their experience of participating in TLT reveal the importance to students of how they are perceived and positioned by prospective teachers.[15] They are proud to be considered, as one student put it, "responsible enough to handle" such responsibility. Taking up that responsibility, they openly share their perspectives, reflect critically on their own education and behaviors as students, and gain insights into teachers' perspectives.

A Forum and Opportunity for Students to Share Their Opinions

Students point out how rarely they have the opportunity to share their perspectives:

> The topics we spoke on are not commonly discussed with students. We don't often get the chance to give the constructive criticism that so many of us have thoughts on.

> This project made me feel that my opinions and beliefs matter in my education, no matter how young I am.

Emphasizing the importance of hearing from multiple, differently positioned students, another student states:

> I enjoyed doing this because I was able to get my opinion out there. It's great that there were several of us [high school students participating] too because the opinions were mixed and not everyone can learn the same way.

An Opportunity to Reflect Critically on Their Own Education and Behaviors as Students

Being invited into a forum to discuss teaching and learning, as well as being listened to, provides students the opportunity to reflect on their own education, behaviors, and needs as students:

> [Participating in this project] made me step back as a student and just look at how everything was going on in the classroom. It made me look at how I was being taught and how teachers worked.

> Being a part of this project helped to make me a better student by reevaluating myself, my study habits, and my teachers' teaching methods.

> The project made me come to my teachers for help if I need [it] because before I thought teachers never cared.

> Not only do I think these [dialogues] will be helpful to the up-and-coming teachers but also to ourselves. They made us reevaluate what is important to us in a learning experience.

An Opportunity to Gain Insights into Teachers' Perspectives

Reflecting on what is important to them as students and what they need as learners positions students not only to offer useful input to preservice teachers, it also helps students think about teachers—and students' relationships with and responsibilities toward teachers—in a different way:

> I think it kind of made me think about how to be a better student almost 'cause it makes you think that, like, a teacher is up there and they worked hard to come up with this lesson plan, and if you're not going to put in a hundred percent then you're letting them down in a way.

> It made me realize the teacher's point of view, like, I never really realized what they go through, that they even care about this.

> It made me realize how much the teachers have to think about what they're doing and that they don't just get up there every day and do their thing. That they actually think about ways that they can improve themselves and they work really hard to do what they do.

Teachers' Experiences of Teaching and Learning Together

Three teachers at several different schools have cofacilitated TLT during the years I have maintained the project.[16] These teachers are already committed to eliciting and responding to student perspectives, to collaborating with students as authorities on their learning, and to reflecting critically on their practice, but participating in TLT gives them more time for discussion with students—time they think it is unlikely they would otherwise find—and the project lets them take their commitments to listening to students to a new level.

Time to Talk with Students

> Once you start teaching, you don't talk education, you do it. There isn't time built into the day to step back and have conversations with students about their experience of schooling.

> [In daily life], I don't have time to process how the students are feeling, if things work. Each year the group is very different, and I have learned a lot as a facilitator.

Within the time for interaction that this project provides, the experienced teachers can engage with students in conversations they otherwise would not have.

Uncommon Conversations

> [The project] provides a whole different opportunity to engage in conversation with the students.

> What's different about this [from my regular interactions with students] is that I get a much broader response and there are no repercussions for what the students say; they can be really honest about their experience.

Listening to students talk about teachers reminds you as a teacher what an impact you have on kids and small things that seem negligible to you are really important to them. It reminds you of how careful you have to be—a glance, a small comment . . . they matter. I was always so surprised at what bothers kids or made them feel good.

Keeping Perspective on What Matters to Students

The conversations themselves are broader [than those you generally have with students]; they go beyond self interest to how the students feel more generally about their education; not just about responding to whether they got the grade they deserved.

Meeting with those students every week keeps you fresh in terms of what kids need and want and their perspectives on what's happening in a classroom.

Deepening Relationships with—and Becoming Better Advocates for—Students

Participating in the project has had an interesting effect on the kids who were also my students. It changed my relationship with them: I felt much more connected with them, I got to know them better, and they saw me differently. Because we had the chance to have this conversation outside of class, outside of a grade, they saw me as a person who was inquiring and eager to hear what they had to say, and I think that changed the way they looked at me as a teacher.

There were times in conversation with colleagues when I was able to reference the students and their perspectives—I call the project my "educational forum"—and I could shed light on things that students were thinking about and share those perspectives with both faculty and administrator colleagues.

Conclusion

As the name of the project implies, Teaching and Learning Together positions everyone involved in the project—high school students, preservice teachers, teacher educators, and school-based teachers—as both teachers and learners. It provides a structure that crosses literal and conceptual boundaries; it forges direct links between those who spend their days in high schools and those who spend their days in college classrooms preparing to reenter schools; and it attempts to foster relationships of mutual respect that will support the ongoing learning and growth in which we all need to engage.

Appendix: Guiding Questions for School-Based Discussions

- Focus on Learners in Social and Cultural Context

    What are some of the most important things to you about your family and community, and how do they affect your experience of school?

- Focus on Learners in Classroom and School Context

  When you are at school, what kinds of things affect your experience within classrooms?

- Getting a Sense of History, Context, and Curriculum Theory

  What do you think students should study in school and why?

- Standards and Curriculum

  Should there be standards for school subjects, and if so, who should decide what students study in school and why?

- Curriculum and Pedagogy: Integrating the Two

  What is the relationship between what you are taught (curriculum) and how you are taught (pedagogy)?

- Classroom Environment and Management

  What qualities in a classroom best support your learning and how should a teacher manage her classroom?

- Pedagogy

  What kinds of learning activities do you like best and why? What aspects of learners' identities (race, class, gender, etc.) should be considered when teaching and why?

- Pedagogy: Differentiation

  How can teachers meet the different learning styles and needs of students in their classes?

- Planning

  How do you like the time during a class period to be divided up and spent?

- Assessment and Evaluation

  What is the best way for you to show a teacher what you have learned in his or her class (tests, projects, papers, performances, or something else)?

Notes

1. For other discussions of this project, see the following articles by Alison Cook-Sather: "What Would Happen If We Treated Students as Those with Opinions That Matter? The Benefits to Principals and Teachers of Supporting Youth Engagement in School," *NASSP Bulletin* 91, no. 4 (2007): 343–362; "Re(in)forming the Conversations: Student Position, Power, and Voice in Teacher Education," *Radical Teacher* 64 (2002): 21–28; "Teachers-to-Be Learning from Students-Who-Are: Reconfiguring Undergraduate Teacher Preparation," in *Stories of the Courage to Teach: Honoring the Teacher's Heart,* edited by Sam M. Intrator (San Francisco: Jossey-Bass Publishers, 2002); "Direct Links: Using Email to Connect Pre-Service Teachers, Classroom-Based Teachers, and High School Students within an Undergraduate Teacher Preparation Program," forthcoming in *Journal of Technology and Teacher Education*; "The 'Constant Changing of Myself': Revising Roles in Undergraduate Teacher Preparation," *The Teacher Educator* 41, no. 3 (Winter 2006): 187–206; "Listening to Students about Learning Differences," *Teaching Exceptional Children* 35, no. 4 (March/April 2003): 22–26; "'A Teacher Should Be . . .': When the Answer Is the Question," *Knowledge Quest* 30, no. 5 (May/June 2002): 12–15.

2. Cook-Sather, 2007b, pp. 11–12.

3. The Bryn Mawr/Haverford Education Program is an undergraduate, secondary teacher preparation program at two selective, liberal arts colleges—Bryn Mawr College and Haverford College—located in the northeastern United States.

4. Ongoing expenses include stipends for the school-based facilitators of the project and stipends for the participating high school students.

5. Cook-Sather, 2002b.

6. As discussed through this sourcebook, raising awareness is a difficult and dangerous responsibility, and it is undertaken in this project with that awareness and by providing a caring and supportive as well as challenging environment for the students.

7. For a discussion of students as authorities on educational practice, see Cook-Sather, 2002, pp. 3–14.

8. See Cook-Sather and Reisinger, 2001.

9. For a variation of this discussion, see Cook-Sather and Youens, 2007.

10. Cook-Sather, 2002a.

11. Cook-Sather, 2002a, p. 8.

12. Cook-Sather, 2001, 2006a.

13. Kamler, 2001, p. 36, quoted in Cook-Sather, 2002, p. 10.

14. Cook-Sather, 2009b.

15. Many of the student statements included here appeared in Cook-Sather, 2007c.

16. A version of this discussion appeared in Cook-Sather, 2007c.

14

Students Mentoring Student Teachers

Listening during Student Teaching

Bernadette Youens

Chapter Overview

Focus of this chapter: The Student Mentor Project, a teacher preparation program based at the University of Nottingham in England that has sought over the past decade to include students' perspectives during the school-based or student teaching phase of the program

Discussed in this chapter:

- Background of the project
- The place of mentoring in teacher preparation in England
- The Student Mentor Project
- Benefits to beginning teachers
- Benefits to students
- Sustainability

Background of the Project

The teacher preparation program described in this chapter is a one-year Postgraduate Certificate in Education (PGCE) course, which is the most common route to qualified teacher status for secondary school teachers in England. All PGCE programs must be planned and taught collaboratively by university departments and schools within formal partnership arrangements and are mandated to be thirty-six weeks in length, with student teachers spending one-third of the course at the university and two-thirds of the course in school placements.[1] The focus of this chapter is how a teacher preparation program based at the University of Nottingham has sought over the past decade to include students' perspectives during the school-based or student teaching phase of the program. The program is called the Student Mentor Project.[2]

The stimulus for the creation of this project was a discussion at a partnership meeting between university staff and staff from partner schools on how classroom teachers should introduce student teachers to their classes. Feedback from a recent training session had revealed a lingering sense of uncertainty among teachers in the schools about how best to describe the beginning teacher's role to students. It was acknowledged that the situation is a delicate one: students, on the whole, agree to comply with a new teacher because they accept the authority vested in the role rather than the personal authority of the individual. However, it was also agreed that most of the students are able to identify a student teacher instantly. The subterfuge of implying that the student is a visiting fully trained teacher therefore operates as a covert declaration of support, offered within a set of classroom discourses that allow it to be understood by all participants in the exchange. The general feeling was that—even when well intentioned—pretense about student teachers' status was unacceptable. Several issues surfaced in the discussion:

- discomfiture about the types of power and authority being employed,
- a strong sense of commitment to authentic relationships between students and teachers, and
- a desire to build trust between the teaching staff and the beginning teacher through collaboration and joint endeavor rather than by offering free rein.

The advantages, to both students and beginning teachers, of developing students' understanding of the process of initial teacher education and involving them in it seemed to become clearer as the discussion proceeded. The benefits to the beginning teacher seemed likely to derive from students' knowledge about how classrooms and the school in general work, and perhaps from their increased understanding of the difficulties inherent in the beginning teacher's role. The benefits to the students seemed likely to come from their chance to use previously untapped expertise and their opportunity to consider what vocational training involves and to observe it at close quarters. The result of this discussion was an exploration of how the student perspective could be integrated into the student teachers' experience of the PGCE course.

The Place of Mentoring in Teacher Preparation in England

As preservice (initial) teacher education in England has moved toward school-based preparation in response to central government directives, this move has been accompanied by the necessary development of the role of teachers in the school-based phases of teacher preparation. Each beginning teacher on a PGCE course is supported in school by an experienced subject-area teacher, and this role is generally referred to as mentoring. Many different conceptions of mentoring in preservice teacher education have developed since the early 1990s, and there is now a considerable body of research and literature in this area.[3] In essence, the role of a mentor is to provide support and guidance to student teachers during the school-based elements of teacher education courses.

The negotiated roles and responsibilities for mentors in the partnership described in this chapter fall into four main areas:

1. managing the student teacher's experience in the school;
2. planning an appropriate program;
3. facilitating professional learning; and
4. assessing the student teacher's performance.

To support this work, university departments of education design and teach tailored mentor development programs for the teachers working with them in partnership. In addition to mentoring in preservice teacher education, there exists a host of other "mentoring" activities in schools involving teachers and students. *Mentoring* is therefore a term that is widely used in schools in England, and after some deliberation it was decided that the best approach to involving students in the preparation of new teachers was to prepare students to themselves act as mentors during the main practicum.

The overarching aim of the Student Mentor Project, therefore, was to provide beginning teachers with structured access to the views of the students they were preparing to teach. To achieve this aim it was hoped that the project would create dialogic spaces within schools where beginning teachers could learn about the particular school they were in and begin to engage in understanding students' perspectives about teaching and learning. In this way we hoped to encourage beginning teachers to consider the views of their students more explicitly when preparing to teach classes.

The Student Mentor Project

Context

The PGCE course at the University of Nottingham includes a thirteen-week practical teaching phase that comprises the middle third of the course. During this teaching practice, student teachers are in school full-time and carry a schedule equivalent to approximately half of a qualified teacher's schedule. In addition to the subject mentor described above, student teachers receive support in school from a senior member of the school staff who has responsibility for managing the school experience of all student teachers in school, referred to in this partnership as the coordinator. A third strand of support for the beginning teacher is provided by a university tutor who works with the student teacher throughout the thirty-six-week course. All university tutors will have been successful classroom practitioners before joining the university and are usually active education researchers as well. The role of the tutor encompasses teaching the university elements of the teacher preparation program, visiting the student teacher regularly during school-based phases of the course, and assessing the student teacher's academic and practical work. Alongside these activities, there are regular individual tutorials that support the student teacher's professional development. In the Student Mentor Project, student teachers working with participating schools also received support from a pair of students, referred to as student mentors.

Selection of Student Mentors

One interesting aspect of the program was how participating schools selected their student mentors. Some schools, after the first few years of working on the project, introduced an application process to try to address issues relating to equity and also to provide a bridge to the world beyond the school community, thus helping to prepare students for later life.[4] Other schools selected students based on a whole variety of criteria, ranging from membership on the school council, to selecting students considering teaching as a career, to providing an opportunity for students who had never visited a university before.

Across the project, though, it was agreed that the mentors would be Year 10 (fourteen- to fifteen-year-old) students and that a pair of student mentors would work with each student teacher throughout the teaching practice. Each year the selected students, together with teachers from their school and their respective student teachers, attended the university for a half-day training session at the start of the teaching practice. The overall aim of the training course was to ensure that all participants understood the rationale for the project and were clear about their roles within the project. The training session followed a similar pattern each year. The introductory session focused on issues of confidentiality and the responsibilities associated with the student mentor role. It involved all participants and was set in the context of the university providing lifelong learning opportunities. In the second part of the training session the students, student teachers, and teachers attended separate workshops, and these are described below.

Student Workshop

During this part of the training program, the students preparing to be the student mentors observe a series of video clips in which student teachers talk about the concerns they have about starting the main teaching practice and also what they are most looking forward to about teaching. After viewing the video clips, students work together in small groups to practice listening and responding to the issues raised. The focus of the session is on encouraging the students to recognize that their perspectives on their school and the learning environment are valid and that the student teachers are learning how to teach and will appreciate constructive advice and guidance from students in the school.

An interesting facet of the program each year has been how students respond to the issues raised by the student teachers. For example, one student teacher was concerned that she looked too young, whereas the students consistently viewed this as a benefit: "I think that works to her advantage." Another student teacher was concerned about how to plan a lesson to fit the allotted time. Student responses included, she "will learn it in time" and she "should include timing in her lesson planning." A third student teacher expressed her anxiety about following school policies that she might disagree with. Students showed that they are prepared to give direct, and quite forthright, advice: "She's *got* to stick with the school policy—if one adult is saying one thing and one another, it's confusing for the students."

A recurrent theme that student teachers are initially very concerned about is the managing of student behavior. In one of the video interviews, a beginning teacher expresses his fears about standing up in front of "a class full of children." Again, students have consistently picked up on the same issues. In this instance his use of the term "children" was objected to by the students: "Don't call us children, because we're not!" and "It's the worst thing anyone can say—calling us children." In addition, the students were concerned that "he seemed to be more bothered about discipline than building a relationship with the students. He shouldn't be so bothered about discipline; talk to the class and get to know them." The notion of communicating with students was also a key issue for the students: "Keep communicating with the students, but remember to follow through on any threats that are made." The students were also able to make some very perceptive comments about the importance of how teachers present themselves to classes: "The worst thing is that he doesn't look confident on the video. A class will know if he's anxious . . . and then the class will play up more. He needs to put on a front until he gets to know the class better." This advice reveals yet again the potential for students not only to analyze teaching in a perceptive way but also to articulate their understandings confidently.

While students are quite prepared to share their perspectives on a wide range of educational issues, an important aspect of the project has also been to make the student teachers aware that the guidance offered by the student mentors is just one perspective, and it will not necessarily be one that they will, or should, agree with. In practice, student teachers responded often to the spirit rather than the detail of the advice proffered, sometimes reinterpreting it in the light of their own developing understanding of the teacher's role.

Student Teacher Group

While the students are meeting in the Student Workshop described above, the student teacher group meets with a university tutor to consider how students might be able to support them during teaching practice and to discuss concerns they have about participating in the project. Once the project is introduced to them, the student teachers are generally positive and can immediately see the potential of talking with students in their placement school. As an example, one student teacher reflected: "I'm constantly thinking, why did I like that teacher and what was it about them that made them good? But I can't pinpoint it as it was so long ago. It would be so nice to have a student that I could say to, on first impression, how do you know whether a teacher is going to be strict or not? And what makes them good? To have that opinion would be good, as I can't remember."

As part of the session, student teachers work in groups to identify their main concerns about being involved in this project and to consider how discussions with students might support their development as teachers. The responses to the first question focus on practical issues, for example, that the "time may cut into our other commitments" and exactly how the project will work in school: "I'm not sure of the structure of the project. I need to know more." Not surprisingly, the student teachers are particularly nervous about issues relating to their role as beginning teachers and to confidentiality. Some of the comments at this stage in the project reveal how insecure the student teachers feel about their status in school; for example: "involvement in this project could undermine our authority"; "students might laugh and talk about us"; "what if they don't take it seriously?" Student teachers describe feeling uncomfortable "about teaching the kids involved," and express concern regarding what happens if "your student mentors are unpleasant characters," the impact of "looking vulnerable in front of students," and "what if they find it difficult to articulate suggestions?" These representative comments demonstrate that in the very early stages of the project, some, although by no means all, of the student teachers underestimate the students, and in some respects hold a deficit view of the understandings students will have about teaching, learning, and schools.

In response to the question about how the students might help them in their development as teachers, the following exemplify the range of areas typically identified in most sessions:

- "feedback on how you appear as a teacher to a student"
- "time management in lessons; how long to plan for each task"
- "how to gain respect"
- "previous mistakes from student teachers"
- "how to make homework more interesting"
- "how do students feel about student teachers?"
- "what happens outside the classroom?"
- "may help you breach the cultural divide between students and teachers/adults"

- "get feedback you wouldn't otherwise get"
- "fresh reaction (fresh eyes)"
- "more aware of school culture"

The third and final workshop of the afternoon is held in school-based groups. The main focus of this part of the training is practical: for all participants in the project to get to know each other in an out-of-school context, for them to learn about administrative arrangements, to pair student mentors and student teachers, and to address other practical issues.

The Project in School

Throughout the project, all student mentors and student teachers are supported by a senior member of the school's teaching staff, usually the partnership coordinator. From discussions during the training sessions it is apparent that issues of confidentiality are of concern, particularly to the student teachers. Over the years, in acknowledgment of the importance of confidentiality, not only has this issue been accorded a high profile during the training session, but all student mentors are issued booklets reminding them of the agreed ground rules for the project:

- Your conversations are private. Don't tell other people about them. Respect the fact that the student teacher is learning to do a difficult and important job.
- If you are worried about something to do with the student mentoring, tell your School Coordinator.
- If you are uncomfortable as a mentor, you can drop out of the scheme. Talk about this with your School Coordinator.
- You aren't responsible if things go wrong for the student teacher. Your job is to give your own views from a student's perspective.
- Be responsible. Keep your appointments. Listen and think. You've got a lot to offer!

The booklets also provide a list of areas for discussion entitled "What shall we talk about?" based on key issues emerging from discussions at the first training sessions. The list of suggestions includes:

- What good teachers do to make lessons enjoyable
- Ideas about what encourages people to behave well
- Advising on how to be a good form tutor (class adviser)
- Marking texts and exams from your point of view
- How you learn best
- What makes lessons boring
- Homework, school uniform, assemblies, and school trips
- The best way for a teacher to give praise or tell someone off
- Bullying from a student's point of view
- Racism or sexism from a student's point of view

How the project is managed at the school level has varied from school to school, depending on the culture of the school and the commitment and expertise of the personnel involved in the project. In one school, for example, the project was managed internally by a vice principal who had overall responsibility for teaching and learning, staff development, and preservice teacher education. Students and student teachers met weekly at lunchtime with the vice principal and another colleague from the appropriate tutor team, which changed annually. The topics were negotiated weekly in advance using the guidance list offered in the booklets. The format of most sessions included whole group discussion and small group discussions between one student teacher and the two student mentors. The timing of the meetings meant that lunch was provided for participants so they finished in time for student teachers to prepare for the next lesson. The main outcomes of the sessions were recorded by one of the teachers and circulated to student teachers, student mentors, and their tutors.

Benefits to Beginning Teachers

One of the main aims of the project was to provide preservice teachers with the opportunity to engage with schools and teaching from the perspective of students. Evaluations of the project have demonstrated that this overarching aim has been achieved each year. The benefits to beginning teachers consistently centered on three main areas, namely:

- Hearing about the school from a student's perspective
- Accessing students' ideas on classroom management, teaching, and learning strategies
- Establishing student-teacher relationships

The student teachers' comments demonstrate how much they learned from being involved with the project:

> I found out what the students liked and disliked about teachers and lessons and was able to implement the ideas.

> The project has significant potential and could give student teachers a valuable insight into teaching and learning in schools as well as wider school issues.

> Students feel as if their views are of value to adults, and student teachers receive advice from those who really know what makes a good teacher. Plus, most of them know what a good teacher is and don't just select their favorite teacher because they are always nice. Consistency and fairness are more important.

> [The project] made you realize how important it is for students to know that as a teacher you care and are interested in students.

> [The student mentors] allowed me to see the school through students' eyes and situations outside the classroom that they have to deal with.

The concerns around confidentiality prove to be largely unfounded as each year student teachers report overwhelmingly that "a relationship of mutual respect was present throughout." In fact, the student teachers consistently remark on how mature and responsible the students were during the project. It appears that the students responded very positively to being placed in positions of trust and responsibility. One of the most significant outcomes of this project is therefore providing experiences that focus on equipping student teachers to work openly and collaboratively with all stakeholders in schools by providing a forum for dialogue about students' perceptions. Reflection on the project helped student teachers to develop their notions of professionalism, particularly acknowledging claims of students in relation to the authority of the teacher.[5]

Benefits to Students

Over the course of the Student Mentor Project a consistent finding was that there were significant benefits not only to the student teachers, which was the initial aim of the project, but also to the students participating in the project. Indeed, the manifest social and personal benefits to students were probably the most significant element in convincing school staff that they wanted to continue working with the Student Mentor scheme further. For example, one student explained that the project "has increased my confidence in talking in front of groups of people and helped our listening skills as we had to listen to different people's opinions." A further finding was that, in general, students felt entrusted with a serious responsibility and they responded accordingly.

Evaluations of the project also revealed that students themselves learned a lot about the job of being a teacher, with four themes consistently replayed in their answers: what hard work it is, how much organization and planning there is to do, how much time it takes, and how difficult it is to plan interesting lessons and to have good ideas.[6] The following are typical of comments made by students on evaluation questionnaires each year:

> I have benefitted from seeing school through the eyes of a teacher. I've realized that it is harder than I first thought and in future I will do my best to make it easier. It [the project] helps teachers find out what it is like for a student and their point of view. Therefore making them better teachers.

> I realize just how difficult it is for a new teacher to make the right impressions—not too strict, not too laid back.

The students also appreciated how valuable it was for the student teachers to have access to students' perspectives on schools and teaching.

In the latter years of the project, student mentors completed lesson observations of the student teachers near the start and the end of the practice, providing that each student teacher agreed. Students were trained how to observe and give written feedback on the lessons. The constructive feedback they offered the student teachers allowed them to develop experience in considering the impact their comments can have on others. We considered that this led to an increasingly professional approach on the part of the student mentors over the teaching practice period.[7] Involvement in the project also helped the student mentors to identify the qualities that they valued in teachers.

Rudduck and Flutter propose that the advocacies for student voice center on three main themes: supporting students in developing their identities and individual voices, involvement of students as "expert witnesses," and the importance of preparing young people to be citizens in a democratic society.[8] The outcomes discussed above demonstrate that, through involvement with this project, all three of the above areas have been addressed. It is clear that the students certainly felt that the project helped them to develop their identities and individual voices. Indeed, this development took place in all the schools involved in the project and was celebrated when the school coordinators met together each year.

Sustainability

That the Student Mentor Project had clear benefits for all participants has been well documented elsewhere.[9] However, after eight years of running the project, it was decided that a different approach was required. The key issue for participating schools has always been one of sustainability and how to expand the principles of the project to other aspects of school life. The schools that chose to participate in the project were self-selecting, and individual staff members invested significant time and energy to ensure that the project was successful each year. Their main motivation in doing this was clearly the positive benefits for the students able to take part in the project. In schools where the culture was supportive of openness and risk taking, staff were keen to harness the expertise developed by the students to support the school's own development agenda.[10]

However, while the Student Mentor Project has been offered to all partnership schools working with the University of Nottingham, only a small proportion of schools has taken up the opportunity. This situation presents us as teacher educators with the dilemma of being committed to the philosophy and principles underpinning the project and knowing the many benefits that preservice teachers derive from participation in it, while also being aware that not all of our preservice teachers have access to the project. The challenge therefore is now to develop alternative pedagogical approaches that embrace the project's underpinning principles and that are accessible to all preservice teachers in our preservice teacher education programs.

Conclusion

Structured interventions like the Student Mentor Project can contribute significantly to helping preservice teachers appreciate the value of knowing one's learners and of understanding the complexities involved in knowing young people as individual learners. The lessons learned from the Student Mentor Project have informed the process of restructuring core elements of one preservice teacher education program to facilitate preservice teachers' engagement in discussion with the range of learners in school-based phases of the course. These lessons offer an alternative, more equitable approach to helping beginning teachers to know those they are learning to teach, as well as to develop their notions of professionalism, particularly regarding acknowledging the claims of students in relation to the authority of the teacher.

Notes

1. DES, 1992.

2. The program is officially called the Pupil Mentor Project, but in keeping with U.S. terminology used through this sourcebook, the term "student" is used.

3. Arthur, Davison, and Moss, 1997; Furlong and Maynard, 1995; Brooks and Sikes, 1997; Hawkey, 1998; Hawkey, 1997; Tomlinson, 1995. For a more detailed discussion of mentoring in initial (preservice) teacher education in England, see Youens and Bailey, 2004.

4. Watts and Youens, 2007.

5. Youens and Hall, 2006, p. 15.

6. Youens and Hall, 2006.

7. See Watts and Youens, 2007, for a more detailed discussion.

8. Rudduck and Flutter, 2004.

9. Cook-Sather and Youens, 2007; Watts and Youens, 2007; Youens and Hall, 2006.

10. See Watts and Youens, 2007, for a more detailed discussion.

Part IV

Conclusions

15

Returning to Perspective and Taking Action

Chapter Overview

Focus of this chapter: To revisit the notion of "perspective" and to recommend action steps educators can take to access and learn from student perspectives

Discussed in this chapter:

- Perspective
- General recommendations about perspective, stance, and interaction
- Action steps for high school teachers, school leaders, and teacher educators

I suggested in my Introduction that this text explores the two meanings of the phrase "learning from the student's perspective." Part I offers multiple examples of students' perspectives on their learning experiences, and Parts II and III feature strategies for and stories of adults learning from student descriptions and analyses of their learning and of acting upon what they learn. I also emphasized in my introduction that students have unique perspectives on teaching, learning, and schooling, and rather than replace all others' perspectives on good teaching or be the sole impetus for revision of educational practices, these perspectives should be included alongside the perspectives of teachers and researchers in conversations about effective teaching. I return to the concept of perspective in this conclusion to reiterate how central it is to learning and, in particular, to learning from students, and I move from a short reflection on the concept of perspective to an enumeration of action steps that teachers, school leaders, and teacher educators might take to move toward making learning from the student's perspective central to their practices.

Perspective

Perspective is, literally, the way things appear to the eye, and it is also, more metaphorically, point of view. Associated definitions suggest that perspective is vision informed by perceptions of distances between things, patterns of relationship, and particular angles of interpretation. In their most basic form, both the literal and the metaphorical definitions of perspective suggest a single position from which one perceives, but it is in fact eyes—plural—that allow for literal perspective, and it is only in relation to *other* points of view that any single one has meaning.

The perspectives presented in this text are neither fixed nor final. They are, instead, new angles on perennial issues that all educators face. They are offered by students in the traditional sense—learners at the high school level—and they are offered as well by learners across the lifespan: recent college students and graduates who coauthored the framing sections of Part I and who wrote the analyses that formed the case studies included in the chapters in that part of the sourcebook; educational researchers and writers committed not only to learning from but also to sharing their knowledge of how to access the perspectives of students; and prospective, beginning, and experienced teachers, school leaders, and teacher educators who have acted on the commitment to make students partners in education.

I conclude this book with a set of recommendations for how to learn from the student perspective in different contexts and from different positions within the educational realm.[1] Like all aspects of this text, these are meant as guidelines with which to begin the necessarily ongoing process of consulting students and working collaboratively with them. They are not prescriptions or approaches that, once taken, constitute the end of consulting students and making them partners in the work of supporting meaningful education.

General Recommendations about Perspective, Stance, and Interaction

Open Yourself to Different Angles of Vision

The capacity to learn from the student's perspective—and from anyone's, for that matter—begins with a willingness to acknowledge that someone looking from a different vantage point might well see something different from what you see. This is obvious in the literal sense, but we tend to forget it when thinking about ideas and not actual angles of vision. Don't assume that being open to other perspectives is necessarily a threat to your own. It's a big world. On the other hand, don't be afraid of the ways you might find yourself moving or changing as a result of this openness. It might entail pain and loss, but it might just as possibly bring joy and renewed energy. There is time for all of this. Be imaginative and conscientious in recognizing that your own angle of vision is socially and culturally embedded.

Recognize That Words Mean Different Things to Different People

Although they may use some of the same words as adults, students might mean different things by the words they use than what adults might mean by or associate with the same words (and students certainly use different words than adults). When engaging in dialogue with students, rather than adhere to assumed meanings and associations, be prepared to explore terms with students—both to learn and to extend what they might mean to students and to us as educators.

Engage in Dialogue with the Goal of Deepening Understanding

As Freire has argued, and as Julie, in Chapter 5, agrees, "without dialogue there is no communication, and without communication there can be no true education."[2] Dialogue with the goal of listening and deepening understanding is dialogue for education. Listening itself can—indeed, must—be active, chosen, agentic (making the listener a producer as well as a product of social systems). Make room in your practice for the power of active listening as a practice itself, as a framework for teaching, not always as a means to an end.[3] And, when you hear something in students' perspectives that challenges you, rather than focusing on how to convince or convert them, becoming defensive or dismissive of other perspectives, and growing frustrated with seeming contradictions or irreconcilable differences, ask yourself what you could do to better understand students' perspectives and help them better understand yours. Such an effort entails acknowledging the emotions of all parties—the forces that make one less, not more, likely to be open to other angles of vision and other meanings.

Regularly Revisit and Revise Your Notions of Responsibility

As discussed in Chapter 5, responsibility is about one's ability (or inability) to respond within the parameters of any given context and relationship, and it is about the action one takes based on one's sense of accountability to others. Consider how responsibility can be shared as well as delegated. Collaborate with students to identify and work toward interpersonal, curricular, and systemic changes in education.

Action Steps for High School Teachers, School Leaders, and Teacher Educators

Take Small and Large Steps in Your Classrooms

Both preservice and experienced teachers can, working within the parameters of their respective schools, take small and large steps with their classrooms to support student voice and participation. Learning to listen, as Darla Himeles (Chapter 8) and Brandon Clarke (Chapter 9) describe, requires commitment, capacity to look hard at one's own experiences and assumptions, and willingness to revise what one believes and what one does. Engaging in these processes is best supported in collegial community: talk with and seek support from others committed to this work. Using some of the strategies included in Part II—questionnaires, discussion questions, and activities—teachers can invite students in a wide variety of ways into dialogue about what works for them, what does not, and what could. Embracing a commitment to working collaboratively with students, as Marsha Rosenzweig Pincus (Chapter 10) illustrates, can become a lifelong process of education for all involved. A first step might be to share with students in your classroom the perspectives that students in Part I of this sourcebook articulate. Talk with your students about how their perspectives confirm or contrast with those perspectives, and discuss together the changes you and they might make to address their learning goals for themselves and your learning goals for them. Consider how these may be built into specific assignments and activities as well as broader classroom discourse.

Create Schoolwide Structures and Mechanisms to Support Student Voice and Participation

Teachers and school leaders can create schoolwide structures and mechanisms, such as Peter Evans's Solon Circle (Chapter 11) and the Eagle Rock School and Professional Development Center (Chapter 12), that support student voice and participation. These can be as simple, but as potentially efficacious, as regular meetings to which all members of the school community are invited, or they can entail a more complex reimagining of roles of those within the educational community, such as we have undertaken at the college level, inviting students to serve as pedagogical consultants to faculty members.[4] As suggested above in reference to classroom practices, you might share with students at your school the perspectives students in Part I of this sourcebook articulate, talk with your students about how their perspectives confirm or contrast with those perspectives, and then think together about implications for reform within your school context.

Advocate for Recognition of Teachers Committed to Student Voice

Consider ways to ensure that teachers who consult students and attend to their perspectives on their learning are acknowledged and rewarded for those efforts. One approach might be to include a question on a standard teaching or administrative evaluation form that asks, did the instructor make changes during the class that were responsive to learning needs expressed by students? Addressing this question, and providing evidence of change based on its answers, could become not only legitimate but also required for review and promotion.[5]

Establish Partnerships between High School and College Faculty

Partnerships can be established between schools with neighborhood colleges or universities or with more distant ones through the use of e-mail, blogs, or other technological media. Programs can invite student input focused in a concentrated way on classroom practices (i.e., creating and maintaining a positive classroom environment, lesson planning, test development) before the student teaching phase of teacher preparation (as discussed in Chapter 13) or during it (as discussed in Chapter 14). Or, programs could be based in courses earlier in preservice teachers' preparation, perhaps focused on multicultural education, special education, urban education, or literacy, in which school-based teachers and groups of students could establish dialogue with preservice teachers that addresses these important issues. An important dimension of such an effort is to provide experiences, as Bernadette Youens suggests in Chapter 14, "that focus on equipping student teachers to work openly and collaboratively with all stakeholders in schools by providing a forum for dialogue about students' perceptions."

Integrate Partnerships into the Culture of the School

Although much can be gained from isolated partnerships, in which individual teachers and programs of teacher preparation work together, much more can be gained from integrating such partnerships into the culture of the school. Ways to accomplish such integration might include these ideas:

- Issue schoolwide invitations to participate and create a sense of seriousness in relation to which teachers and students will be selected to participate.
- Make time and provide support for orientation to the collaboration. Sponsor a daylong or half-day orientation on-site at which participants discuss the rationale and premises of the collaboration, invite past participants to share their insights and advice, and generally create continuity across years of participation.
- Integrate opportunities for participation into the regular school schedule (as opposed to having them squeezed after school between classes and sports or clubs) and, by extension, into the curriculum.
- Plan professional development days around student input and lessons from the collaboration and around what teachers learn through their participation in such projects. Have teachers and students co-present at these events, thus highlighting student voice as well as what teachers can learn from students.
- Invite student and teacher participants to share their insights at faculty, school board, and PTA meetings or in other forums of school- and district-wide discussion. Either in teams, as suggested above, or in groups within the same constituency, teachers and students could provide firsthand accounts like those included here, which effectively convey to others the power of this kind of experience.
- Support and train teacher leaders at the school site who are committed to student voice and engagement.

It is my hope that the general recommendations about perspective, stance, and interaction and the action steps for high school teachers, school leaders, and teacher educators included in this penultimate chapter will provide some guiding principles and concrete steps that educators can take toward supporting and engaging in learning from the student's perspective. In the final chapter, I introduce a metaphor—translation—I have used elsewhere to analyze the processes of education, school reform, and educational research, this time focusing on how schools and educators need to translate and be translated.[6]

Notes

1. For other versions of this discussion, see Cook-Sather, 2007c and 2009b.
2. Freire, 1990, p. 81.
3. Schultz, 2003.
4. Cook-Sather, 2008, 2009a.
5. Cook-Sather, 2002a.
6. Cook-Sather, 2002a, 2006, 2007a, and 2009b.

16

Translating Schools and Educators

What It Takes to Learn from the Student's Perspective

Chapter Overview

Focus of this chapter: To introduce a metaphor intended to facilitate the thinking about and practice of change in schools and educators
Discussed in this chapter:

- Translation: A metaphor for change
- Translating schools
- Translating educators

In this final chapter, I draw upon a metaphor I have developed elsewhere to argue for education as a process of translation through which the learner is both the translator and the thing translated.[1] I suggest that we also need to translate schools into places—and educators into people—that support a process of education as translation. I make this argument to educators, school leaders, teacher educators, and others who have the power and the desire to make these needed changes.

Translation: A Metaphor for Change

While "translate" is most often understood to mean the making of a new version of a text by rendering it in one's own or another's language, the term has other powerful meanings that carry it beyond the realm of textual rendering. To translate can mean to bear, remove, or change from one place or condition to another. It can also mean to change the form, expression, or mode of expression of, so as to interpret or make tangible, and thus to carry over from one medium or sphere into another. And to translate can mean to change completely, to transform.[2] If we conceptualize education both literally and metaphorically in terms of the range of definitions of translation, with the learners understood as both the translators and the subjects of their own translation,[3] all learners who genuinely engage in an educative process change condition, make themselves comprehensible to others in a new sphere, make new versions of themselves, and are transformed. These processes are never finished; they are always open to further revision and always lead to further renderings. In any translation, one preserves something of the original or previous versions, and one renders a new version appropriate to a new context and to the relationships within that context.

The most obvious learner within this framework is the student with the teacher as an active, engaged supporter of student translations, but a teacher must also be a perpetual learner engaged in ongoing translations, as the authors of the chapters in Part III of this sourcebook illustrate. In my use of translation as a metaphor for the process of self-transformation in which learners engage, I have emphasized the importance of the learners themselves being the ones to effect the translation.[4] In other words, I do not use the metaphor to suggest that teachers translate students within classrooms. Likewise, I would not want to see the metaphor applied to school reform along the same lines: as policymakers translating teachers, students, or schools into new versions of those entities. Rather, I would like to see the various more nuanced meanings of translation—to bear, remove, or change from one place or condition to another; to change the form, expression, or mode of expression of, so as to interpret or make tangible, and thus to carry over from one medium or sphere into another; or to change completely, to transform—inform our thinking about educational reform as a never-finished process of change that enables a reform ideal to be newly accessible to comprehension and communication *and* re-rendered in relation to the ideals of those who spend their days in classrooms; and I would like those processes to be effected by teachers and students as much as by policymakers.[5] Any such process requires deviation from an established standard—in other words, it requires change—and that change is both prompted and effected more meaningfully when more people are involved in those processes.

One of the results of adhering to prevailing structures and commitments in U.S. schools is a focus on—even an obsession with—fixedness in the production and "finishedness" as an outcome of that education: educational contexts are structured toward achieving finishedness, and success is evaluated in terms of finishedness. But as Freire points out, "It is our awareness of being unfinished that makes us educable."[6] Gregory Rabassa's words about translation can be a reminder of this important lesson regarding education: "A translation is never finished. . . . It is open and could go on to infinity. . . . This matter of choice in translation always leaves the door open to that other possibility. . . . The translator can never be sure of himself, he must never be."[7] As long as neatness, tidiness, efficiency, and uniform standards are the goals of education in the United

States, supported by federal policies such as No Child Left Behind, the traditions, structures, programs, and processes that have defined education until now will endure. Alternatively, we could reconceptualize schools as spaces within which teachers and students might cocreate conditions for translation and support all learners as they change their condition, make themselves comprehensible to others in a new sphere, make new versions of themselves, and are transformed. Honoring students' perspectives and agency and the complexity of the realities they face in their classrooms requires and entails transforming structures that are limiting, oppressive, and disempowering into ones that better support teachers and students. Such reform requires those who work within schools to translate themselves—a process that I name as the goal of education.

Translating Schools

Much of the mainstream thinking about schools is informed by what Tyack and Cuban call the "grammar of schooling" and by a related metaphor: "Education is production."[8] These ways of thinking seem not only to underlie the structural problems that we face, they also ensnare the reformers who want to make changes but are not able to break free of the power of those structures. One particular area of blindness that these two metaphors encourage is that toward the centrality of the lives, thoughts, and critiques of students, who are the most centrally poised to understand and to offer ways of thinking about teaching and learning. Translation as I define it above places students at the center not only of education but also of educational reform and thus might offer a way out of this enduring deadlock.

Tyack and Cuban coined the phrase "the grammar of schooling" to describe the ways schools divide time and space, classify students, "splinter knowledge into 'subjects,'" and award "grades and 'credits' as evidence of learning."[9] With this metaphor, Tyack and Cuban illuminate the institutionalized structures and practices of schooling in contemporary North America in an effort to show some of the underlying logic of the system and the way this logic constrains the possibilities for change. The basic elements and principles of the grammar they describe took hold as a result of policymakers' and school leaders' embrace of the "cult of efficiency"[10] in the early twentieth century and have persisted regardless of context, of individuals teaching and learning within any given context, and of differences among the ways those individuals engage in the process of education. Tyack and Cuban suggest that the grammar of schooling has endured in part because it allows teachers to "discharge their duties in a predictable fashion" and to "cope with the everyday tasks" that those in charge expect them to perform: "controlling student behavior, instructing heterogeneous pupils, and sorting people for future roles in school and later life."[11]

The language that Tyack and Cuban use here is consistent with the lexicon of that second metaphor, which can be discerned in a wide variety of discussions of schools: "education is production." Within this conceptual framework, schools are factories or sorting machines; teachers are factory workers, machines themselves, or managers of the assembly line; and students are products of the factory that is the school.[12] As a cog in the machine, a teacher implements "teacher-proof materials,"[13] functions as "a well-ordered machine,"[14] or "regulates the content and the activities of the learner."[15] As products, "students enter the factory as raw material and are somehow 'assembled' as persons,"[16] expected to conform to certain objectively determinable characteristics, normally those that strengthen the national ability to produce wealth and thus secure a position of global power and also those that strengthen the position of some groups and weaken the position of others.

When one analyzes the related logic of these two metaphors, the efficiency, control, and systematic production that characterize both, it is no surprise that schools seem intractable to reform driven by other premises. Fixed structures and notions of production are rarely conducive to change of any kind, but certainly not change that calls basic assumptions and practices into question. Translation offers a more responsive, dynamic, and generative way to think about schooling and the experiences of teachers and students within schools—a way of thinking that could, if acted upon, lead to changes in the structures and goals of schooling. Rather than focusing on the structures and function of schools, as the notions of "the grammar of schooling" and "education is production" do, translation as a conceptual framework focuses on the processes and relationships within schools—those aspects of schooling emphasized by students in Part I of this text. The inclusion of students' voices in discussions of educational reform could both constitute and facilitate change because new voices, new and different ways of speaking, prompt someone who has been speaking unconsciously and without self-awareness—and who listens—to rethink what he has been saying and how he says it. Any previously monolingual speaker who has learned a second language is familiar with this phenomenon. It is certainly challenging for those who work within the existing metaphorical frameworks for schooling to find language and ways of thinking that get outside those old ways. However, raised awareness, openness to different forms of expression, and critical thinking about how to redefine previously uninterrogated premises all help meet that challenge.

Educators are uniquely positioned within schools and not only have the potential to contribute to school reform but also to support students in debates about that reform, although the ways in which their knowledge and visions are generally unheeded limit that potential. Educators are, according to Jean Anyon, in a strong position to build a constituency for change because they have continual access to parents and students, and they thus "have a unique opportunity to engage residents and youth in political conversations and activity" and to "help students appreciate their own value, intelligence, and potential as political actors."[17] As this sourcebook illustrates, the different position from which students experience schooling and, more generally, from which they experience the world makes their contributions to discussions of school reform essential. Including new voices with different ways of speaking in ongoing conversations about school reform can prompt new ways of thinking because even when those new voices say familiar things, they sound different coming from differently positioned people.

I dedicated this book to one of the pioneers of the student voice movement, the late Jean Rudduck, who has pointed out that

> school reform is not a question of a quick makeover to meet the requirements of the moment. It is not about a bit of liposuction to improve the school's grades profile. It is, instead, about reviewing the deep structures of schooling that hold habitual ways of seeing in place. We need urgently to review the goodness of fit between schools and young people—and their commentaries on what helps them to learn in school and what gets in the way of their learning will help.[18]

Including students in discussions of school reform in ways described in this sourcebook has the potential to translate schools in a fundamental way: those who are traditionally sorted and produced become active collaborators in their own education, thus changing the nature of that education. Such a translation is a form of reform in and of itself, as it positions students in different ways within the established structures of schools—not only such that they derive greater benefits from those existing structures but also so that they can be active participants in a process of negotiation with teachers and others to transform schools and further to translate themselves.

Translating Educators

The process of translating schools is inextricably connected with translating educators.[19] In this final section, I apply this metaphor to teachers, school leaders, and teacher educators; I outline the qualities of a translating educator not as a set of fixed features but rather as a collection of flexible qualities that should be further reinterpreted, revised, and enacted over time.

- A translating educator seeks out and works to translate concepts and terms that signal powerful ideas associated with schools. Terms such as "relationships," "respect," and "responsibility" that are so central to students' experiences of school need to be understood in students' terms. I do not suggest that we replace adult definitions with student definitions but rather that we let the terms be more variously defined, more complicated, less fixed. I urge educators to identify, interrogate, and translate other such ideas that evoke educational (and, more generally, social) values, structures, and practices.
- A translating educator calls into question simple, fixed, or established understandings and invites a more nuanced, variously informed, and more respectful interpretation of identities, such as

"teacher" and "learner." Such educators work with students toward a better understanding of how those identities get constructed both by those who hold them and by those who interact with those who hold them. Resisting monolithic categories, normalization, and simplistic notions of identity formation, translating educators challenge us to come to understand that any interpretation of identity must be informed by multiple sources and undertaken from various angles and to reconsider in particular the perspective and experience of the person claiming or being labeled with a particular identity. As with translations of terms and concepts, translations of identity are not about replacing one version with another. Rather, they are about informing new versions of any given identity with both existing and new meanings.

- A translating educator strives to redefine institutional roles and thus responsibilities and relationships within classroom and school contexts. The roles of teacher and student warrant particular kinds of translation—shifts from one "form" (of teacher or student) to another with something of previous versions remaining within the new. This translation does not entail the replacement of one set of relationships and responsibilities with another but rather requires a reconsideration of the basic purpose and focus of the relationships assumed and implied by particular roles.

- A translating educator strives to translate as well the context within which the ideas, identities, and roles relevant to the context are shaped and enacted: school. Because it is an institution, this term and entity is the most fixed (and thus limiting), the most inflexible, the most in need of translation. Translating educators must think of ways to rethink school as a bounded entity, to understand difference and diversity in new ways, to review the "deep structures of schooling that hold habitual ways of seeing in place."[20] Because ways of framing—boundaries, differences, ways of seeing—have a direct bearing not only on what can be seen but also on what can happen within those frames, we need a new version of school, as discussed in the first part of this chapter—one that is more resonant and meaningful than previous versions and more open and inclusive.

- A translating educator not only works to complicate existing understandings—of concepts, identities, roles, and institutions—but also strives to redistribute power and agency among participants in education. These are threatening challenges for those who would preserve the status quo, but the risk of not facing them is, I suggest, greater than the risk of taking them on. Educators are particularly well positioned to engage in and call for translations that have the potential to change the nature of the teacher-student relationship and therefore the ways schools and participation within them are structured.

- A translating educator brings to her practice an attitude that is open to translation of and in response to students' experiences and perspectives. Like teachers who embrace constructivist models of learning, educators who are open in this way "follow the learner."[21] To be open like this to young people is to redefine the relationship between young people and adults and, as a result, classrooms and schools.

- A translating educator attempts to open himself to unanticipated and unexpected findings and dilemmas not only regarding students' experiences but also regarding the educational approach or process itself. Specifically, such educators translate the invisible or unacknowledged forces that inform any educational approach, such as assumptions and expectations. Although we cannot—and should not—eliminate assumptions and expectations, we can make the educational approaches that are inevitably informed by these tendencies into ongoing, unfinishable processes. Letting young people challenge educators' assumptions and expectations and have those challenges accepted constitutes a form of translation of the basic premises of constructivist, student-centered practices into a different version of itself.

- A translating educator has to face numerous issues that Rudduck identifies: time, institutional commitment, anxiety generated by the change in power relations, authenticity, and inclusion.[22] Because teachers might feel threatened by the loss of their power and authority—a loss which may be necessary to afford students some of their own power and authority—some educators might be loath, consciously or unconsciously, to relinquish their power and authority, as illustrated by the exchange between a student and a teacher in Chapter 11. This issue highlights the concerns some educators have about trusting students as authorities: "How authentic is [student] voice and how do we know?" query MacBeath, Myers, and Demetriou.[23] And finally, the issue of inclusion highlights questions of who gets consulted: are only certain students' experiences accessed and documented, and, therefore, are representations of students' experiences of school skewed?

- A translating educator faces a somewhat ironic if not contradictory force: the conserving influence of some students themselves. The more radical or transformative forms of translation can find resistance or rejection among students who do not necessarily embrace the kind of empowered place advocated for them by some of these translating educators. This ironic situation may not just be a result of students who are used to their more passive place in the system being unable to rise above their historically subservient lot in (school) life. Rather, some students consciously choose this more conservative location (based largely on their view of schools and teachers). In these circumstances, then, educators who are faithful to working with students may be constrained in their more transformative intent by their commitment to negotiate a shared interpretive space, their views tempered by the need to find some kind of agreed perspective with students who may not share the educators' more democratic and equitable goals. This challenge and potential conflict is analogous to that posed by some theorists: that liberatory pedagogy can be impositional.[24]

- A translating educator is committed to knowing students in all their complexity. Because students' experiences and perspectives are constructed; individually varied, situated, or contextually bounded; and negotiated in the sociopolitical realities of classroom and school life, translating educators acknowledge and act on the understanding that consultation must find ways of accessing that complexity.

- Translating educators not only listen to what students have to say, but they also, as Dennis Thiessen puts it, "listen for when students 'have a say' in what classrooms and schools do on their behalf." Like researchers of student voice, a translating educator "examines where, under what circumstances, in what form, and to what degree the voices of students matter to decisions about how schools work and improve."[25]

- A translating educator strives to develop an awareness of the choices she has regarding how much of former versions of herself to keep as she forges new versions. There are always play and movement in the rendering of herself, different choices made in different moments and contexts that highlight how the researcher herself is always changing and evolving as a meaning-maker.

Translation as I discuss it here can be a source of rejuvenation, growth, and development—a profoundly life-affirming experience for all involved. If education "is a process of enabling a person to become different,"[26] and engaging in consultation of and entering into partnership with students are forms of education, then engaging in consultation of students to translate schools, educators, and students themselves should enable those involved to become different. Change and growth are the hallmarks not only of survival but also of vitality. Poet and translator David Constantine's claim about language holds true for any vital thing: it is living "only in so far as it can move and change."[27] So too for education and those who engage in it.

Notes

1. This chapter draws on Cook-Sather, 2002a, 2006, 2007a, and 2009c.
2. *Webster's New International Dictionary,* 2nd ed.
3. Cook-Sather, 2003, 2006.
4. Cook-Sather, 2006, 2007a.
5. *Webster's New International Dictionary,* 2nd ed.
6. Freire, 1998, p. 58.
7. Rabassa, 1989, pp. 7, 12.
8. Tyack and Cuban, 1995. For an extended version of this discussion, see Cook-Sather, 2009c.
9. Tyack and Cuban, 1995, p. 85.

10. Callahan, 1962.

11. Tyack and Cuban, 1995, p. 86.

12. Cook-Sather, 2006, 2003; Callahan, 1962; Fenstermacher and Soltis, 1992; Schlechty, 1991; Spring, 1976.

13. Schlechty, 1991, p. 23.

14. Efron and Joseph, 2001, p. 78.

15. Fenstermacher and Soltis, 1992, p. 16.

16. Fenstermacher and Soltis, 1992, p. 16.

17. Anyon, 2005, pp. 178, 179.

18. Rudduck, 2007, p. 587.

19. For a different version of this discussion, see Cook-Sather, 2007a, pp. 829–871.

20. Rudduck, 2007.

21. See discussion of constructivism in the Introduction.

22. Rudduck, 2007.

23. MacBeath, Myers, and Demetriou, 2001, p. 80.

24. Cook-Sather, 2007b.

25. Thiessen, 2007, p. 54.

26. Greene, 2001, p. 5.

27. Constantine, 1999, p. 15.

Appendix

Research Support for Consulting Students

International Models for Listening to Students

The democratic school movement represents one effort to enact genuine participatory democracy that includes listening to students and positioning them as active agents in their learning. Developed according to Dewey's notion that "all those who are affected by social institutions must have a share in producing and managing them," this movement acts on the premise that such an "all" includes students.[1] Within this movement, schools adhere to and enact democratic principles; in other words, those principles are embodied, not simply espoused.[2] Democratic schools can be found around the world.

A movement that focuses on student participation across contexts has come to be known as the student voice movement. Researchers who helped to generate the student voice movement focused their attention on student perspectives on and participation in a wide variety of school settings. Writing in England in the late 1970s, Meighan pointed out that "there are only a few studies of schooling from the point of view of the learners," and writing in the United States in the early 1990s, Erickson and Shultz argued that "virtually no research has been done that places student experience at the center of attention."[3] Questions about the absence of students' perspectives in conversations about education were posed in Canada as well, where Fullan asked, "What would happen if we treated the student as someone whose opinion mattered?"[4] Since the 1960s, prompted by observations and questions such as these and inspired by their conviction that what students have to say "is not only worth listening to but provides an important—perhaps the most important—foundation for thinking about ways of improving" teaching, learning, and schooling, some educational researchers have attempted to develop an understanding of life in classrooms and schools that includes the perspectives of students and to develop processes through which students can play more active roles in shaping what happens there.[5] One among these researchers, I have argued that "it is time that we count students among those with the authority to participate both in the critique and in the reform of education."[6] With this text I extend that argument: it is now time for more educational institutions in the United States and teacher education programs around the world to count students among those with the authority to participate in more processes of educational reform and, specifically, to take an active role in teacher preparation.

While researchers in Australia, Canada, England, and the United States have developed frameworks for consulting students, educators in the first three of those countries are far ahead of the United States in efforts at integrating students into discussions about and processes of reform in K–12 schools.[7] In Australia, researchers[8] have developed frameworks for attending to students' perspectives[8] and blueprints for schools based on what students argue they need,[9] and there are examples of schools that include students as active participants in constructing their education.[10] In Canada, the deputy minister of education for the province of Ontario designed and implemented a provincewide reform strategy that firmly places student perspectives and students in active roles at the center. Not only did he assert that the most promising reform strategies involve treating students as capable persons, capitalizing on their knowledge and interests, and involving them in determining goals and learning methods, he acted on these assertions.[11] And in England, policies such as Every Child Matters: Change for Children set out a national framework for local change programs to build services around the needs of young people to maximize opportunity and minimize risk for all youth, and the appointment of a children's commissioner for England has the stated aim of giving all young people, but particularly the most vulnerable in society, a voice in government and in public life.[12] Alongside these general initiatives are national frameworks intended to guide educational practices, such as the Department for Education and Skills (DfES) consultation paper *Working Together: Giving Children and Young People a Say* (2004) or the Office for Standards in Education (OfSTED) framework *Evaluating Educational Inclusion* (2000), which assert the "rights of children and young people to have a voice and an active role in decision making and planning in education."[13] Although researchers in England have argued for more than thirty years that students have a role to play in teacher education, the idea of including students' perspectives and voices in teacher education in the United States is a rare phenomenon.[14] Some projects consist of university students and their school partners holding weekly exchanges focused on traditional subject areas, such as literature or writing as a tool for learning across the curriculum.[15] Others focus on student teachers providing encouragement and support for students, and still others on preservice teachers learning about the particular needs of a given population, such as second-language learners.[16] While these projects bring preservice teachers into contact with school students, they do not necessarily position students as authorities on educational practice. Very few projects position students as teacher educators.[17]

Research Findings on Listening to Students

The research literature cited above, as well as studies conducted by other scholars, tells us that when adults listen to and learn from students, teachers can teach better and students can learn better: a focus on student participation in processes of analyzing and revising teaching and learning approaches "can enhance [student] progress in learning."[18] In particular, consulting with, listening to, and working with students help teachers build relationships with students, access the student experience of school, learn what facilitates student learning, and begin to address deeply entrenched social inequities.

Building Relationships That Promote Engagement and Learning

The development of relationships between students and teachers and of collaborative forms of engagement based on those relationships improves student experiences and learning at school.[19] As discussed extensively in Chapters 1 and 4, as well as throughout the sourcebook, when teachers make the effort to get to know students and let students know them, and when a relationship of mutual respect emerges as a result of that process, students are more willing to learn and open to learning, and they are also more willing to enter into a collaborative relationship with teachers. Such forms of caring and engaged relationships are particularly important for students who feel alienated from mainstream school culture, such as those at risk of cutting class or dropping out of school, but they are important for all students.[20] When students are taken seriously and attended to as knowledgeable participants in conversations about teaching and learning, when they have collegial relationships with adults, they feel empowered and motivated to participate constructively in their education.[21]

Such motivation and participation can move students—and teachers—toward a more collaborative approach to education, which is in keeping with a cultural shift toward more collaborative, participatory processes in the workplace. A commitment to learning from the student's perspective can contribute to the conceptualization of teaching, learning, and the ways we study them as more collaborative processes.[22] Rudduck and McIntyre explain that the teachers who consulted students about their learning needs discovered "ways in which classroom teaching and learning can become not only more effective, more meaningful, and more enjoyable but a task that teachers and [students] can undertake collaboratively."[23] For students, Rudduck and McIntyre continue, this participation in developing and revising pedagogical practices is "about their development individually and in groups as they come better to understand their own learning and take control of their work, and as they come to believe that they can contribute to improve the conditions of learning in their school."[24]

Accessing the Student Experience of School— and Making School More Accessible

When teachers listen to and learn from students, they can begin to see the world from those students' perspectives.[25] Treating students as legitimate informants on their learning experiences gives us access to what ethnographers call students' "meaning perspectives"—the perspectives from which students make meaning and thus that influence any meaning made regarding what works, what does not work, and what could work in their learning. Gaining access to those perspectives can help teachers make what they teach more accessible to students and make sure that what they teach is relevant.[26] In a rapidly changing world infused with and altered by multiple technologies, such perspective gaining is essential if we are to keep students engaged in their work and prepare them for productive participation in the global society. The perspectives that students offer in Chapters 1 through 5 can guide educators in that preparation.

Addressing Social Inequities

Many of society's inequities are structured into schools and play out in both visible and invisible ways in students' lives.[27] Listening to students and building teaching around themes that are relevant to and that emerge from students' own lives can be transformative for students both personally and politically.[28] Genuinely listening to students and respecting what they say can counter discriminatory and exclusionary tendencies in education.[29] And finally, when students develop voice—particularly when that voice does not belong or conform to the dominant culture—they develop a sense of power, and "[with power] the locus of learning and creation of knowledge becomes a dialogical process in which the teacher and students alike can be cocreators."[30] One of the challenges of this work is learning the difference between having a sense of power and having actual power. While the capacity for empowerment through such dialogic processes is undeniable, there is potential for students to shut down when they encounter constrictions or impediments in their progress toward empowerment. Educators and students committed to addressing social inequities must be prepared for long-term investment and engagement, working as allies within larger structures of inequity.

As this growing body of research indicates, student "commentaries on teaching and learning in school provide a practical agenda for change that can help fine-tune or, more fundamentally, identify and shape improvement strategies."[31] Inviting students to be partners in developing, enacting, and assessing educational approaches is the best—perhaps the only—way to create learning opportunities that students want to take up and truly benefit from embracing.[32] For their part, as addressed in Chapter 5, students need to meet their adult educational partners halfway, taking up the responsibilities such consultation affords while also progressing on their own individual and shared learning trajectories. As I indicated in the Introduction, to be empowered in the ways explored in this text is not to sacrifice traditional success; rather, a collaborative approach can further individual achievement while also striving toward collective empowerment.

Notes

1. Dewey, quoted from his 1937 lecture, "Democracy and Educational Administration," excerpt in Joseph Ratner, ed., *Intelligence in the Modern World: John Dewey's Philosophy* (New York: Modern Library, 1939), pp. 400–401.

2. Apple and Beane, 2007; Gutmann, 1999; Miller, 2002.

3. Meighan, 1977, p. 91; Erickson and Shultz, 1992, p. 467.

4. Fullan, 1991, p. 170.

5. Rudduck, Chaplain, and Wallace, 1996, p. 1. For overviews of this work, see Rudduck and McIntyre, 2007; and Thiessen and Cook-Sather, 2007.

6. Cook-Sather, 2002a, p. 3.

7. Fielding, 2001a, 2001b, 2004b; Hart, 1997; Holdsworth, 2000; Lodge, 2005; Mitra, 2007; Thomson and Holdsworth, 2003; Thiessen, 1997.

8. Holdsworth, 2000.

9. Smyth, 2007.

10. Thomson, 2007.

11. Levin, 1994, 2000; Pekrul and Levin, 2007.

12. DfES, 2004b.

13. Quoted in Cruddas and Haddock, 2003, p. 5.

14. Meighan, 1977; Hull 1985; McKelvey and Kyriacou, 1985.

15. Randolph, 1994; Sullivan, 1998; Sipe, 2000.

16. Bowman and Edenfield, 2000; Hadaway, 1993.

17. Cook-Sather, 2002b; Cook-Sather and Youens, 2007; Donohue, Bower, and Rosenberg, 2003; Youens and Hall, 2006.

18. Rudduck and Flutter, 2004, p. 11.

19. Cook-Sather and Shultz, 2001; Dennison, 1969; Meier, 1997; Cothran and Ennis, 1997; Hull, 1985.

20. Dei, Mazzuca, McIsaac, and Zine, 1997; Schussler and Collins, 2006; Smyth et al., 2004; Sanon et al., 2001.

21. Hudson-Ross, Cleary, and Casey, 1993; Colsant, 1995; Oldfather et al., 1999; Sanon et al., 2001; Shultz and Cook-Sather, 2001.

22. Corbett and Wilson, 1995; Nicholls and Thorkildsen, 1995; Oldfather and Thomas, 1998; Shor, 1992.

23. Rudduck and McIntyre, 2007, pp. 9–10.

24. Ibid., p. 10.

25. Clark, 1995; Duckworth, 1987; Finders, 1997; Heshusius, 1995; Rodgers, 2002, 2006; Schultz, 2003; Shultz and Cook-Sather, 2001.

26. Commeyras, 1995; Dahl, 1995; Davies, 1982; Lincoln, 1995; Johnston and Nicholls, 1995.

27. Mac an Ghaill, 1988; Willis, 1977.

28. Hull, 1985; Freire, 1990; McLaren, 1989; Shor, 1987, 1992.

29. Banks, 1996; hooks, 1994; Ladson-Billings, 1994; Nieto, 1994, 2000.

30. Dias-Greenberg, 2003, p. 78.

31. Rudduck and Flutter, 2004, p. 29.

32. This text focuses on inviting students to be partners within their classrooms. An important related activity not taken up in this text is students as researchers. For more information, please consult the growing literature on students as researchers, including Fielding and Bragg, 2003; Fine et al., 2007; SooHoo, 1993; Thiessen and Cook-Sather, 2007.

References

Anyon, J. 2005. *Radical Possibilities: Public Policy, Urban Education, and a New Social Movement.* New York: Routledge.

Apple, M. W., and J. A. Beane. 2007. *Democratic Schools: Lessons in Powerful Education,* 2nd ed. Portsmouth, NH: Heinemann.

Arnot, M., D. McIntyre, D. Pedder, and D. Reay. 2004. *Consultation in the Classroom: Developing Dialogue about Teaching and Learning.* Cambridge, UK: Pearson.

Bains, L. 2008. "Youth Learning on Their Own Terms." *Teachers College Record* (February 14). http://www.tcrecord.org, ID Number: 15000. Accessed March 14, 2008.

Banks, J., ed. 1996. *Multicultural Education, Transformative Knowledge, and Action: Historical and Contemporary Perspectives.* New York: Teachers College Press.

Barr, D. D., and P. Vergun. 2000. "Using a New Method of Gathering Patient Satisfaction Data to Assess the Effects of Organizational Factors on Primary Care Quality." *Joint Commission Journal on Quality Improvement* 26, no. 12: 713–723.

Bates, D., N. Chase, C. Ignasiak, Y. Johnson, T. Zaza, T. Niesz, P. Buck, and K. Schultz. 2001. "Reflections: A Middle School Play about Race Relations." In *In Our Own Words: Students' Perspectives on School,* edited by J. Shultz and A. Cook-Sather, pp. 127–148. Lanham, MD: Rowman and Littlefield.

Berlin, J. 1990. "The Teacher as Researcher: Democracy, Dialogue, and Power." In *The Writing Teacher as Researcher: Essays in the Theory and Practice of Class-Based Research,* edited by Donald A. Daiker and Max Morenberg, pp. 3–14. Portsmouth, NH: Boynton/Cook.

Bowman, C., and R. Edenfield. 2000. "Becoming Better Together through Collaboration and Technology." *English Journal* 90, no. 2 (November): 112–119.

Bragg, S. 2001. "Taking a Joke: Learning from the Voices We Don't Want to Hear." *Forum* 43, no. 2: 70–73.

Brendtro, L., M. Brokenleg, and S. Van Bockern. 1990. *Reclaiming Youth at Risk: Our Hope for the Future.* Bloomington, IN: National Educational Service.

Bruhn, J. G. 2001. "Equal Partners: Doctors and Patients Explore the Limits of Autonomy." *Journal—Oklahoma State Medical Association* 94, no. 2: 46–54.

Burnaford, G. E., and D. Hobson. 2001. "Responding to Reform: Images for Teaching in the New Millennium." In *Images of Schoolteachers in America,* 2nd ed., edited by P. B. Joseph and G. E. Burnaford, pp. 229–244. Mahwah, NJ: Lawrence Erlbaum Associates.

Burnard, P. 2002. "Investigating Children's Meaning Making and the Emergence of Musical Interaction in Group Improvisation." *British Journal of Music Education* 19: 157–172.

Buss, E. 1999. "Confronting Developmental Barriers to the Empowerment of Child Clients." *Cornell Law Review* 84: 895.

Calkins, L. 1994. *The Art of Teaching Writing.* Portsmouth, NH: Heinemann.

Callahan, R. E. 1962. *Education and the Cult of Efficiency: A Study of the Social Forces That Have Shaped the Administration of the Public Schools.* Chicago, IL: University of Chicago Press.

Clark, C. 1995. *Flights of Fancy, Leaps of Faith: Children's Myths in Contemporary America.* Chicago, IL: University of Chicago Press.

Cochran-Smith, M., and S. Lytle. 1993. *Inside/Outside: Teacher Research and Knowledge.* New York: Teachers College Press.

Colsant, L. 1995. "Hey, Man, Why Do We Gotta Take This . . . ? Learning to Listen to Students." In *Reasons for Learning: Expanding the Conversation on Student-teacher Collaboration*, edited by J. G. Nicholls and T. A. Thorkildsen, pp. 62–89. New York: Teachers College Press.

Commeyras, M. 1995. "What Can We Learn from Students' Questions?" *Theory into Practice* 43, no. 2: 101–106.

Condon, D. 2008. "From the Inside Out: Eagle Rock School Producing a New Generation of CES Teachers." *Horace* 24 (Spring): 1.

Constantine, D. 1999. "Finding the Words: Translation and Survival of the Human." *Times Literary Supplement*, May 21, 14–15.

Cook-Sather, A. 2001. "Translating Themselves: Becoming a Teacher through Text and Talk." In *Talking Shop: Authentic Conversation and Teacher Learning*, edited by Christopher M. Clark, pp. 16–39. New York: Teachers College Press.

———. 2002a. "Authorizing Students' Perspectives: Toward Trust, Dialogue, and Change in Education." *Educational Researcher* 31, no. 4 (May): 3–14.

———. 2002b. "Re(in)forming the Conversations: Student Position, Power, and Voice in Teacher Education." *Radical Teacher* 64: 21–28.

———. 2003. "Movements of Mind: *The Matrix*, Metaphors, and Re-imagining Education." *Teachers College Record* 105, no. 6 (August): 946–977.

———. 2006. *Education Is Translation: A Metaphor for Change in Learning and Teaching.* Philadelphia: University of Pennsylvania Press.

———. 2007a. "Translating Researchers: Re-imagining the Work of Investigating Students' Experiences in School." In *International Handbook of Student Experience in Elementary and Secondary School*, edited by D. Thiessen and A. Cook-Sather, pp. 829–871. Dordrecht, the Netherlands: Springer.

———. 2007b. "Resisting the Impositional Potential of Student Voice Work: Lessons for Liberatory Educational Research from Poststructuralist Feminist Critiques of Critical Pedagogy." *Discourse* 28, no. 3 (September): 389–403.

———. 2007c. "What Would Happen If We Treated Students as Those with Opinions That Matter? The Benefits to Principals and Teachers of Supporting Youth Engagement in School." *NASSP Bulletin* 91, no. 4: 343–362.

———. 2008. "'What You Get Is Looking in a Mirror, Only Better': Inviting Students to Reflect (on) College Teaching." *Reflective Practice* 9, no. 4 (November): 473–483.

———. 2009a. "From Traditional Accountability to Shared Responsibility: The Benefits and Challenges of Student Consultants Gathering Midcourse Feedback in College Classrooms." *Assessment and Evaluation in Higher Education* 34, no. 2 (April): 231–241.

———. 2009b. "'I Am Not Afraid to Listen': Prospective Teachers Learning from Students to Work in City Schools." *Theory into Practice* 48, no. 3.

———. 2009c. "Translation: An Alternative Framework for Conceptualizing and Supporting School Reform Efforts." *Educational Theory* 59, no. 2 (June).

Cook-Sather, A., and O. Reisinger. 2001. "Seeing the Students behind the Stereotypes: The Perspectives of Three Pre-Service Teachers." *The Teacher Educator* 37, no. 3: 91–99.

Cook-Sather, A., and J. Shultz. 2001. "Starting Where the Learner Is: Listening to Students." In *In Our Own Words: Students' Perspectives on School*, edited by J. Shultz and A. Cook-Sather, pp. 1–17. Lanham, MD: Rowman and Littlefield.

Cook-Sather, A., and B. Youens. 2007. "Repositioning Students in Initial Teacher Preparation: A Comparative Descriptive Analysis of Learning to Teach for Social Justice in the United States and in England." *Journal of Teacher Education* 58, no. 1 (January–February): 62–75.

Cooper, P., and D. G. McIntyre. 2000. *Effective Teaching and Learning: Teachers' and Pupils' Perspectives*, 2nd ed. Buckingham, UK: Open University Press.

Corbett, H. D., and R. L. Wilson. 1995. "Make a Difference with, Not for, Students: A Plea for Researchers and Reformers." *Educational Researcher* 24, no. 5: 12–17.

Cothran, D. J., and D. Ennis. 1997. "Students' and Teachers' Perceptions of Conflict and Power." *Teaching and Teacher Education* 13, no. 5: 541–553.

Cothran, D. J., P. H. Kulinna, and D. A. Garrahy. 2003. "'This Is Kind of Giving a Secret Away . . .': Students' Perspectives on Effective Class Management." *Teaching and Teacher Education* 19: 435–444.

Cruddas, L., and L. Haddock. 2003. *Girls' Voices: Supporting Girls' Learning and Emotional Development*. Stratfordhire, England: Trentham Books.

Cushman, K. 2003. *Fires in the Bathroom: Advice for Teachers from High School Students*. New York: New Press.

Dahl, K. 1995. "Challenges in Understanding the Learner's Perspective." *Theory into Practice* 43, no. 2: 124–130.

Davies, B. 1982. *Life in the Classroom and Playground: The Accounts of Primary School Children*. Boston: Routledge.

Davis, B., and D. Sumara. 2002. "Constructivist Discourses and the Field of Education: Problems and Possibilities." *Educational Theory* 52, no. 4: 409–428.

Dei, G., J. Mazzuca, E. McIsaac, and E. Zine. 1997. *Reconstructing Drop-Out: A Critical Ethnography of the Dynamics of Black Students' Disengagement from School*. Toronto: University of Toronto Press.

De Jesus, A. 2003. "'Here It's More Like Your House': The Proliferation of Authentic Caring as School Reform at El Puente Academy for Peace and Justice." In *Critical Voices in School Reform: Students Living through Change*, edited by B. Rubin and E. Silva, pp. 132–151. London: RoutledgeFalmer.

Dennison, G. 1969. *The Lives of Children: The Story of the First Street School*. New York: Random House.

DES. 1992. "Initial Teacher Training (secondary phase)." Circular number 9/92. London: Department for Education.

Dewey, J. 1964. "My Pedagogic Creed." In *Dewey on Education*, edited by R. D. Archambault, pp. 427–439. Chicago, IL: University of Chicago Press.

DfES (Department for Education and Skills). 2004a. "Working Together: Giving Children and Young People a Say." DfES Consultation Paper. http://www.dcsf.gov.uk/consultations/downloadableDocs/239_2.pdf.

———. 2004b. Every Child Matters: Change for Children. http://www.hertsdirect.org/infobase/docs/pdfstore/ECMCFCsummary.pdf.

Dias-Greenberg, R. 2003. *The Emergence of Voice in Latino High School Students.* New York: Peter Lang.

Donohue, D. M., J. Bower, and D. Rosenberg. 2003. "Learning with and Learning From: Reciprocity in Service Learning in Teacher Education." *Equity and Excellence in Education* 36, no. 1: 15–27.

Dreier, O. 2003. "Learning in Personal Trajectories of Participation." In *Theoretical Psychology: Critical Contributions,* edited by Niamh Stevenson, H. Lorraine Radtke, Renè Jorna, and Henderikus J. Stam, pp. 20–29. Toronto: Camptus.

Duckworth, E. 1987. "The Virtues of Not Knowing." In *"The Having of Wonderful Ideas" and Other Essays on Teaching and Learning,* pp. 64–79. New York: Teachers College Press.

Dunderdale, K., S. Tourscher, R. J. Yoo, O. Reisinger, and A. Cook-Sather. 2001. In *In Our Own Words: Students' Perspectives on School,* edited by J. Shultz and A. Cook-Sather, pp. 57–72. Lanham, MD: Rowman and Littlefield.

Easton, L. B. 2002. *The Other Side of Curriculum: Lessons from Learners.* Portsmouth, NH: Heinemann.

———. 2008. *Engaging the Disengaged: How Schools Can Help Struggling Students Succeed.* Thousand Oaks, CA: Corwin.

Efron, S., and P. Joseph. 2001. "Reflections in a Mirror: Metaphors of Teachers in Teaching." In *Images of Schoolteachers in America,* 2nd ed., edited by Pamela M. Joseph and Gail E. Burnaford, pp. 75–92. Mahwah, NJ: Lawrence Erlbaum Associates.

Entwistle, N., B. Koseiki, and H. Tait. 1989. "Students' Perceptions of School and Teachers." *British Journal of Educational Psychology* 59: 326–339.

Erickson, F., and J. Shultz. 1992. "Students' Experience of Curriculum." In *Handbook of Research on Curriculum,* edited by Philip W. Jackson, pp. 465–485. New York: Macmillan.

Fenstermacher, G. D., and J. F. Soltis. 1992. *Approaches to Teaching.* New York: Teachers College Press.

Fielding, M. 1999. "Target-Setting, Policy, Pathology, and Student Perspectives: Learning to Labour in New Times." *Cambridge Journal of Education* 29: 277–287.

———. 2001a. "Students as Radical Agents of Change." *Journal of Educational Change* 2, no. 3: 123–141.

———. 2001b. "Beyond the Rhetoric of Student Voice: New Departures or New Constraints in the Transformation of 21st Century Schooling?" *Forum* 43, no. 2: 100–110.

———. 2004a. "Transformative Approaches to Student Voice: Theoretical Underpinnings, Recalcitrant Realities." *British Educational Research Journal* 30, no. 2 (April): 295–311.

———. 2004b. "'New Wave' Student Voice and the Renewal of Civic Society." *London Review of Education* 2, no. 3 (November): 197–217.

Fielding, M., and S. Bragg. 2003. *Students as Researchers: Making a Difference.* Cambridge, UK: Pearson.

Finders, M. 1997. *Just Girls: Hidden Literacies and Life in Junior High.* New York: Teachers College Press.

Fine, M., ed. 1994. *Chartering Urban Reform: Reflections on Public High Schools in the Midst of Change.* New York: Teachers College Press.

Fine, M., M. E. Torre, A. Burns, and Y. Payne. 2007. "Youth Research/Participatory Methods for Reform." In *International Handbook of Student Experience in Elementary and Secondary School,* edited by D. Thiessen and A. Cook-Sather, pp. 805–828. Dordrecht, the Netherlands: Springer.

Flutter, J., J. Rudduck, H. Addams, M. Johnson, and M. Maden. 1999. "Improving Learning: The Students' Agenda." A report for secondary schools supported by the Nuffield Foundation, 1997–1998.

Freire P. 1987. "The Importance of the Act of Reading." In *Literacy: Reading the Word and the World,* edited by P. Freire and D. Macedo, pp. 29–36. Westport, CT: Bergen and Garvey.

———. 1990. *Pedagogy of the Oppressed.* New York: Continuum.

———. 1998. *Pedagogy of Freedom: Ethics, Democracy, and Civil Courage.* Translated by P. Clarke. Lanham, MD: Rowman and Littlefield.

Fullan, M. G. 1991. *The New Meaning of Educational Change.* London: Cassell.

———. 2002. *Leading in a Culture of Change.* San Francisco: Jossey-Bass.

Goswami, D., and P. R. Stillman, eds. 1987. *Reclaiming the Classroom: Teacher Research as an Agency for Change.* Upper Montclair, NJ: Boynton/Cook.

Greco, M., A. Brownlea, J. McGovern, and M. Cavanagh. 2000. "Consumers as Educators: Implementation of Patient Feedback in General Practice Training." *Health Communication* 12, no. 2: 173–193.

Greene, M. 1973. *Teacher as Stranger: Educational Philosophy for the Modern Age.* Belmont, CA: Wadsworth.

———. 1988. *Dialectic of Freedom.* New York: Teachers College Press.

———. 2001. "Defining Aesthetic Education." In *Variations on a Blue Guitar: The Lincoln Center Institute Lectures on Aesthetic Education,* pp. 5–6. New York: Teachers College Press.

Groundwater-Smith, S. 1998. "Students as Researchers: Two Australian Case Studies." Paper presented at the British Education Research Association, University of Sussex, September.

Gutmann, A. 1999. *Democratic Education.* Princeton, NJ: Princeton University Press.

Hadaway, N. 1993. "Encountering Linguistic Diversity through Letters: Preparing Preservice Teachers for Second Language Learners." *Equity and Excellence in Education* 26, no. 3: 25–30.

Hannam, D. 2001. "Attitudes, Attendance, and Exclusion in Secondary Schools That Take Student Participation Seriously: A Pilot Study." Paper presented to ESRC Project, Cambridge, October 15.

Hart, R. 1997. *Children's Participation.* London: Earthscan.

Hartup, W. W. 1995. "The Three Faces of Friendship." *Journal of Social and Personal Relationships* 12: 569–574.

Heshusius, L. 1995. "Listening to Children: 'What Could We Possibly Have in Common?'—From Concerns with Self to Participatory Consciousness." *Theory into Practice* 43, no. 2: 117–123.

Holdsworth R. 2000. "Schools That Create Real Roles of Value for Young People." *UNESCO International Prospect* 3: 349–362.

hooks, b. 1994. *Teaching to Transgress: Education as the Practice of Freedom.* New York: Routledge.

Horn, I. S. 2003. "Helping, Bluffing, and Doing Portfolios in a High School Geometry Classroom." In *Critical Voices in School Reform: Students Living through Change,* edited by B. Rubin and E. Silva, pp. 92–110. London: RoutledgeFalmer.

Hudson-Ross, S., L. Cleary, and M. Casey. 1993. *Children's Voices: Children Talk about Literacy.* Portsmouth, NH: Heinemann.

Hull, C. 1985. "Pupils as Teacher Educators." *Cambridge Journal of Education* 15, no. 1: 1–8.

Hurder, A. J. 1996. "Negotiating the Lawyer-Client Relationship: A Search for Equality and Collaboration." *Buffalo Law Review* 44: 71.

James, A., and A. Prout. 1997. *Constructing and Reconstructing Childhood*. London: Falmer.

Johnston, P., and J. Nicholls. 1995. "Voices We Want to Hear and Voices We Don't." *Theory into Practice* 43, no. 2: 94–100.

Judon, Q., J. Cohen-Dan, T. Leonard, S. Stinson, T. Colson, J. Cohen, and D. Brown. 2001. "Speaking out Loud: 'Every Woman for Herself.'" In *In Our Own Words: Students' Perspectives on School*, edited by J. Shultz and A. Cook-Sather, pp. 39–56. Lanham, MD: Rowman and Littlefield.

Keiser, D. L., and S. Stein. 2003. "'We Have a Motion on the Floor': Montclair High School and the Civics and Government Institute." In *Critical Voices in School Reform: Students Living through Change*, edited by B. Rubin and E. Silva, pp. 171–187. London: RoutledgeFalmer.

Kravitz, R. L. 2001. "Measuring Patients' Expectations and Requests." *Annals of Internal Medicine* 134, no. 9, Pt. 2: 881–888.

Ladson-Billings, G. 1994. *The Dreamkeepers: Successful Teachers of African American Children*. San Francisco: Jossey-Bass.

Levin, B. 1994. "Educational Reform and the Treatment of Students in Schools." *Journal of Educational Thought* 28, no. 1: 88–101.

———. 2000. "Putting Students at the Centre of Education Reform." *Journal of Educational Change* 1, no. 2: 155–172.

Lincoln, Y. 1995. "In Search of Students' Voices." *Theory into Practice* 43, no. 2: 88–93.

Lodge, C. (2005). "From Hearing Voices to Engaging in Dialogue: Problematising Student Participation in School Improvement." *Journal of Educational Change* 6, no. 2 (June): 125–146.

Lofquist, W. A. 1996. *The Technology of Development: A Framework for Transforming Community Cultures*. Tucson, AZ: Development Publications.

Mac an Ghaill, M. 1988. *Young, Gifted, and Black: Student-Teacher Relations in the Schooling of Black Youth*. Philadelphia: Open University Press.

MacBeath, J. 1999. *Schools Must Speak for Themselves: The Case for School Evaluation*. London: Routledge.

MacBeath, J., and P. Mortimore, eds. 2001. *Improving School Effectiveness*. Buckingham, UK: Open University Press.

MacBeath, J., D. Mearns, and M. Smith. 1986. *Home from School*. Glasgow: Jordanhill College of Education.

MacBeath, J., H. Demetriou, J. Rudduck, and K. Myers. 2003. *Consulting Pupils: A Toolkit for Teachers*. Cambridge, UK: Pearson.

MacBeath, J., K. Myers, and H. Demetriou. 2001. "Supporting Teachers in Consulting Pupils about Aspects of Teaching and Learning and Evaluating Impact." *Forum* 43, no. 2: 78–82.

MacBeath, J., M. Schratz, D. Meuret, and L. Jakobsen. 2000. *Self-Evaluation in European Schools: A Story of Change*. London: RoutledgeFalmer.

Mann, L., and D. Chambers. 2001. "Designing a Consumer-Friendly Practice." *Australian Family Physician* 30, no. 3: 241–244.

Martin, N. 1987. "On the Move: Teacher-Researchers." In *Reclaiming the Classroom: Teacher Research as an Agency for Change*, edited by Dixie Goswami and Peter R. Stillman, pp. 20–28. Portsmouth, NH: Boynton/Cook.

Marzan, S., A. Peterson, C. Lewis, S. Christian, and E. Gold. 2001. "An Education for What? Reflections of Two High School Seniors on School." In *In Our Own Words: Students' Perspectives on School*, edited by J. Shultz and A. Cook-Sather, pp. 93–104. Lanham, MD: Rowman and Littlefield.

Mayall, B., G. Bendelow, P. Storey, and M. Veltman. 1996. *Children's Health in Primary Schools.* London: Falmer.

McGilchrist, B., K. Myers, and J. Reid. 1997. *The Intelligent School.* London: Paul Chapman.

McKelvey, J., and C. Kyriacou. 1985. "Research on Pupils as Teacher Evaluators." *Educational Studies* 11, no. 1: 27–31.

McLaren, P. 1989. *Life in Schools: An Introduction to Critical Pedagogy in the Foundations of Education.* New York: Longman.

Meier, D. R. 1997. *Learning in Small Moments: Life in an Urban Classroom.* New York: Teachers College Press.

Meighan, R. 1977. "The Pupil as Client: The Learner's Experience of Schooling." *Educational Review* 29: 123–135.

Meredith, L. S., et al. 2001. "Are Better Ratings of the Patient-Provider Relationship Associated with Higher Quality Care for Depression?" *Medical Care* 39, no. 4: 349–360.

Miller, R. 2002. *Free Schools, Free People: Education and Democracy after the 1960s.* Albany: State University of New York Press.

Mitra, D. 2001. "Opening the Floodgates: Giving Students a Voice in School Reform." *Forum* 43, no. 2: 91–94.

———. 2004. "The Significance of Students: Can Increasing 'Student Voice' in Schools Lead to Gains in Youth Development?" *Teachers College Record* 106, no. 4 (April): 651–688.

———. 2007. "Student Voice in School Reform: From Listening to Leadership." In *International Handbook of Student Experience in Elementary and Secondary School,* edited by D. Thiessen and A. Cook-Sather, pp. 727–744. Dordrecht, the Netherlands: Springer.

Moje, E. 2000. *"All the Stories That We Have": Adolescents' Insights about Literacy and Learning in Secondary Schools.* Newark, DE: International Reading.

Morgan, C., and G. Morris. 1999. "Good Teaching and Learning: Pupils and Teachers Speak." *Educational Research* 41, no. 3: 357–358.

Nicholls, J., and T. Thorkildsen. 1995. *Reasons for Learning: Expanding the Conversation on Student-teacher Collaboration.* New York: Teachers College Press.

Nieto, S. 1994. "Lessons from Students on Creating a Chance to Dream." *Harvard Educational Review* 64, no. 4: 139–148.

———. 2000. *Affirming Diversity: The Sociopolitical Context of Multicultural Education,* 3rd ed. Needham Heights, MA: Longman.

Noddings, N. 1997. "Caring." In *Classic and Contemporary Readings in the Philosophy of Education,* edited by S. Cahn. New York: McGraw-Hill.

Oakes, J., and M. Lipton. 2007. *Teaching to Change the World,* 3rd ed. New York: McGraw-Hill.

Office for Standards in Education (OfSTED). 2000. *Evaluating Educational Inclusion: Guidance for Inspectors and Schools.* http://www.ofsted.gov.uk.

Oldfather, P. 1995. Introduction to "Learning from Student Voices." *Theory into Practice* 43: 84–87.

Oldfather, P., and S. Thomas. 1998. "What Does It Mean When Teachers Participate in Collaborative Research with High School Students on Literacy Motivations?" *Teachers College Record* 90, no. 4: 647–691.

Oldfather, P., S. Thomas, L. Eckert, F. Garcia, N. Grannis, J. Kilgore, et al. 1999. "The Nature and Outcomes of Students' Longitudinal Research on Literacy Motivations and Schooling." *Research in the Teaching of English* 34: 281–320.

Orlich, D., R. J. Harder, R. C. Callahan, M. S. Trevisan, and A. H. Brown. 2001. *Teaching Strategies: A Guide to Effective Instruction*, 7th ed. Boston: Houghton Mifflin.

Packer, M. 2001. *Changing Classes: School Reform and the New Economy (Learning in Doing: Social, Cognitive, and Computational Perspectives)*. New York: Cambridge University Press.

Pekrul, S., and B. Levin. 2007. "Building Student Voice for School Improvement." In *International Handbook of Student Experience in Elementary and Secondary School*, edited by D. Thiessen and A. Cook-Sather, pp. 711–726. Dordrecht, the Netherlands: Springer.

Phillips, D. 1995. "The Good, the Bad, and the Ugly: The Many Faces of Constructivism." *Educational Researcher* 24, no. 7 (October): 5–12.

Pincus, M. 2005. "Learning from Laramie: 'Urban High School Students Read, Research, and Reenact *The Laramie Project*.'" In *Going Public with Our Teaching: An Anthology of Practice*, edited by T. Hatch et al. New York: Teachers College Press.

Pope, D. 2003. *Doing School: How We Are Creating a Generation of Stressed-Out, Materialistic, and Miseducated Students*. New Haven, CT: Yale University Press.

Rabassa, G. 1989. "No Two Snowflakes Are Alike: Translation as Metaphor." In *The Craft of Translation*, edited by J. Biguenet and R. Schulte, pp. 1–12. Chicago, IL: University of Chicago Press.

Randolph, R. 1994. "Writing across Institutional Boundaries: A K–12 and University Collaboration." *English Journal* 83, no. 3: 68–74.

Rodgers, C. 2002. "Redefining Reflection: Another Look at John Dewey and Reflective Thinking." *Teachers College Record* 104, no. 4 (June): 842–866.

———. 2006. "Attending to Student Voice: The Role of Descriptive Feedback in Learning and Teaching." *Curriculum Inquiry* 36: 2.

Rodriguez, A. P. 2003. "'There's Not Really Discussion Happening': Students' Experiences of Identity-Based Curricular Reform." In *Critical Voices in School Reform: Students Living through Change*, edited by B. Rubin and E. Silva, pp. 56–72. London: RoutledgeFalmer.

Rose, M. 1989. *Lives on the Boundary: The Struggles and Achievements of America's Underprepared*. New York: Free Press.

Rosenthal, D. E. 1974. *Lawyer and Client: Who's in Charge?* New York: Russell Sage Foundation.

Rubin, B. 2003a. "On Different Tracks: Students Living Detracking Reform at a Diverse Urban High School." In *Critical Voices in School Reform: Students Living through Change*, edited by B. Rubin and E. Silva, pp. 31–55. London: RoutledgeFalmer.

———. 2003b. "'I'm Not Getting Any F's': What 'At Risk' Students Say about the Support They Need." In *Critical Voices in School Reform: Students Living through Change*, edited by B. Rubin and E. Silva, pp. 188–207. London: RoutledgeFalmer.

Rubin, B., and E. Silva, eds. 2003. *Critical Voices in School Reform: Students Living through Change*. London: RoutledgeFalmer.

Rudduck, J. 1998. "Student Voices and Conditions of Learning." In *Didaktikk: Tradisjon og Formyelse*, edited by B. Karseth, S. Gudmundsdottir, and S. Hopmann, pp. 131–146. Oslo, Norway: Universitetsforlaget.

———. 2007. "Student Voice, Student Engagement, and School Reform." In *International Handbook of Student Experience in Elementary and Secondary School*, edited by D. Thiessen and A. Cook-Sather, pp. 587–610. Dordrecht, the Netherlands: Springer.

Rudduck, J., R. Chaplain, and G. Wallace. 1996. *School Improvement: What Can Pupils Tell Us?* London: David Fulton.

Rudduck, J., and J. Flutter. 2004. *How to Improve Your School: Giving Pupils a Voice.* London: Continuum.

Rudduck, J., and D. McIntyre, D. 2007. *Improving Learning through Consulting Pupils.* London: Routledge.

Sanon, F., M. Baxter, L. Fortune, and S. Opotow. 2001. "Cutting Class: Perspectives of Urban High School Students." In *In Our Own Words: Students' Perspectives on School,* edited by J. Shultz and A. Cook-Sather, pp. 73–91. Lanham, MD: Rowman and Littlefield.

Sarason, S. B. 1991. *The Predictable Failure of Educational Reform.* San Francisco: Jossey-Bass.

Schlechty, P. C. 1991. *Schools for the 21st Century: Leadership Imperatives for Educational Reform.* San Francisco: Jossey-Bass.

Schultz, K. 2003. *Listening: A Framework for Teaching across Differences.* New York: Teachers College Press.

Schussler, D. L., and A. Collins. 2006. "An Empirical Exploration of the Who, What, and How of School Care." *Teachers College Record* 108, no. 7: 1460–1495.

Shapiro, A. 2002. "The Latest Dope on Research (about Constructivism): Part I— Different Approaches to Constructivism—What It's All About." *International Journal of Educational Reform* 11, no. 4 (Fall): 347–361.

———. 2003. "The Latest Dope on Research (about Constructivism): Part II—On Instruction and Leadership." *International Journal of Educational Reform* 12, no. 1 (Winter): 62–77.

Shor, I. 1987. *Freire for the Classroom: A Sourcebook for Liberatory Teaching.* Portsmouth, NH: Heinemann.

———. 1992. *Empowering Education: Critical Teaching for Social Change.* Chicago, IL: University of Chicago Press.

Shulman, L. S. 2008. "Talk on Teacher Integrity." Carnegie Foundation. http://www .carnegiefoundation.org/files/elibrary/integrativelearning/assets/ilp_lsclips.mov.

Shultz, J., and A. Cook-Sather, eds. 2001. *In Our Own Words: Students' Perspectives on School.* Lanham, MD: Rowman and Littlefield.

Silva, E., and B. Rubin. 2003. "Missing Voices: Listening to Students' Experiences with School Reform." In *Critical Voices in School Reform: Students Living through Change,* edited by B. Rubin and E. Silva, pp. 1–7. London: RoutledgeFalmer.

Sipe, R. B. 2000. "Virtually Being There: Creating Authentic Experiences through Interactive Exchanges." *English Journal* 90, no. 2 (November): 104–111.

Sizer, T., and N. F. Sizer. 1999. *The Students Are Watching: Schools and the Moral Contract.* Boston: Beacon.

Smyth, J. 2007. "Toward the Pedagogically Engaged School: Listening to Student Voice as a Positive Response to Disengagement and 'Dropping Out'?" In *International Handbook of Student Experience in Elementary and Secondary School,* edited by D. Thiessen and A. Cook-Sather, pp. 635–658. Dordrecht, the Netherlands: Springer.

Smyth, J., and R. Hattam, with J. Cannon, J. Edwards, N. Wilson, and S. Wurst. 2004. *"Dropping Out," Drifting Off, Being Excluded: Becoming Somebody without School.* New York: Peter Lang.

SooHoo, S. 1993. "Students as Partners in Research and Restructuring Schools." *Educational Forum* 57: 386–393.

Spring, J. 1976. *The Sorting Machine: National Educational Policy since 1945.* New York: McKay.

Stern, D. 1995. *Teaching English So It Matters: Creating Curriculum for and with High School Students.* Thousand Oaks, CA: Corwin.

Stewart, M. 2001. "Towards a Global Definition of Patient-Centred Care: The Patient Should Be the Judge of Patient-Centred Care." *British Medical Journal* 322, no. 7284: 444–445.

Stewart, M., et al. 1995. *Patient-Centered Medicine: Transforming the Clinical Method.* Thousand Oaks, CA: Sage.

Stiggins, R. 2001. *Student-Involved Classroom Assessment*, 3rd ed. Upper Saddle River, NJ: Prentice-Hall.

———. 2005. "From Formative Assessment to Assessment FOR Learning: A Path to Success in Standards-Based Schools." *Phi Delta Kappan* 85, no. 4 (December): 324–328.

Strong, R., H. F. Silver, and A. Robinson. 2001. "What Do Students Want (and What Really Motivates Them)?" In *Kaleidoscope Readings in Education*, edited by K. Ryan and J. M. Cooper, pp. 85–90. Boston: Houghton Mifflin.

Strosser, M., and N. Patterson, executive producers. 1993. *I Used to Teach English* (film). Philadelphia, PA: Stockton Rush Bartol Foundation.

Strucker, M., L. N. Moise, V. Magee, and H. Kreider. 2001. "Writing the Wrong: Making Schools Better for Girls." In *In Our Own Words: Students' Perspectives on School*, edited by J. Shultz and A. Cook-Sather, pp. 149–164. Lanham, MD: Rowman and Littlefield.

Sullivan, J. 1998. "The Electronic Journal: Combining Literacy and Technology." *Reading Teacher* 52, no. 1 (September): 90–93.

Thiessen, D. 1997. "Knowing About, Acting on Behalf of, and Working with Students' Perspectives: Three Levels of Engagement with Research." In *Children and Their Curriculum*, edited by A. Pollard, D. Thiessen, and A. Filer, pp. 184–196. London: Falmer Press.

———. 2007. "Researching Student Experience in Elementary and Secondary School: An Evolving Field of Study." In *International Handbook of Student Experience in Elementary and Secondary School*, edited by D. Thiessen and A. Cook-Sather, pp. 1–76. Dordrecht, the Netherlands: Springer.

Thiessen, D., and A. Cook-Sather, eds. 2007. *International Handbook of Student Experience in Elementary and Secondary School.* Dordrecht, the Netherlands: Springer.

Thomson, P. 2007. "Making It Real: Community Activism, Active Citizenship, and Students' Learning." In *International Handbook of Student Experience in Elementary and Secondary School*, edited by D. Thiessen and A. Cook-Sather, pp. 775–804. Dordrecht, the Netherlands: Springer.

Thomson, P., and R. Holdsworth. 2003. "Theorizing Change in the Educational 'Field': Re-readings of 'Student Participation' Projects." *International Journal of Leadership in Education* 6, no. 4: 371–391.

Tyack, D., and L. Cuban. 1995. *Tinkering toward Utopia: A Century of Public School Reform.* Cambridge, MA: Harvard University Press.

Wade, B., and M. Moore. 1993. *Experiencing Special Education: What Young People with Special Educational Needs Can Tell Us.* Buckingham, UK: Open University Press.

Webster's New International Dictionary. 1951. Unabridged 2nd ed. Springfield, MA: G. and C. Merriam.

Weis, L., and M. Fine, eds. 1993. *Beyond Silenced Voices: Class, Race, and Gender in United States Schools.* Albany: State University of New York Press.

Wiggins, G., and J. McTighe. 2005. *Understanding by Design*, 2nd ed. Alexandria, VA: ASCD.

Willis, P. 1977. *Learning to Labour: How Working Class Kids Get Working Class Jobs.* London: Saxon House.

Wilson, B. L., and H. D. Corbett. 2001. *Listening to Urban Kids: School Reform and the Teachers They Want.* New York: State University of New York Press.

———. 2007. "Students' Perspectives on Good Teaching: Implications for Adult Reform Behavior." In *International Handbook of Student Experience in Elementary and Secondary School*, edited by D. Thiessen and A. Cook-Sather, pp. 283–314. Dordrecht, the Netherlands: Springer.

Wing, J. Y. 2003. "The Color Line in Student Achievement: How Can Small Learning Communities Make a Difference?" In *Critical Voices in School Reform: Students Living through Change*, edited by B. Rubin and E. Silva, pp. 152–170. London: RoutledgeFalmer.

Wortham, S. 2004. "The Interdependence of Social Identification and Learning." *American Educational Research Journal* 41, no. 3 (Fall): 715–750.

Yonezawa, S., and M. Jones. 2007. "Using Student Voices to Inform and Evaluate Secondary School Reform." In *International Handbook of Student Experience in Elementary and Secondary School*, edited by D. Thiessen and A. Cook-Sather, pp. 681–710. Dordrecht, the Netherlands: Springer.

Youens, B., and C. Hall. 2006. "Incorporating Pupil Perspectives in Initial Teacher Education—Lessons from the Pupil Mentoring Project." *Teacher Development* 10, no. 2: 197–206.

Acknowledgments

Many thanks go to Jody Cohen, Alice Lesnick, and Elliott Shore, my colleagues at Bryn Mawr College, who read drafts of the manuscript and offered invaluable feedback, and to Laura Perry for help with the index. Thanks go as well to former students, now colleagues, Ben Daley (Haverford 1995, former physics teacher and currently chief academic officer, High Tech High, San Diego) and Maeve O'Hara (Bryn Mawr 2008, mathematics teacher, Bodine High School, Philadelphia) for their thoughtful feedback, and to a new colleague, Ted Domers (teacher at Freire Charter School in Philadelphia and school-based collaborator for Teaching and Learning Together), for very detailed and constructive comments.

At Paradigm Publishers thanks go to Beth Davis, former editor for education; Melanie Stafford, project editor; Shena Redmond, copyeditor; Ann Hopman, editorial and business associate; and Dean Birkenkamp, founder and publisher, for their confidence in this project and their good ideas about how to shape the book. Thanks to Dean, especially, for his support of my work over the years.

I also wish to thank all the students, particularly those who have participated in Teaching and Learning Together between 1995 and 2008, as well as all those students who shared their perspectives with researchers and teachers in Australia, England, and the United States. In addition, I wish to thank all the teachers, school leaders, and researchers who are committed to learning from the student's perspective who do not appear in these pages but who nonetheless are engaged in this important work.

Finally, thanks go to my husband, Scott, and my daughter, Morgan, for their patience, love, and support.

Index

About the Author
and Contributors

Brandon Clarke completed his certification in social studies through the Bryn Mawr/Haverford Education Program in 2008 and took part in the Teaching and Learning Together program. He graduated from Haverford College in 2005 with a degree in history and has taught English in China, at an elementary level as well as in a university.

Daniel Condon has worked with several hundred nonprofit organizations and schools since the early 1990s. Selected as one of twenty young visionaries of 1996 by *Who Cares* magazine, he serves as a faculty member with Public Allies, Inc.'s Leadership Practice in collaboration with Northwestern University's Asset Based Community Development Institute. He is a Critical Friends Group Coach through the National School Reform Faculty and founded the Public Allies Teaching Fellowship Program in Colorado, a teacher preparation and licensure initiative, embraced by the Obama administration. He is also a Google Certified Teacher and is interested in using social media to further education renewal and reform. Currently, he is the associate director of professional development at the Eagle Rock School and Professional Development Center, a nonprofit subsidiary of the American Honda Motor Company.

Alison Cook-Sather is professor of education and coordinator of the Teaching and Learning Initiative at Bryn Mawr College. A former high school English teacher, she holds a Ph.D. from the University of Pennsylvania, and since 1995 she has taught core courses for students seeking state certification to teach at the secondary level and worked with faculty, students, and staff on various teaching and learning efforts. Her research interests focus on critical, creative, and collaborative approaches to teacher education and metaphors for teaching and learning, on which she has published thirty articles, ten book chapters, and four books. With a grant from the Andrew W. Mellon Foundation, she has developed a program at Bryn Mawr and Haverford colleges through which students serve as pedagogical consultants for faculty members (http://www.brynmawr.edu/tli).

Kathleen Cushman is a writer who has specialized in education and school reform for almost two decades. Her work has appeared in the *Harvard Education Letter, Educational Leadership, Phi Delta Kappan*, the *Atlantic Monthly*, the *New Yorker*, and many other national magazines. Cushman has been writer and editor of two school reform journals, *Horace* and *Challenge Journal*. She is the author or coauthor of eleven books, including *Practice* (in press), *First in the Family* (2005, 2006), *Fires in the Bathroom: Advice for Teachers from High School Students* (2003), *Schooling for the Real World* with Adria Steinberg and Rob Riordan (2000), and *The Real Boys Workbook*, with William S. Pollack (2001). She lives in New York City.

Helen Demetriou is a research associate at the University of Cambridge, England. She holds a Ph.D. in developmental psychology from the Institute of Psychiatry, University of London, and worked at Homerton College since 1998 in the Research Department as research associate with Jean Rudduck. During this time she has also lectured in developmental psychology in the Social and Political Sciences Department of the University of Cambridge. She has authored and coauthored numerous publications.

Lois Easton works as a consultant, coach, and author. She is particularly interested in learning designs for adults and for students. She recently retired as director of professional development at Eagle Rock School and Professional Development Center, Estes Park, Colorado. Easton was director of Re:Learning Systems at the Education Commission of the States (ECS) from 1992 to 1994. Re:Learning was a partnership between the Coalition of Essential Schools (CES) at Brown University in Providence, Rhode Island, and ECS. Prior to that, Easton served in the Arizona Department of Education. A middle school English teacher for 15 years, Easton earned her Ph.D. at the University of Arizona. Easton has been a frequent presenter at conferences and a contributor to educational journals. She is author of *The Other Side of Curriculum: Lessons from Learners* (2001); *Engaging the Disengaged: How Schools Can Help Struggling Students Succeed* (2007), selected as the 2009 education book of the year by Delta Kappa Gamma; and *Protocols for Professional Learning* (2009). She is editor of *Powerful Designs for Professional Learning* (2004, 2008).

Peter M. Evans, principal of Montpelier High School in Montpelier, Vermont, holds an Ed.D. from the University of Vermont's College of Education and Social Services and has thirty years of experience as a teacher, assistant principal, and principal. He currently is involved with other Vermont educators in bringing the issue of student voice to the forefront through a statewide initiative, "Youth and Adults Transforming Schools Together." The primary goal of the project is to expand and deepen student voice in school decisionmaking. Peter is also on the faculty at the graduate school of Saint Michaels' College, Colchester, Vermont, where he facilitates classes on school leadership for aspiring principals. In addition to this work, Peter has represented Vermont principals on several statewide projects and served as president of the Vermont Principals' Association. He was recently named Vermont Principal and was a nominee for National Principal of the Year.

Jossi Fritz-Mauer graduated from Haverford College in 2006. He spent some time teaching middle- and high-schoolers in Namibia while trying to live up to his ideals of privileging student voices in (and out of) the classroom.

Darla Himeles is coordinator of staff education at Bryn Mawr College, in Bryn Mawr, Pennsylvania. In this role, she works with staff, students, and faculty on various teaching and learning projects, including student-mentored computing classes for staff and faculty, staff-student continuing education partnerships, and staff-taught technology classes. Her work focuses on supporting colleagues across college constituencies in developing and teaching classes that are collaborative (in development, instruction, and learning) and that are responsive to learners' input and feedback. She is a graduate of Bryn Mawr College's undergraduate English Department and Education Program, where she graduated summa cum laude and earned her Pennsylvania teaching certification in secondary education. Darla is coauthor (with Jody Cohen and Alice Lesnick) of the article "Temporary Anchors, Impermanent Shelter: Can the Field of Education Model a New Approach to Academic Work?" (2007). A published poet, Darla is currently pursuing her MFA in poetry.

Jessica Mitra Mausner graduated from Haverford College in 2006 with a major in English and minor in education and educational studies. Her interest in education developed in high school, where she served as an advocate at the school and district levels for student involvement in decision-making processes. After college she worked as an English teacher, arts teacher, and caretaker at Lovedale Foundation's orphanage in Bangalore, India. Most recently, she worked with youth as a program coordinator at a Philadelphia nonprofit, where she created a school- and community-based peer health education program to control tobacco use. She hopes to continue her work in literacy, arts, and health education domestically and abroad.

Marsha Rosenzweig Pincus taught English and drama in the School District of Philadelphia between 1974 and 2008. A teacher-consultant for the Philadelphia Writing Project and Philadelphia Young Playwrights, she has been the recipient of the Rose Lindenbaum Award and the Ruth Wright Hayre Teacher of the Year Award. Her work has appeared in *Inside/Outside: Teacher Research and Knowledge* (Lytle and Cochran-Smith, eds.) and *Going Public with Our Teaching: An Anthology of Practice* (Hatch, Lieberman, et al., eds.). She has also been the subject of an award-winning documentary entitled "I Used to Teach English." She is a fellow of the Carnegie Academy for the Scholarship of Teaching and Learning, and her teacher-research is featured on the Carnegie Foundation's Gallery of Teaching and Learning (www.gallery.carnegiefoundation .org).

Bernadette Youens is a lecturer in the School of Education, University of Nottingham, England, and is currently director of Initial Teacher Education. She joined the School of Education as a teacher fellow in science education in 1998 and was appointed to her current post in 2001. Since then Bernadette has taught preservice teachers in a range of teacher preparation courses as well as supervised graduate and Ph.D. students. Her research interests include teacher education and student voice.